THE INVERTED CONQUEST

THE INVERTED Conquest

The Myth of Modernity and the Transatlantic Onset of Modernism

Alejandro Mejías-López

Vanderbilt University Press

NASHVILLE

Nashville, Tennessee 37235

First Edition 2009

Publication of this book has been supported by a generous subsidy from the Program for Cultural Cooperation between Spain's Ministry of Culture and United States Universities.

Library of Congress Cataloging-in-Publication Data
Mejías-López, Alejandro.
The inverted conquest : the myth of modernity and the transatlantic onset of modernism / Alejandro Mejías-López.
p. cm.
Includes bibliographical references and index.
ISBN 978-0-8265-1677-0 (cloth : alk. paper)
1. Spanish American literature—19th century—History and criticism. 2. Spanish American literature—20th century—History and criticism. 3. Modernism (Literature)—Latin America. 4. Modernism (Literature)—Spain. 5. Spanish literature—Latin American influences. I. Title.
PQ7081.M3845 2010
860.9'98—dc22
2009006557

To Missy and Lyra.
To my mother.
To my father, in memoriam.

Contents

Acknowledgments

There are many whose insight, encouragement, and material help have made the writing of this book possible. I am grateful to my colleagues and graduate students at the University of North Carolina, Indiana University, and elsewhere for their always stimulating conversation, their intellectual generosity, and their friendship. I am particularly thankful to Andrew Anderson, Deborah Cohn, Santiago Colás, Stuart Day, Patrick Dove, Cedomil Goic, Carl Good, Emily Maguire, John Nieto-Phillips, Gabriela Nouzeilles, Edurne Portela, Andrew Reynolds, María Salgado, and Steven Wagschal. I would like to thank Michael Ames, director of Vanderbilt University Press, for his unwavering support of this book and his insight, diligence, and patience throughout the process. It has been a pleasure working with him and everyone at the press, especially its managing editor, Jessie Hunnicutt. I would also like to thank the anonymous readers of the manuscript for their enthusiasm and their extremely helpful comments.

I would like to thank the *Arizona Journal of Hispanic Cultural Studies* for permission to reprint portions of Chapter 3, which first appeared in print, with slight variations, as part of my article "*Modernismo*'s Inverted Conquest and the Ruins of Imperial Nostalgia: Rethinking the Hispanic Atlantic in Contemporary Critical Discourse," *AJHCS* 12 (2008) 1–23.

I am most deeply grateful to my partner, Melissa Dinverno. Her brainpower and intellectual honesty are difficult to match and have helped keep me on my toes and not take things for granted. Her reading of many drafts and her many insightful comments have been instrumental in making this a better book. For her love, emotional support, and generosity with her time, I cannot thank her enough. Without her, this book would simply not have been written. Finally, I want to thank our daughter, Lyra, for being who she is and for renewing the meaning of awe on a daily basis. Her help in the first months of her life was, if unaware, no less important. Her ease with transatlantic travel and her love of books would have made many a modernist proud.

THE INVERTED CONQUEST

Introduction

> Modernism in literature and art does not refer to any particular artistic or literary school. It is rather a profound spiritual move carried out by artists and writers from dissimilar schools.
>
> —Manuel Díaz Rodríguez, *The Way of Perfection*

> There is little doubt that of all the concepts used in discussing and mapping twentieth-century Western literature, "modernism" has become the most important. . . . One must of course be aware that until quite recently, "modernism" was not a widespread concept.
>
> —Astradur Eysteinsson, *The Concept of Modernism*

> As a concept, neocolonialism is as disempowering as the conditions it portrays.
>
> —Robert Young, *Postcolonialism*

In 1965, an English speaker interested in learning about modernist poetry might have turned to the then recently published *Princeton Encyclopedia of Poetry and Poetics* and found, perhaps to her surprise, that the entry on "modernism" described a Hispanic literary movement spanning the last decades of the nineteenth and early decades of the twentieth centuries. She would have learned that "a cosmopolitan perspective, a new concinnity of language, and a new poetic diction" were "the main contributions of modernism to Western literature" (Preminger 527). Let's imagine the same reader going back to the *Encyclopedia* in 1974, after the publication of the second edition, and discovering that, although the term remains in its English form in the page header, the only entry on the subject appears now under its Spanish name, *modernismo*. Since the entry remains the same, however, she does not think twice about it. Twenty years later, in 1993, our imaginary reader goes back to the library to consult what is now called the *New Princeton Encyclopedia of Poetry and Poetics*. "Modernism" has returned to its pages as an entry (now accompanied by "Postmodernism"), but the Hispanic literary movement that so caught her attention almost thirty years back is not to be found anywhere in that entry. In fact, the entry mentions no Hispanic poet. Puzzled, she remembers the odd change of language in the previous edition and, sure enough, finds what she is looking for under the Spanish term *modernismo*. In the updated entry, however, the assessment of modernismo's contributions to Western literature is no longer there.

This persistent imaginary reader is not the unsuspecting witness of a progressive move toward multiculturalism; on the contrary, she has traced through the years a critical operation of exclusion. As modernism came to be the object of increasing theorization in the Anglo American academy and beyond, reaching its peak with the advent of the postmodernism debate, Hispanic modernism (perhaps never more than a curiosity in those same circles) was rapidly set aside, not as a result but as a precondition of that theorization.[1] Hispanic "modernism," the first movement to coin and theorize the term, may be condemned to remain untranslatable, italicized, and often accompanied by an explanatory note to reassure any unsuspecting reader that indeed modernismo is *not* modernism.

Matei Călinescu stands out as an important exception to the rule, insightfully identifying modernismo as the first instance of an aesthetic theorization that was able to see beyond the "parochial squabbles" (70) of contemporary schools and movements. It is a testament to the power of the critical process of exclusion that, despite his book's remaining an important reference for the study of modernism, Călinescu's comments have fallen on deaf ears. It is a sign of the speedy naturalization of the process of exclusion that, by 1998, Perry Anderson could find it "contrary to conventional expectation" that modernism was born "in a distant periphery rather than at the center of the cultural system of the time" (*Origins* 3), while in 2002, Fredrick Jameson could refer to the "scandal of Spanish usage" (100), perhaps anticipating the reaction of his readers when he told them, as he was about to, that modernism was indeed first coined in Spanish America.[2]

The "otherization" of modernismo, however, has not been exclusive to Anglo American and European studies. Spanish American criticism itself, having naturalized a certain understanding of Anglo European modernity, often either has questioned the very existence of nineteenth-century modernity in Spanish America or has considered it imperfect, defined by what it lacked rather than by what it was.[3] As a result, modernismo's story has turned into the tale of an attempt by writers to be modern, a wishful thinking, an unfulfilled desire, when not simply a story of ghosts. The Anglo European self is confirmed by Spanish America's neocolonial or postcolonial otherness. Thus, the two narratives complement and corroborate each other: modernism can keep being defined, without guilt, by the exclusion of modernismo, and modernismo remains safely contained, unable to challenge the alleged neocoloniality of Spanish American literature.[4] Whatever does not fit the requirements of these plots is discarded or simply overlooked; alternate plots are deemed unthinkable.

Yet, as Jorge Luis Borges said, "There are ten or twelve plots for a story; each one has to tell itself in its own way, with slight variations that are, of course, precious. Supposing that everything has already been said is an error" ("Conversation"). This book tells the story of both modernismo and modernity with the conviction that other plots are not only possible but also desirable. The neocolonial plot has been a powerful one, to be sure, but at the expense of rendering Spanish America powerless. As an explanatory system, this narrative has advanced our understanding of both modernismo and modernity by unveiling forces that were previously hidden, but it has done so by consistently overlooking many other forces that did not conform to the expectations of the plot. A variation of the neocolonial plot has been the postcolonial, which has brought a wealth of new theoretical insights into the narrative, but only by confirming and even furthering Spanish American marginality.

To dismantle the many myths of Anglo European modernity and begin to explore its heterogeneity, the plot of *The Inverted Conquest* incorporates new elements with those that did not fit earlier narratives. It opens the study of modernismo and Spanish American modernity to a more accurate and, indeed, less punitive understanding. When American literatures from North and South were having to cope with the issue of European distinction (in Bourdieu's interconnected sense of both difference and superiority), Spanish American modernismo successfully challenged European authority. This is, thus, a thoroughly transatlantic story that neither the neo- nor the postcolonial framework has been able to tell for, although a story of conquest, it is that of an inverted conquest.

Modernismo, in its strictest sense, lasted roughly from 1880 to the late 1920s. It defies definitions and classifications largely due to its own self-awareness as a radical break from academicism, its unabashed eclecticism, the wide array of its manifestations, and the diversity of its members, many of whom resisted identification with the name "modernismo"—a resistance that was itself a *modernista* gesture. For a century, the origins, nature, and scope of modernismo have been the subject of debate. Even in relation exclusively to form and style, the understanding of modernismo has always been mediated by geopolitics. Studied for many years mostly in its poetic production and considered by most a transposition of French Symbolism and Parnassianism, as well as a movement aloof and unconcerned with Spanish American reality, modernismo experienced an important critical reevaluation in the 1970s, when critics like Ángel Rama and Octavio Paz began to give serious consideration to the relationship between modernismo and the conditions of Spanish American modernization, between the movement and the social and economic conditions of the region at the end of the nineteenth century. Since the 1980s, scholarship on modernismo has also sought to expand the critical focus on poetry to other areas of the movement's vast literary production, most notably the journalistic writings, or *crónicas*, and, to a lesser extent, the novels. One of the scholarship's most significant blind spots has been the transatlantic dimension of the movement, which is all the more striking given that modernismo originated in Spanish America and was exported to Spain. Often mentioned in passing, this fact has received scant critical attention. It is fair to say that modernismo has been largely studied as if it were two separate phenomena, one on each side of the Atlantic, with anecdotal commonalities.

In this book, I propose a new reading of Spanish American modernismo as the most transatlantic literary enterprise of the nineteenth century and, arguably, of the twentieth. By "transatlantic" I mean not only a connection between localities on both sides of the Atlantic, but also a way of thinking of the Atlantic as a cultural, social, and political space crisscrossed by a thick network of discourses and historical events that cannot be fully understood in isolation. In this sense, transatlanticism is consubstantial to modernismo, and many of the modernista writers were among the first, if not the first, to theorize the Atlantic. They were also the first to coin the term "modernism," in a conscious effort to bring about an aesthetic revolution against academicism and realism and foreground the self-conscious constructedness of literature. They were the first to theorize not just Hispanic, but "Western" modernism and the problematic relationship of literature and art to the changing environments brought about by modernization, which they believed threatened the very drive for human knowledge and progress they thought central to modernity itself since the Renaissance.

Using the concepts of symbolic capital and literary field developed by sociologist Pierre Bourdieu, and expanding them from the national to the transnational context, I argue that modernismo created a continental Spanish American literature, actively engaged the international cultural and political arena, and became the only postcolonial literature to wrest cultural authority from its former European metropolis.[5] Far from a case of mere literary influence, Spanish American modernismo radically altered Spain's literary field, transformed and modernized literary expression in Spanish, and stripped Spain of linguistic authority, the very core of its (imperial) identity. In doing so, modernismo moved the cultural center of the Hispanic Atlantic westward to America.

This sequence of events is embodied in the title of this book, *The Inverted Conquest*, a term coined a century ago by Venezuelan novelist Manuel Díaz Rodríguez. He employed it to describe this unparalleled reversal of influence in the context of literary debates in Spain, which were heavily coded in postimperial and postcolonial language. Modernismo also challenged the increasingly dominant racial discourse of Anglo-Saxon modernity by refusing to let either Spanish America *or* Spain be written out of the modern. Through the study of Spanish American modernismo, this book opens a critical space that enables us to uncover political, economic, and cultural differences within what is usually presented as a monolithic imperial tandem Europe/United States. It thus allows a more nuanced and dynamic understanding of the circulation of culture and its relationship to power.

Postindependence Latin American history has been largely written under the rubric "neocolonialism," a term that originated in the post–World War II era in the context of the African decolonization process. Although originally an economic concept, this theoretical model has also marked profoundly the study of Latin American literature and culture, resulting, explicitly or implicitly, in the widely held view that, as Charles Hale has rightly pointed out, "independence was formal and superficial and that dependence was the deeper and more significant experience of the region." Thus, Latin America's independence, born out of some of the first liberal revolutions against the ancient regime and giving birth to some of the earliest sustained efforts to establish liberal republics, has become virtually irrelevant and Latin America's cultural production perpetually understood in colonial or neocolonial terms. Hale is certainly right, then, when he states that "to dismiss or downgrade these political and social ideas as 'imitative' or 'derivative,' or as mere rationalisations for the economic interests of a dependent governing class, is to make insignificant what was regarded then as of great importance, and to distort our understanding of Latin American history" (368). It is indeed striking how much not only Latin American history, but also the study of its literary and cultural production and the very status of its modernity in the nineteenth century have been mediated by the concept of neocolonialism; how often Latin America is measured against an assumed original and perfect metropolitan center rather than on its own terms. Cultural theories of transculturation, dependency, hybridity, and parody, while undoubtedly seeking to empower Latin American cultural production through difference, have ultimately perpetuated, in one way or another, the imperial sameness of the metropolitan center under critique. Moreover, when dealing with the nineteenth century, scholarship has wielded the notion of metropolitan center in quite a problematic way. "Metropolitan centers," "the West," "Western hegemony," and "Western modernity" are all terms commonly used to signify the tandem "Europe and the United States," as if in the course of the long nineteenth century both regions had been evenly modernized, and consistently and equally powerful. A glance at this period, however, reveals unprecedented changes and shifting power struggles in both Europe and the Americas, not the clear-cut opposition that the neocolonial plot tends to portray.

The Atlantic (and indeed the world) was profoundly transformed between 1776 and 1914. The status of the old metropolitan centers was hardly stable, and new kinds of metropolitan centers were emerging: in the course of the century, the most vast and powerful empire hitherto known, the Spanish, lost most of its territory and entered into the same relation of economic dependency on northern European capital as its ex-colonies, while some recently independent colonies in North America built a new type of imperial project that would eventually affect the entire world. To subsume the complexity and richness of nineteenth-century transatlantic conflicts and developments under a monolithic block of an ever-the-same imperial "West" from which only Latin America is excluded and relegated to an equally monolithic neocolonial periphery is to distort our understanding of Latin America, as Hale has pointed out. It is also, I would argue, to distort our vision of European and North American histories, modernities, and cultural production, as well as of the history of nineteenth-century transatlantic relations.

The history of the Americas and their relationship to Europe—that is, a large part of transatlantic history—is unique. Under European colonial rule since the fifteenth century, by the early nineteenth most of the American continent had become home to independent republics. This was a drastic change and an unprecedented political experiment, since at that time, outside of the Americas, only France had experienced a short-lived republican system and liberal democracy was but a project everywhere else. By 1820, not only was most of Europe still under monarchic rule, but also some regions (e.g., what today are Germany and Italy) had yet to become nation-states, while others (e.g., Ireland and Norway) were still colonies and would remain so until the twentieth century. Thus, in many ways, the political changes in the Americas were radically new and experimental, without a tradition or solid models on which to rely. That many of the philosophical and political ideas behind American independence were European in origin holds true for both North and South America and should not be surprising, since the revolutionary movements were carried out by Creoles of European descent, as Jorge Klor de Alva has rightly noted. This, however, does not take away from the fact, on the one hand, that these ideas were transformed in the Americas and, on the other, that their concrete implementation, as Mary Louis Pratt has reminded us (*Imperial Eyes* 175–76), was very much uncharted territory. If they developed differently in the United States than in the Latin American republics, so did they in different European regions, where the political development of countries such as England, France, Italy, and Spain could not have been any more different. The swiftness with which literary scholars sometimes bypass Latin American independence and seamlessly move from a colonial to a neocolonial Latin America while leaving Europe an unchanged imperial center—after a mostly perfunctory acknowledgment of the decline of the Iberian empires—does not do justice to the complexity of the transformations taking place at the time that would affect the future configuration of power across the Atlantic, and indeed the world.

At the start of the nineteenth century, Spain and Portugal, until then the dominant European empires, found themselves occupied by a foreign power and fighting their own wars of independence from Napoleonic occupation (known in English as the Peninsular War). Moreover, Portugal, renamed the United Kingdom of Portugal, Brazil, and the Algarve, was ruled for over a decade from Rio de Janeiro, which became the de facto capital of the empire, stripping Lisbon of that title while Portugal itself was governed mostly by British forces. Spain and Portugal, which had begun their own processes of state rationalization and modernization under the enlightened monarchic regimes of Charles III and Joseph I respectively, saw those processes altered by the Napoleonic invasion and the ensuing wars. From then on, amid regime changes and bloody civil wars between liberals and conservatives, Spain and Portugal would struggle with an idea of modernity that was already inevitably mediated by foreignness ("afrancesados" versus "patriotas") and by the peninsula's new subordinate position in the global political order.[6] Latin American independence came about, then, in the aftermath of its metropolitan centers' own wars of "independence." In Robert Young's definition, "neocolonialism denotes a continuing economic hegemony that means that the postcolonial state remains in a situation of dependence on its former masters, and that the former masters continue to act in a colonialist manner towards formerly colonized states" (45). This term is, then, clearly insufficient and even misleading when used to explain the case of Spanish America, especially taking into account that one reason for the independence movements was precisely to expand the region's economy beyond the monopoly imposed by the Spanish crown. Spanish American nations entered the global economy dependent on foreign capital and investments, but not those of their former masters. In fact, the former masters themselves were in a similar "neocolonial" condition with regard to new masters. For most of the nineteenth century, Spain and Portugal remained economically dependent on northern European capital, mainly British. In the North, while Canada remained a colony of Britain, the United States went from a collection of British colonies to an emerging imperial power by century's end, although not without first waging another war against Britain (1812–1815), curiously enough itself a by-product of the Peninsular War. The so-called War of 1812 helped the United States consolidate its sense of independence and, perhaps more importantly, its growing military might.[7] The imperial trajectory of the United States would still require a genocidal campaign against its Native American population, the annexation of over half of Mexico's territory, the devastation of a terrible civil war, and the opening of the country to massive immigration.

By the end of the nineteenth century, things in the Americas looked dramatically different from its beginning. The United States had intervened in the Cuban war of independence and defeated Spain in 1898, taking away its last American and Pacific colonies. Moreover, the United States had surpassed in economic, political, and military power its own former metropolis, Britain. To the south, countries like Argentina, Uruguay, Venezuela, and Chile had far stronger economies than their former metropolis, Spain. In fact, by 1913 Argentina had a larger per capita income than not only that of Spain, but also those of France, Germany, and the Netherlands (Della Paolera and Taylor 3). It is hardly a surprise, then, that scores of Europeans were emigrating to the Americas in search of a better life. In Latin America, the exhilaration of making history as the wars of independence gave way to the new American republics; the political, economic, social, and cultural transformations taking place across the continent; the increasing mobility of peoples, ideas, and material goods; and a growing sense of cosmopolitanism held tremendous significance. These lay behind both a sense of superiority with regard to their European ex-metropolis and other regions, and a conviction that in some ways Latin Americans were among the world's avant-garde. This situation gave many Latin Americans—modernista writers among them—a sense of entitlement that one should not dismiss.

This book takes a new look at both modernismo and the way transatlantic modernities took shape in the nineteenth century. This requires taking Spanish American independence as the groundbreaking event it was and recognizing not only that modernity began in the sixteenth century, as Enrique Dussel and Walter Mignolo have argued, but also and as importantly that it did not suddenly end in 1810, as they have also implied: modernity was behind the revolutionary acts sweeping the continent from north to south and their subsequent republican political experiments of nation building. Likewise, this project entails dismantling the myths of European modernity and examining both the historical changes that took place across the Atlantic during the century and the significance of their impact at the time. This means accepting that Latin American independence is one of the defining events of nineteenth-century modernity. To say, as is common practice, that Latin American independence was "inspired by the revolutions which had transformed Europe and the USA" (Hobsbawm, *Revolution* 32) is, at best, only relatively true and does little for our understanding of the region in the nineteenth century, reducing Latin America to the status of the merely derivative and hence of little significance.[8] Yet, by the time of the Argentine May Revolution and the Mexican Grito de Dolores in 1810, the only European revolution available for "inspiration" was that of France, which was still far from transforming Europe itself. Interestingly enough, one of the first turning points in European politics after the French Revolution was the political experiment of the Cortes of Cadiz in Spain, which, with the participation of Spanish American delegates, gave birth to the term "liberalism." The Latin American revolutionary wars and the liberal projects that ensued were an integral part of "Western modernity." As we shall see, to consider them otherwise is to consider them ahistorically and from the point of view of a concept of the modern that is defined by exclusion: that is, when only the specific manifestations of mostly British and Anglo American (and to a lesser extent French) modernities are used to define a concept that is then universalized and turned into the gold standard of modernity.

Dismantling the myths of modernity further opens the study of the nineteenth century to the possibility of making connections that remain hidden otherwise. One such connection is that the historical development of Latin America finds many parallels with developments taking place in southern Europe. The notion of a monolithic Europe hides rather than illuminates these connections and, in so doing, prevents us from examining them and their implications. In fact, southern Europe's modernization processes often followed patterns similar to those in Latin America. Not coincidentally, there is another factor uniting these two regions of the West: the progressive racializing of modernity that took place in the nineteenth century and that effectively divided *both* Europe *and* the Americas between a Protestant Anglo-Germanic "modern" North and a Catholic Latin "backward" South. This, as we shall see, was particularly the case in the opposition between the Anglo-Saxon and the Spanish "races."[9] This racial distinction with religious undertones, which is arguably anecdotal today in Europe but still central in the imaginary of the Americas, was powerful enough to have significant economic, political, social, and cultural effects—powerful enough, in fact, to profoundly mediate from the start the way modernity took shape in the nineteenth century in these regions and the way modernity would come to be defined from then on.

Although the North-South divide proved to be more powerful in the long run, the relationship between the Atlantic's East and West resulting from their colonial past was, in contradictory ways, still very much alive in the long nineteenth century. Latin American Creoles, as Carlos Alonso has argued, understood themselves through a "narrative of futurity" (*Burden* 8) that separated them both from their former European masters and the indigenous and African subalterns, all of whom were figured as belonging to the past. Although Alonso does not say it, this narrative was also at work in the United States. In both cases, it was powerful enough to break political ties with their metropolis, but certainly not so strong as to counter the hegemony of a European cultural tradition that, to a very large extent, still defined the identity of northern and southern Creoles and exercised its authority over their cultural production. North and South American Creoles spent the rest of the century grappling with the anxiety of European influence. Indeed, as I argue in this book, Spanish American modernismo was to become the first instance in which the anxiety of European influence was not only overcome, but its directionality actually reversed, as modernismo imposed itself in Spain and, removing its literary authority, left its former European metropolis coming to terms with the unprecedented anxiety of (Latin) American influence.

Cultural theoretical models based on an economic neocolonial concept have tended to reduce the nineteenth century to a binary opposition of metropolitan Europe and United States versus neocolonial and colonial Latin America that does not correspond to the changing complexities of historical (political, cultural, social) events along the long century. Thus, they cannot do justice to Spanish America's experience of modernity nor to the remarkable achievements of its cultural production. This is particularly so at a time when language, literature, and culture were considered in symbiotic relationship with national and transnational identities, and when politics and economics were fueled by "civilizing" missions.

Postcolonial studies, although closely tied to neocolonial frameworks, have offered a more nuanced understanding of the relationship between culture and power in postcolonial contexts. However, since the 1990s when Klor de Alva famously argued against the use of the term "postcolonial" to describe the (Latin) American experience after independence (which he thought better understood as a civil war between Europeans than as a war for independence by colonial subjects), and Lawrence Buell and Peter Hulme pushed in the opposite direction for the inclusion of the United States within the postcolonial (based on the cultural power differential between Creoles and British), the concept of postcoloniality has had a troubled relationship with the Americas. I believe that the reason behind these troubles can be found largely in the fact that postcolonial theory finds its ultimate horizon in a limited and limiting concept of modernity, the one born out of the ethnoreligious division between North and South that took place in the long nineteenth century. This is quite clear in the following definition by one of postcoloniality's most influential theorists, Gayatri Chakravorty Spivak: "Let us learn to discriminate the terms *colonialism*—in the European formation stretching from the mid-eighteenth to the mid-twentieth centuries—*neocolonialism*—dominant economic, political, and culturalist maneuvers emerging in our century after the uneven dissolution of the territorial empires—and *postcoloniality*—the contemporary global condition, since the first term is supposed to have passed or be passing into the second" (172).

Spivak effectively leaves the Americas out of the global postcolonial condition since, according to her definitions, colonialism did not even begin until the mid-eighteenth century and evolved into neocolonialism in the twentieth. For Spivak, then, North and South American colonization and decolonization processes are not even on the map. As is implicit in Spivak's chronology, the United States enters colonial history as a metropolitan/imperial nation whose own colonial past is erased. Latin America, however, remains unaccounted for in her scheme, since by the time colonial history is supposed to have begun, most of Latin America was no longer a colony, yet not a metropolitan center either. Nonetheless, even if very briefly, Spivak does include Latin America within the contemporary global condition of postcoloniality in her book (117–18). The place of Latin America in Spivak's text, as in a large part of postcolonial studies, is thus a paradoxical one: postcoloniality without colonialism. Spivak's gesture is symptomatic of the founding fallacy of postcolonial theory: its central concept, "colonialism," is defined exclusively from the concrete experience of the second wave of British (and, to a far lesser extent, French) imperialism. This historically determined and geopolitically specific experience is universalized and considered the *origin* of *all* colonial, neocolonial, and hence postcolonial conditions.[10] It is ironic that Spivak compels us to both historicize and read critically: "We might want to help ourselves by a greater effort at historical contextualization. Yet this too, if unaccompanied by the habit of critical reading, may feed the Eurocentric arrogance in Sartre's declaration: 'there is always some way of understanding [the other] if one has sufficient information'" (173). The problem here is that one cannot read critically what one does not know; one cannot historicize what one already considers outside history.[11] This is, ultimately, the problem with the way postcolonial studies have been carried out in the past decades, a problem that is a result of the archive from within which postcolonial theory was formulated. While Joseba Gabilondo opts for considering the entire "Hispanic Atlantic" a space different from the West (introduction 112), my argument here is that this is precisely how it has been constructed for the last two hundred and some years. I find it more productive, instead, to explore how the Hispanic Atlantic, as an integral part of "the West," can help expose the biased and skewed ways in which "Western" history has been written.

Modernity and coloniality—inseparably linked, as Dussel and Mignolo have argued—began with the Iberian colonization of the Americas in the sixteenth century. In the mid-eighteenth century, however, northern European discourse began to monopolize the concept of the modern, writing that date as its origin and erasing more than two centuries of modernity and coloniality. As a result, Hispanic history and cultural and intellectual production were excluded from the "modern" archive, despite having made that archive possible; as a consequence, Spanish ceased to be considered a language of knowledge and scholarship.[12] In the last few decades, postcolonial studies have reenacted that same process. The silence of postcolonial studies on Latin America is simply the effect of having as their intellectual horizon the imperial archive of north European modernity/colonialism, the postcolonial critique of which simultaneously reaffirms it. My point is not, of course, to substitute one imperial claim (the British) for another (the Spanish) but to explore the hidden links between both and to start working toward a better understanding of the wide diversity of imperial, colonial, and postcolonial dynamics since 1492 and the multiple connections, continuities, and discontinuities among them.

Many events that reshaped the Atlantic in the nineteenth century were not detached and unrelated to developing events in other areas of the globe. As I discuss in this book, they gave birth to concepts that are central to the way we understand the world today, but that, although historically grounded, have become naturalized as always already there. Among these are an idea of "Western" modernity/modernization that uncritically generalizes, and covers up, what once were very concrete manifestations of specifically British and Anglo American developments; an idea of Europe that reduces its southern half to oblivion; and an idea of America that considers its North as always already Western, while its South is neither West nor quite anything else, and remains in its own kind of limbo. The history of the Atlantic in the nineteenth century also had less abstract repercussions. As the first anticolonial wars, the revolutions in the Americas served as an inspiration to other struggles and acts of resistance. On the other hand, as Marshall, Young, and others have noted, the independence of the United States had a significant impact on the way Britain would think of itself as empire, forcing it to reconsider its new imperial policies elsewhere. Similarly, if perhaps less obviously, Latin American independence also played a part in the construction of the British imperial imaginary, in which it became renewed evidence for the centuries-old Black Legend about Spain. Indeed, it can be argued that the British idea of a commonwealth of nations was, in part at least, born in opposition to the "tyranny" of the Spanish empire. As one of the founders of the Colonial Society (today the Royal Commonwealth Society) said in 1858, showing a certain amnesia about the events of 1776: "The Australian colonies stood in the same relation to England . . . that Latin America had stood to 'Old Spain.' But the Australian colonies would always remain a part of the British Empire, while most of Spain's colonies had proved eager to break away. This came from the wonderful way that England treated her colonies, so unlike the way that Spain had treated hers" (Beasley 58–59).[13] Furthermore, across the Atlantic from Britain, as María DeGuzmán has shown, the United States also began to imagine itself as "the 'good' empire that is not one" (xii) precisely against figures of Spain.

My study aims, then, both to break away from the limitations of neocolonial interpretive frameworks and to expand postcolonial thinking by beginning to explore the constitution of the nineteenth-century "modern" archive and to open it to other texts, in particular those written in Spanish. In an insightful discussion about Edward Said's *Culture and Imperialism*, Mary Louise Pratt suggested that "the difference in chronology with respect to colonization and decolonization seems to be one of the main reasons the Americas have remained almost entirely off the map of the colonial discourse movement and colonial studies in general (though in less charitable moments, *one suspects that the main barrier has been the need to learn so unprestigious a language as Spanish*)" (Robbins 4; my emphasis). I find Pratt's aside about prestige (or lack thereof) extremely relevant and a productive place to begin the study of modernismo and nineteenth-century modernity in a transatlantic context, for, as I argue in this book, the struggle for symbolic capital and prestige in the transnational cultural field and within the larger field of power was a defining element of the nineteenth-century Atlantic. It was precisely the place of the Spanish language and Hispanic cultures within a changing global order that became a central preoccupation of Spanish America's first groundbreaking postcolonial literary project: modernismo.

The reason modernismo remains such a difficult movement to explain, despite the vast critical attention it has received, resides in the frameworks from which it has been mainly approached. Comparing Spanish American modernity to a fictionally perfect European modernity has meant either placing modernismo and Spanish America outside the modern from the start, or looking for reasons why their modernity was imperfect. By both undoing the myth of a homogenously modern nineteenth-century Europe and exploring the formation, power, and pervasiveness of the racial discourse of modernity, we can begin to understand the complexity of the period and its consequences for today. Modernismo confronted the irony of being modern but excluded from modernity. The fact that its many and far-reaching achievements remain understudied today and entirely absent from discussions of modernism and postcoloniality beyond Hispanic studies speaks to the lasting influence of the exclusionary discourses they faced.

CHAPTER I

The Myths of European Modernity

> There is a radical difference between Europeans and Spanish Americans: when Baudelaire indicts progress as "a grotesque idea," or when Rimbaud denounces industry, their experiences of progress and industry are real, direct, whereas those of Spanish Americans are derivative.
>
> —Octavio Paz, *Children of the Mire*

> It is also necessary to bear in mind . . . that by 1913 France . . . was not an industrial or truly industrialized country. . . . France remained fundamentally a peasant-based rural economy.
>
> —François Crouzet, "The Historiography of French Economic Growth in the Nineteenth Century"

> What is more significant in all these cases is that the modernity of the states in question is a modernity for other peoples, an optical illusion nourished by envy and hope, by inferiority feelings and the need for emulation.
>
> —Fredric Jameson, *A Singular Modernity*

The late nineteenth century in Spanish America was saturated with writers who were coming to grips with the changes in the texture of life brought about by modernization, depicting an environment of transformations and uncertainty full of possibilities and paths of exploration. In 1882, Cuban José Martí addressed the profound effects of the times on art, the artist, and society at large in his famous prologue to Juan Antonio Pérez Bonalde's "Poema del Niágara," while Mexican Manuel Gutiérrez Nájera had an ironic flâneur hop onto a trolley and gaze at a growing Mexico City in his "La novela del tranvía" (The Novel of the Trolley). In 1888, Nicaraguan poet Rubén Darío first coined the literary term "modernismo," and Spanish critic Juan Valera saw all the main issues of "modern life" addressed in Darío's collection *Azul* . . . (Blue . . . ; hereafter referred to as *Azul*). In 1895, Amado Nervo's novel *El bachiller* caused quite a stir in Mexico and a year later, Colombian José Asunción Silva and Uruguayan Carlos Reyles wrote novels that explicitly addressed a new kind of reading public. That same year, José Enrique Rodó, also Uruguayan, published an essay about this new literature in which he strived to convey what almost a century later Marshall Berman would label "the experience of modernity": "el espectáculo de una cultura en cuyo seno hierven a un tiempo todas las ideas y todas las pasiones, en cuyo ambiente se entrechocan todas las resonancias del Deseo, del Entusiasmo y del Dolor, concurso extraño de aspiraciones sin armonía, de dudas sin respuesta, de contradicciones sin solución, de voces de esperanza y de angustia" (164) [the spectacle of a culture at the center of which all ideas and all passions are boiling at once, in whose milieu all the echoes of Desire, Enthusiasm, and Pain are crashing together, a strange confluence of aspirations without harmony, of doubts without answer, of contradictions without solution, of voices of hope and of anguish].[1]

It is striking then that despite the clear modernista connection with the modern, the critical discourse on modernismo has generally been skeptical—when not dismissive—of that connection, considering it derivative, imperfect, or phantasmagoric. Despite recognizing modernismo's many literary achievements, scholarship has had a propensity to highlight the movement's "debts" to European literature. Even when traditional formalist criticism, largely focused on identifying elements of European artistic trends in modernista texts, gave way to contemporary approaches that have placed the movement in its sociohistorical context, the question of European influence has continued to hold center stage in Spanish American modernista studies. To be sure, by reading modernismo in relation to economic, political, and social forces in the context of the global economy at the turn of the century, contemporary approaches have advanced tremendously our understanding of modernismo and provided a more nuanced vision of its complexities and its relationship to both American and European cultures.[2] Yet, when exploring the relationship between modernismo and nineteenth-century modernity, critics have tended to doubt the concepts and experiences articulated so forcefully by the writers themselves. For some decades, critics have asked variations of the same question: Was there *really* an experience of modernity to speak of in Spanish America? Were Martí, Darío, Rodó, and their many peers *actually* experiencing modernity themselves or were they simply living it vicariously, "derivative[ly]," as Octavio Paz put it early on (*Hijos* 132; *Children* 91), acting *as if* they were modern, in Aníbal González's view? Was Spanish America "forced," as Marshall Berman quickly and anachronistically assumes, "to build on fantasies and dreams of modernity," (232) hence revealing its modernity as fundamentally rhetorical, a cultural discourse in a perpetual state of self-contradiction, as Carlos Alonso has argued? Or was it a real but imperfect experience that generated an irreducibly heterogeneous discourse, as Julio Ramos believes? Was modernismo an act akin to transculturation, as Ángel Rama suggested, and Latin American modern culture a peculiar hybrid, as Néstor

García Canclini has famously formulated? In this regard, past and present critical approaches to modernismo and Spanish American modernity seem to share a similar view, as they consider both phenomena adoptions of European models and thus either simply rhetorical or unevenly and imperfectly adjusted to Spanish American reality.[3] Having assumed a somehow imperfect modernity in Spanish America, then, and despite their insights and their enrichment of modernista and modernity studies, these critical works implicitly or explicitly begin with the assumption of a perfect modernization process elsewhere to which the modernista experience cannot ever live up, a point of departure that undercuts the complexities of the movement, its achievements and implications. To a large extent, the critical view that Spanish American modernistas lived a mirage has rendered modernismo itself ghostly, written out of discourses of modernity and modernism. Where does this assumption of Spanish America's imperfect modernity come from, and what are the consequences for our understanding of modernismo and nineteenth-century Spanish America?

In this chapter, I argue that most approaches to Spanish American literature and culture and the way in which research questions have been formulated have been affected by the myths of European modernity, which have prevented scholars from thinking of modernismo beyond a colonial matrix that, in many instances, they set out to critique in the first place.[4] In other words, scholarship has followed the unidirectionality of European discourses that establish the existence of a perfect and even modernity in a homogeneously singular Europe, in comparison to which Spanish American modernity is always and necessarily imperfect, imitative, or derivative, when not simply inexistent. Spanish American neocolonial difference thus is made possible only by affirming European imperial sameness. Instead, I propose foregrounding both Europe's own heterogeneity and modernity's inherent strangeness to itself. This allows us to look at the nineteenth-century Atlantic as a complex space of shifting power and cultural relations that redrew the dividing lines between North and South, East and West, and that, in the process, redefined the concept of modernity.

From Edmundo O'Gorman's seminal *La invención de América* (1958) to the critical insights of poststructural and postcolonial theory to the liberation and decolonization projects of Enrique Dussel, Aníbal Quijano, and Walter Mignolo, we have learned that Europe needed to define its other in order to define itself. Europeans could believe themselves to be modern only by telling its others that they were not. Thus, European discourse imposed a vision of modern time that worked not only diachronically but also synchronically across space: its others were, at best, Europe's past.[5] However, while the effects of this process have been thoroughly explored in the colonial world, their implications for our understanding of Europe's own modernization have not. As a consequence, the idea that nineteenth-century Spanish America somehow missed the train of modernity while a homogeneous

Europe was traveling in first class is, despite different theoretical approaches to the period, the most pervasive notion determining our view of modernismo. In other words, we may have learned to distrust European discourse on its others, but we may still be caught in the trap of trusting European discourse on itself.

The Myths of (European) Modernity

From Modernity to Modernization

The first and possibly most difficult question to answer is what we mean when we speak of modernity. As we shall see later in this chapter, there are at least two separate but intimately connected definitions of modernity, which Enrique Dussel dubbed the worldly, or first modernity, and the provincial, or second modernity. Although both are imperial/colonial in origin, the first made possible the second, so that, in fact, they ultimately are but two stages of a single modernity. Understood this way, modernity is a process that began in the colonial act that "created" America for Europe in 1492, and thus America has always been modern. Indeed, it was America's very coming into being in Western discourse and economic and social fabric that made modernity possible: "Amerindia forms part of 'modernity' since the moment of the conquest and colonization (the mestizo world in Latin America is the only one that is as old as modernity), for it contained the first 'barbarian' that modernity needed in its definition" (Dussel, "Beyond" 18). Marshall Berman, author of the influential *All That Is Solid Melts into Air* and one of the most widely cited theorists of modernism, acknowledges this long history of the concept of modernity when he affirms that "although most of the people have probably experienced modernity as a radical threat to all their history and traditions, it has, in the course of five centuries, developed a rich history and a plenitude of traditions of its own." In the spirit of such a long history and experiential variety, Berman explains his intention "to explore and chart these traditions, to understand the ways in which they can nourish and enrich our own modernity" (16). Alas, despite such a promising beginning, Berman soon forgets this temporal and spatial scope, and radically limits modernity to post-Enlightenment "Europe" and the United States. In other words, Berman circumscribes it to the provincial, or second, concept of modernity. According to this formulation, modernity began in the eighteenth century so is but two centuries old. Although connected at first to aesthetics and philosophy, in the nineteenth century this concept of modernity became associated almost exclusively with (northern) European material, technological, and, to a lesser degree, political changes, understood as the necessary result of "modern" (i.e., Enlightened) reason. In the 1950s, this concept of modernity was renamed "modernization," a term born in the social sciences and linked to the idea of development. Jürgen Habermas, perhaps the most influential theorist of (the second) modernity, offers a classic definition of modernity/modernization:

> The concept of modernization refers to a bundle of processes that are cumulative and mutually reinforcing: to the formation of capital and the mobilization of resources; to the development of the forces of production and the increase in the productivity of labor; to the establishment of centralized political power and the formation of national identities; to the proliferation of rights of political participation, of urban forms of life, and of formal schooling; to the secularization of values and norms; and so on. (*Philosophical Discourse* 2)[6]

In current scholarly discussions about modernism (or virtually any other topic, literary or otherwise), "modernity" and "modernization," "modern" and "modernized," have become virtual synonyms. It is this second modernity, or modernization, that for Berman is the condition sine qua non for the development of modernism. For Berman, then, the "experience of modernity" is the "dialectics of modernization and modernism" (16). This second stage of modernity (i.e., modernization) is also the central concept in the critical tradition on Spanish American modernismo and modernity, and thus questions regarding the relationship between modernismo and modernity in Spanish America have been formulated and answered from within this framework.[7]

Reproducing the Myth: The Legacy of Octavio Paz

In Octavio Paz's *Los hijos del limo* (1974; published in English as *Children of the Mire* [1974]), which Aníbal González has rightly called the first sustained study on modernity in Spanish (*Crónica* 8), we find a foundational instance of this critical tradition. Octavio Paz helped establish a way of looking at Spanish American modernization that captured the critical imagination of modernista studies.[8] Also, and perhaps unfortunately, Paz's vision of an absent Spanish American modernization process has had an uncommon influence on scholarship outside Hispanic studies. In *Los hijos del limo*, Octavio Paz offered a devastating view of nineteenth-century Spanish America, the negative of Europe in almost every aspect:

> Un feudalismo disfrazado de liberalismo burgués, un absolutismo sin monarca pero con reyezuelos: los señores presidentes. Así se inició el reino de la máscara, el imperio de la mentira. Desde entonces la corrupción del lenguaje, la infección semántica, se convirtió en nuestra enfermedad endémica; la mentira se volvió constitucional, consustancial.... El positivismo en América Latina no fue la ideología de una burguesía liberal interesada en el progreso industrial y social como en

> Europa, sino de una oligarquía de grandes terratenientes. . . . Hay una diferencia radical entre los europeos y los hispanoamericanos: cuando Baudelaire dice que el progreso es "una idea grotesca" o cuando Rimbaud denuncia a la industria, sus experiencias del progreso y de la industria son reales, directas, mientras que las de los hispanoamericano son derivadas. . . . La realidad de nuestras naciones no era moderna: no la industria, la democracia y la burguesía, sino las oligarquías feudales y el militarismo. (126, 127, 132)

> [Feudalism disguised as bourgeois liberalism, absolutism without a monarch but with petty kings—the presidents. And so the kingdom of the mask was born, the empire of lies. From then on the corruption of language, the semantic infection, became an endemic malady; lies became constitutional, consubstantial. . . . Positivism in Latin America was not the ideology of a liberal bourgeoisie interested in industrial and social progress, as it was in Europe, but of an oligarchy of big landowners. . . . There is a radical difference between Europeans and Spanish Americans: when Baudelaire indicts progress as "a grotesque idea," or when Rimbaud denounces industry, their experiences of progress and industry are real, direct, whereas those of Spanish Americans are derivative. . . . The reality of our nations was not a modern one: not industry, democracy, or bourgeoisie, only feudal oligarchies and militarism. (86, 87, 91)]

Powerful and effective as Paz's writing always is, his appraisal of nineteenth-century modernity in Spanish America, of its process of modernization, is more poetic than historical. Paz considers Spanish American cultural history "delayed" with respect to Europe's and considers modernismo Spanish America's true romanticism. In this regard, Carlos Alonso has rightly argued that Paz's study is contaminated by modernity itself, "marked by the dialectical, chronological drive at the heart of modernity that he so thoroughly exposed in his study" (*Regional* 21). Paz's text is also contaminated by modernity in a different but related manner, not only temporally but spatially, the other side of the same coin, that is, Paz assumes a vision of European space (from which the Iberian Peninsula is excluded) as harmoniously and homogenously modern, against which Spanish American modernity cannot even begin to compare. The general opposition between Europe and Spanish America as perfect/imperfect that permeates Paz's assessment of nineteenth-century modernity represents fairly well the assumptions about "development" and "periphery" that implicitly or explicitly continue to operate today.

Discursive Tensions and the Persistence of the Myth

Carlos Alonso's *The Burden of Modernity* (1998) is one of the two most important book-length studies on Spanish American nineteenth-century modernity to come out since Octavio Paz's pioneering work. (The other is Julio Ramos's *Desencuentros de la modernidad en América Latina* [1989; *Divergent Modernities* (2001)], discussed in Chapter 2.) Alonso argues that Spanish American nineteenth-century cultural modernity (as well as late twentieth-century "postmodernity") has been fundamentally rhetorical. He proposes that the articulation of Spanish American cultural discourse is marked by the tension between identification and rejection of the modern. According to Alonso, Creoles based their fight for independence, cultural difference, and authority to speak about themselves on what he calls a narrative of futurity, which established Spanish America as the realm of the future, while it relegated both Europe and Native America to the past. Yet, as Spanish America became independent, Europe's increasing claim over modernity (i.e., futurity) threatened to undo America's distinctiveness and authority: "Hence, at the precise moment when Spanish American intellectuals moved to assert their specificity or made a claim for cultural distinctness, they did so by using a rhetoric that unavoidably reinforced the cultural myths of metropolitan superiority" (20). In this way, Alonso characterizes the Spanish American discursive practice as in perpetual contradiction with itself, much like a sentence whose predicate negates its subject, both identifying with and rejecting the modern, searching for ways to preserve an authority to speak that always seems to slip away. Alonso builds a compelling argument, to be sure, and his work is moved by a salutary effort to think Spanish American literature beyond the limits of dependency models.

Alonso's own text, however, is an example of the very rhetorical tension he analyzes: his thesis about Spanish American difference is threatened by the possibility that Spanish American cultural discourse may not be so different from Europe's after all. Citing Paul de Man's analysis of the inherent contradiction of literary modernity and Matei Calinescu's classic definition of the tension between cultural and material modernities (reworked by Berman as the dialectic between modernism and modernization), Alonso is faced with a dilemma not unlike the one faced by Spanish American Creoles after independence: "For it would appear that the problematic that I have identified as intrinsic to the Spanish American rhetorical situation in fact characterizes the experience of modernity in metropolitan circles as well, thereby complicating if not outright disallowing its viability as a marker of discursive specificity" (*Burden* 30). Finding himself in a bind, Alonso is compelled to fall back on Paz's argument: the lack of Spanish American modernization sets it apart from the metropolitan center. Appealing to Berman's "modernism of underdevelopment" (itself reminiscent of Paz's ideas), Alonso renders Spanish American modernization ghostly: "In Spanish America the appropriation of the discursive modalities of metropolitan modernity have had to contend with the absence of its material antagonist in its midst, or more precisely, with its phantasmatic presence as the always distant and assumed reality of the metropolis" (32).[9] Aware of the dangers of this move, Alonso breaks with Paz and Berman (as well as other theories of dependency and transculturation that Alonso places under critique) in one important way: he does not seem to take European modernization at face value, but suggests instead that it was "assumed" by Spanish Americans regardless of its real existence. Referring to Dussel, Alonso speaks of the "myth of modernity" as one of the prevalent narratives of legitimacy in nineteenth-century Spanish America, that is, "the belief that there were metropolitan foci out of which the modern emanated and which by means of a rippled and delayed expansion through time and space would eventually transform the material and cultural orders of those societies that languished in the outer confines of the system" (19).

In this way, Alonso resolves the problem by textualizing it. Modernization is ultimately irrelevant outside the text that imagines it, "regardless of the relative level of advancement of the writer's society at any given time." It is a rhetorical place, not a geopolitical location, Alonso says: "The 'somewhere else' where the modern is thought to reside for the Spanish American intellectual should not be construed as a discrete place or concrete set of historical and economic circumstances, but rather as what, in effect, it was: a conceptual and rhetorical category" (32). Ultimately, Alonso cannot completely resolve the tension of his own text and concludes his argument affirming that the Spanish American rhetorical situation is "to be sure, founded on the historical and economic reality of Spanish America as a neocolonial, peripheral zone, . . . since the inconsistent modernity of the region is a direct result of its economic subservience to and dependence on the metropolis" (48). Thus, Alonso falls prey to the very myth of modernity that he identified, as he imagines the existence of a "consistent" modernization "somewhere else," which now rather than a conceptual category turns out to be the very concrete geopolitical space of the metropolis. In this way, Alonso's argument does not diverge substantially from theories like Paz's or Berman's, or, as we shall see, from Julio Ramos's notion of "uneven modernity."[10] Nonetheless, in its very rhetorical tension, Alonso's study opens a compelling space to begin exploring the implications of the many myths of modernity.

When Alonso mentions Latin America's economic dependence on the metropolis, he is referring to neither Spain nor Portugal, of course. In fact, in a very insightful note to the main text, Alonso briefly suggests a parallel between Spanish America and its former metropolitan center, Spain. Bringing up Spain's troubled relationship with modernity and its similarities with the Spanish American case, he identifies a common experience of economic and material dependence. Thus, in Spain "the rhetorical dialectics that I describe . . . were also set into motion; that is, even in those texts that would seem to argue for the unbridled adoption of the program of modernity, there was simultaneously the expression of a desire to distance oneself from the modern, an affirmation of the incommensurableness of the local by the . . . instruments of modernity" (*Burden* 185). Unfortunately, Alonso does not take this insight any further nor does he examine the implications that such connection may have for both his argument about Spanish America and for our understanding of modernity at large.[11]

Jesús Torrecilla in *La imitación colectiva* (Collective Imitation) had discussed the existence of a similar tension to the one identified by Alonso for Spanish America in nineteenth-century Spanish literary discourse: "Los autores españoles conscientes de pertenecer a una sociedad atrasada experimentan una tensión irresoluble entre su deseo de ser originales en un sentido temporal (escribir algo nuevo o moderno) y su necesidad de ser originales en un sentido espacial (escribir algo auténticamente español)" (226). [Spanish authors, aware of belonging to a backward society, experienced an unresolvable tension between their desire to be original in a temporal sense (to write something new or modern) and their need to be original in a spatial sense (to write something authentically Spanish).][12] More recently, Michael Iarocci, in his groundbreaking examination of Spanish romanticism, *Properties of Modernity*, revisited Spain's peripheral position within "modern Europe" and the problematic but insightful relationship of Spanish cultural discourse with "European modernity." Iarocci challenges notions of "perfect" or "even" modernities and rightly argues that European modernity may be understood as "one of the West's big lies" (39), a myth, or a language game; nonetheless, he adds: "what can be easily overlooked by adopting such options, however, is the impact of the narrative of the modern as a centuries-long representational legacy not easily forgotten, dismissed, or analyzed away by those who were not the subjects of the celebratory tale" (40). In spite of this observation and in a vein similar to Alonso's, Iarocci does not pursue this line of thought and prefers to leave the myth standing unquestioned, finding it more productive, instead, to ask "whether peripherally modern cultures might not be privileged rather than deficient sites for inquiry into the modern" (176–77).

The problem with this approach is threefold. First, it performs a simple inversion of values, favoring now the "periphery" as the privileged site of enunciation over that of what remains a homogeneous "center" without further inquiry into the validity of the categories themselves and investing "Europe's other" with an aura of insight by the mere fact of being other.[13] Second, this critical position cannot but perpetuate the myth and its already established damaging effects for those "not the subjects of the celebratory tale," for it would be naïve to think that the myth of modernity has lost its power over them or over those on the celebratory side. Third, perpetuating the myth is a testament to its persistent power to determine the way in which scholarly discourse approaches the modern, preventing it from seeing the unsuspected, that which does not fit the established "tale"; consequently, it prevents us from formulating other possible narratives, not only about the "periphery," but also about the "center" itself, and attaining in the process a better understanding of the modern.[14]

The myth of modernity is, thus, more pervasive than Alonso or Iarocci assume. It affected not only the self-perception of many Spanish Americans (and

Spaniards, among many others, including north Europeans themselves), but also our own critical analysis of the conditions of Spanish American and European modernities. It has led scholars to disbelieve perceptions that *do not* conform to (or that expose) this myth and, therefore, to either ignore them or explain them away. The case of Spanish American modernismo is a perfect example: by turning into fact the perception of a lack of modernization that many nineteenth-century intellectuals had, scholars have denied the modernistas the experience of modernity that they so clearly claimed for themselves and the region on the assumption that *their* perception *must* be wrong.[15]

Furthermore, a central aspect of the myth of nineteenth-century modernity, that is, the belief that the modern was "somewhere else," is not exclusive to the Spanish American experience (or the Spanish), nor does the modern seem to have always been located in the "metropolitan center." After all, it was not the Spanish Americans who migrated massively to Europe in the nineteenth and early twentieth centuries, but the other way around. If modernity implies a narrative of futurity, as Alonso says, for hundreds of thousands of Europeans (and hundreds of thousands from other regions across the world) the perception was that the modern, the future, was somewhere else too, and that somewhere else was in Spanish America. Argentine writer and statesman Domingo F. Sarmiento might represent the epitome of the Spanish American intellectual fallen prey to the myth that modernity resides somewhere else in the metropolitan center. However, in the 1840s while Sarmiento was seeing barbarism all over the Argentine interior, a Parisian in Honoré de Balzac's *Paysans* was seeing barbarism all over the French countryside: "You don't need to go to America to see savages" (qtd. in E. Weber 3). Indeed, as far as the perception of modernization is concerned, while most people across the globe in the nineteenth century thought that France was the very center of the modern, many French intellectuals perceived the modernization process brought about by the Second Empire as an external imposition, "the latest blow in what amounts to the Americanization of France" (Mathy 274).[16] For Parisian intellectuals, then, the modern also resided somewhere else, this time in the United States, and they decried its coming home. In negative or positive terms, the "somewhere else" of the modern, as we shall see, might turn out to be consubstantial to modernity itself.

Reconsidering European and American Modernization

Independence in the Americas: Breaking New Ground

A cursory look at the development of nineteenth-century European politics and social life hardly shows the easy, straightforward, and peaceful transition from ancient regime to industrialized well-functioning parliamentary democracies that

Octavio Paz and virtually everybody else dealing with the "third world" would have us believe and that we have tacitly accepted. If anything, modernization is a process, not a state of being that could be achieved overnight. I do not intend here to dwell on the intricacies of modern European history, much less to propose a celebration of Spanish America's modernization process. Rather, I want to stress the complexities of the historical situation at a time when the agents could neither know the future nor turn to any point of comparison or reference in the past. For, as Pratt has rightfully reminded us,

> one does not need to identify with the interests and prejudices of the creole elites to recognize the challenges South Americans faced at the moment of decolonization. "Independence" was not a known process, but one being improvised in the Americas even as they wrote. The words "decolonization" and "neocolonialism" did not exist. In both North and South America, this first wave of decolonization truly meant embarking on a future that was quite beyond the experience of European societies (as it remains today). . . . In this sense, Spanish America at independence was indeed a New World on its way down a path of social experimentation for which the European metropolis provided little precedent. The elites empowered to construct new hegemonies in America were challenged to imagine many things that did not exist, including themselves as citizen-subjects of republican America. (*Imperial Eyes* 175–76)

As obvious as this might seem after reading Pratt, her assessment of the radical novelty of the Spanish American experience stands as an important and necessary corrective to a critical tendency to look at the nineteenth century with the benefit of hindsight. Reading Pratt, it is difficult to imagine, in fact, a more fitting moment in which to acutely experience the modern than postindependence America.[17] From this point of view, Spanish America was indeed undergoing a radically new experience, a political experiment in self-governance and liberal republicanism that few nations were attempting at the time, including those of Europe. The sense of futurity that Alonso identifies as central to the Creole project of independence and nation building in the nineteenth century was clearly warranted. With most of Europe still under the ancient regime, modern liberalism was indeed primarily an American phenomenon.[18]

Liberalism and Nation Building

The experiment in nation building and constitutional government in the new Spanish American republics was far from smooth, but so it was in Europe and the United States. Neither Germany nor Italy achieved national unity until late in the nineteenth century and, even then, their commitment to the liberal state was certainly not without major problems.[19] This is not even taking into account their devastating totalitarian regimes, led by Hitler and Mussolini, only a few decades into the twentieth century. Ireland remained a colony of Britain until the twentieth century, and Norway was first part of Denmark and then of Sweden after a failed attempt at independence. In the South, Greece followed a troublesome constitutional path after fighting for its independence from the Ottoman Empire. Spain and Portugal spent much of the nineteenth century engulfed in bloody conflicts between liberals and conservatives after regaining their independence from Napoleonic France, itself a nation with a tumultuous postrevolutionary political trajectory.[20] Finally, most of central Europe was subsumed under the Austro-Hungarian empire, where, "inhabited by different races—German, Czechs, Poles, Ukrainians, Slovenes, Croats, Italians, and others—and with widely differing levels of economic development, it was the emperor and the imperial army and administration which alone gave it a sort of unity" (Joll 9). To this series of difficult national trajectories we should add the proliferation of serious transnational conflicts between European nations, most notably the Napoleonic and the Franco-Prussian wars, seeds of far worse horrors to come in the twentieth century. Politically, the success of liberalism and the consolidation of the modern liberal state were far from simple processes anywhere in the West, even in the United States, the poster child of liberalism.[21] There, Native Americans were largely exterminated or confined to reservations and subjected to a project of assimilation that failed to grant them citizenship (until 1924) or any political participation or power. Indeed, they were unable to vote in some states until the mid-twentieth century. Additionally, even after a traumatic civil war and the official abolition of slavery, African Americans generally remained disenfranchised until the Civil Rights and Voting Rights Acts a century later, particularly in the southern states, where slavery gave way to forced labor, debt peonage, and other forms of pseudo-feudal relations.

Within this context, then, nineteenth-century Spanish American politics may not seem less troubled, but certainly less exceptionally so, and definitely less "radically different," as Paz would have it. As Bushnell and Macaulay explain, Spanish America "opted for an essentially liberal model of development, in principle not unlike that adhered to by Great Britain, the United States, and, most of the time, also France. . . . Latin Americans embraced the model in question selectively, for they did not find all "liberal" precepts equally adaptable to their needs." Nevertheless, liberalism "did come as close as anything to serving as a dominant ideology" (12).[22]

Indeed, if liberalism is one of the pillars of nineteenth-century modernity, the Spanish American republics were "modern" sooner than most other nations across Europe and across the globe. The very term "liberalism" was born, not in England or France, but in Spain during the Cortes de Cádiz of 1812, with the active participation of Spanish American delegates. The Cortes were also the birthplace of the third constitution—after those of the United States and France—and the most liberal. The constitution of 1812 was meant to rule not only over Spain but over the entire empire, and although it never went into effect in America because of independence, it was an influential point of reference for the new American constitutions. Thus, the liberal constitution was short-lived in Spain, but in America liberalism fueled the end of the Spanish empire and the birth of the Spanish American republics.[23] Moreover, as Álvarez Junco has noted, the use of the term "War of Independence" to refer to the Spanish war against Napoleonic France did not come into existence and become solidified in Spain until the 1830s and 1840s; in other words, it was only *after* the Spanish American wars of independence that Spaniards imagined their uprising against the French as *their own* war of independence—a war which, let us remember, is considered a foundational moment in constructions of Spanish national identity. As Joseba Gabilondo has rightly noted: "The founding myth of Spanish nationalism is therefore a reaction against a French invasion and a surrogate form of the Latin American war of colonial independence" ("Historical" 259).[24] It becomes obvious, then, that this sequence of events could not be any more complex, more unusual, and indeed more fascinating.

Yet all this is lost when history is narrated only in binary terms of center-periphery, the significance of Spanish American independence ignored in favor of the always already (neo)colonial, and Europe's heterogeneity dismissed. Interestingly enough, in Bushnell and Macaulay's quoted description, Britain and the United States appear as the only consistent liberal models (since liberalism was apparently inconsistent in France and selective in Latin America), implying the Anglo Atlantic as the final measure of all other experiences, inevitably set up for failure or deviation from the assumed (Anglo American) norm. A more productive and historically accurate way of looking at these processes, however, might be to think of liberalism as a theoretical political and economic model that was implemented in a variety of different ways according to the diversity of national and regional contexts, none of which ultimately, as I have shown, came close (at first and for quite a while, if ever) to matching theory and practice. Not only is such an approach less normative, and hence less punitive, but also it allows us to establish interesting and fruitful connections between similar patterns in different regions, such as Latin America, France, and southern Europe.

The Social Composition of Modernity

The social composition of Spanish American liberalism is one of the elements most often mentioned by critics as evidence of the region's imperfect modernization. According to these critics, liberalism in Spanish America was the political project of only a small Creole elite. Yet, according to Hobsbawm—whose unapologetically Eurocentric vision of world history cannot possibly be doubted—the fight against the ancient regime was not so widespread in Europe, where "all revolutionaries regarded themselves, with some justification, as small elites of the emancipated and progressive operating among, and for the benefit of, a vast and inert mass of the ignorant and misled common people, which would no doubt welcome the liberation when it came" (*Revolution* 114–15). A recurrent form that revolutionary ideas would take in southern Europe in particular was that of the "secret insurrectionary brotherhood" (115) like the Italian-born *Carbonari*, whose influence reached from Greece to France and Spain. These so-called brotherhoods were the origin of the military uprisings or *pronunciamientos*, which Hobsbawm calls "'pure' insurrection" and would become "regular features of the Iberian and Latin American political scenes" (116). Seen in this context, instead of under the explicit or implicitly punitive light of comparing Latin America to a theoretically fulfilled Anglo American liberal model, the Creole revolutionary and liberal causes of the Spanish American republics, rather than exceptional, were similar to those in other regions and certainly more successful, since Latin America gained independence and established constitutional governments while much of Europe, including Germany, Austria, Italy, Spain, and at times even France, was still under the Old Regime.

Paz's vision of a failed modernization and his radical opposing of an all-powerful Spanish American landowning class (a remnant of the colonial past) and an industrial and progressive European liberal bourgeoisie are also skewed. Powerful landowners were not exclusive to Spanish America's postindependence but were a reality in Europe as well: "Over much of Europe . . . the power of the old landowning class was unchallenged in the countryside; and even those landlords who introduced scientific farming methods and equipment did little to alter the social organization on their estates" (Joll 32–33). Paz's picture of a European revolutionary bourgeoisie taking over power and progress while Latin America's social composition remained as it had been since the sixteenth century bears little resemblance to historical developments. On the contrary, as Álvarez Junco and Shubert explain, "there was a great deal of continuity in the social composition among European elites between the second half of the eighteenth and the first half of the nineteenth centuries" (35). The notion that modernization is inseparable from an all-powerful "liberal bourgeoisie" in Europe is also questionable, since "no country in Europe, with the exception of England, had a bourgeoisie strong enough to independently impose its own political agenda before 1850" (34–35).[25] The social composition, economic development, and political participation in Europe did not radically and immediately metamorphose in the post-Enlightenment period. Conversely, the new Spanish American republics were not merely a continuation of "the old colonies" either (Paz, *Hijos* 125; *Children* 85). Instead, Latin America was far more socially mobile and egalitarian than ever before. As Bushnell and Macaulay argue: "There is little justification for casting Latin American history as a struggle between the elites and the masses. . . . The masses were composed of many interest groups. This is no less true of the elites . . . , many of whom sprang from the masses. . . . The contest was not between the elites and the masses but among interest groups whose membership often cut across class lines" (53–54). Along these lines, Peter Guardino has shown that "Mexico's peasantry entered the national political stage in 1810 and was not even temporarily excluded until after 1876. Many peasants participated actively in the political and ideological conflicts of the period. The 'elite' political struggles of early-nineteenth-century Mexico were never substantially detached from the concrete realities of Mexican society" (6).[26] It was ironically because of the diversity of Mexico's social and political composition that many in the United States argued against its annexation after the war of 1848. U.S. senator and vice president John Calhoun, for instance, affirmed: "The greatest misfortunes of Spanish America are to be traced to the fatal error of placing these colored races on an equality with the white race. That error destroyed the social arrangement which formed the basis of society." For Calhoun, the "problem" of Spanish America consisted of both biological and political miscegenation. The irony cannot be overlooked for, in this case, Spanish America's problem was *too much* democracy, as it were. As U.S. politics have changed, so has this vision been reversed.

A Tale of Many Cities

The last third of the nineteenth century brought a period of relative peace and prosperity across the Atlantic, a time of rapid growth and exponential increase in modernizing processes. As in much of Europe and the United States, the pace of modernization picked up dramatically in Spanish America beginning in the 1870s. This period brought sweeping changes in the texture of life in the region in what Leslie Bethell has defined as a "Golden Age" of "material prosperity . . . , ideological consensus and, with some notable exceptions like Mexico during the Revolution (1910–1920), political stability" (preface 4:xv). Much as everywhere else in the West, in Latin America the transformation of life became increasingly rapid in the last third of the nineteenth century: "Massive changes occurred, changes that affected the lives of everyone, rich and poor, urban and rural. Major Latin American cities lost their colonial cobblestones, white plastered walls, and red-tiled roofs. They became modern metropolises, comparable to urban giants anywhere. Streetcars swayed, telephones jangled, and silent movies flickered from Montevideo and Santiago to Mexico City and Havana. Railroads multiplied fabulously" (Chasteen 179).

Generalizations such as Paz's that claim that at the time of modernismo "the reality of our nations was not a modern one" (91) are completely untenable. Life throughout Spanish America underwent striking political, economic, social, material, and cultural changes in the last third of the nineteenth century, and not surprisingly, it was in the continent's principal cities that those changes were more immediately apparent and had a stronger impact on everyday life. Urban development and expansion are some of the processes associated with modernization, and this was a period of extraordinary urban growth across the West, as capital cities became large urban centers and small towns became cities. As in other regions, "the urban landscape of Latin America was completely transformed by a number of different but interconnected factors. . . . And nearly everywhere the capital cities came to possess striking similarities to, and enjoyed many of the amenities of, the major European and North American cities" (Scobie 237).[27] Inverting the terms of Scobie's comparison, that is, reversing the direction of our thinking, it could also be said that many Latin American cities enjoyed amenities that many European cities did not. At the end of the century, Buenos Aires could not compete with Paris, to be sure, but it certainly was a larger, more "modernized" city than almost any other in France. In fact, Buenos Aires had a larger population than did Rome, Madrid, and Lisbon *combined*. It was the fourth-largest city on the entire American continent after New York, Chicago, and Philadelphia, while capitals such as Mexico City and Santiago were approximately the same size as Madrid and Rome. Furthermore, according to Claudio Véliz, around 1890, Venezuela, Chile, Argentina, and Uruguay were more urban countries than the United States (cited in Rotker 31). Not only did capital cities grow significantly, but also other cities and ports underwent rapid changes; for example, Valparaiso, Chile—where Darío lived and first published *Azul*—multiplied its population forty times over during the nineteenth century, going from a small town of 5,000 people in 1810 to a thriving port of about 200,000 in 1900.[28]

Certainly, the generalizations that accompany most studies of Spanish American modernismo conjure an image of Europe as one large extension of Paris, ignoring not only the rest of still largely rural France, but also the rest of a very unevenly urbanized continent. Hardly ever is it mentioned that, as France entered the last third of the nineteenth century and at the peak of its worldwide cultural prestige, two-thirds of its population was rural, or that by 1914 the urban populations of France and Argentina were the same, about 50 percent of their national populations (Joll 14).[29] The reality of Spanish American nations was indeed very much "modern," but as with virtually any region at the time, this did not mean modernized in equal measure everywhere in the continent, or everywhere in each nation. The difference between urban centers and rural areas was vast in much of the American continent (both North and South), but this difference was not unique to the Americas. In other words, what was taking place in the Paris of Baudelaire and Rimbaud that Paz found so paradigmatic of European modernity bore little resemblance to what the rest of a still largely rural European continent was experiencing: "These urban improvements . . . hardly affected the mass of the peasantry who remained, even after the coming of the railway, in a condition which had changed little since the end of the eighteenth century. The industrial revolution touched them very little and in some areas, such as the south of Italy, methods and equipment had not changed since antiquity" (Joll 32).[30] Finally, even within the urban sectors, change and the spread of new ideas were not immediate or equally accepted. As Joll states: "Most of the members of the ruling classes of Europe before 1914 were acting on ideas and assumptions formulated twenty or thirty years before, and took little interest in advanced ideas and advanced artistic developments" (164). During the nineteenth century and the first third of the twentieth, at the very least, modernization in Europe coexisted with traditions in a manner very close indeed to the hybrid modernity that García Canclini has found definitive of the Latin American experience.

The Economics of Modernization and the Facts of Immigration

If liberalism, nation formation, and other processes such as urban growth developed unevenly across Europe, so did the economic means through which various countries and regions took the path to modernization. The incorporation of Latin America into the world market in the last third of the nineteenth century is generally considered as opening the "neocolonial period," in which Latin America became reliant on foreign capital and entered the market mainly as exporter of primary goods and importer of manufactured commodities. It is this dependent economic situation that marked Spanish American modernization and within which modernismo has been understood. Yet, when using neocolonialism and dependency to describe both this period and the Spanish American experience of nineteenth-century modernity, it is inaccurate to say, as is generally done, that this relationship was established with Europe, since large parts of Europe itself followed a similar pattern. Most relevant to my discussion here is the case of Spain, both for the obvious reason that it had been the metropolitan center of Spanish America until quite recently and because of its implications for the study of modernismo. In an uncommon but significant reversal of the usual pattern of comparison, historian Raymond Carr explains the development of nineteenth-century Spain via a comparison to Latin America: "Like Latin American nations, Spain had become an export economy supplying raw materials to the developed West" (27).

One of the most important components of economic development and commerce was transport, particularly the creation and expansion of the railroad. It is well known that much of Spanish America's railroad system was built by British and U.S. capital, a circumstance often mentioned as a sign of its neocolonial condition. It is worth considering, then, that the Spanish rail system was to a large extent equally tied to foreign capital, mostly British, and most often at the expense of Spain's own economic interests.[31] In fact, the railway system was designed to favor a type of trade and economy in Spain that it is frequently associated with nineteenth-century Latin American economic history, that is, the export of primary materials to "developed" countries: "The radial pattern did facilitate the export of raw materials, especially minerals, and the import of foreign manufactures, especially to Madrid" (Shubert 18).

Furthermore, agricultural exports from Spain and Spanish American countries like Argentina often competed for the same northern European markets (García de Cortázar and González Vesga 475–76). Economic development based on the export of raw materials and primary goods was not only the case of Latin America, Spain or even Southern Europe, nor did it necessarily signal a lack of modernization. Northern European countries such as Denmark, Norway, and Sweden went through modernization processes largely based on the export of primary materials. Bushnell and Macaulay draw striking parallels between the economic development of Argentina and Denmark: "Denmark in the nineteenth century experienced political turmoil, multiple constitutions, secessionist movements, foreign wars, invasion, and dismemberment. Through it all, the Danish economy, based on agricultural exports, maintained its long-term growth. . . . Denmark, like Argentina, had achieved a high level of socioeconomic development by the beginning of the twentieth century without industrialization" (290). It is important to remember that as the nineteenth century ended, as modernismo was asserting its presence in Spanish America and Spain and Rubén Darío was hailing Buenos Aires, not Madrid, as the true capital of the Hispanic world, Argentina was one of fastest growing and richest economies in the world, ahead of most European countries. Spain, then, the imperial power of yesteryear, in the nineteenth century had become economically dependent on other European powers, and some of its ex-colonies enjoyed an economic growth and level of modernization beyond that of their former European metropolis. Given this historical context, the critical separation of an imperial Europe from a neocolonial Latin America, an unbridgeable gap between developed and undeveloped, does not correspond to economic, social, and cultural reality.

In the final analysis, perhaps nothing reflects better how misleading are the common views of nineteenth-century Spanish America and Europe than the facts of immigration. The last third of the nineteenth century witnessed a massive movement of people from Europe to America, both North and South, a phenomenon familiar to us today when discussions about third-world immigration to the United States and Europe are central to the concept of globalization, and exclusionary laws are being passed and walls being built. As Bushnell and Macaulay point out: "The eagerness of large numbers of people from other regions to migrate to Latin America in the late nineteenth century indicates the widespread perception, at least, that conditions of employment, health, and education were, on balance, better in Argentina, southern Brazil, Uruguay, Chile, and Cuba than in the lands whence the immigrants came" (289). To a considerable extent, these lands were in Europe, and the perception that it was better to live in Latin America than in Italy, Spain, Germany, or France was powerful enough to mobilize hundreds of thousands in the nineteenth century.

In sum, if the experience of modernity in the nineteenth century is related to the variety of processes that constitute what we call modernization, then there should be no doubt that there was nothing vicarious or ghostly in the Spanish American experience so forcefully and insightfully described by modernista writers from Martí to Rodó. That these processes in Latin America differed from those in Europe and the United States (which also differed from each other) may be true, but in the nineteenth century (at the very least) "different" becomes an almost empty signifier; modernization was ultimately different *everywhere from everywhere else* and without fixed directionality. The experience of the modern may have been stronger in London than in Bogotá or La Paz, but it was also certainly stronger in Buenos Aires than in Madrid, Dublin, or Bordeaux. Spanish American nations might have been dependent on northern European capital, but so was most of southern Europe. Moreover, some northern Atlantic regions, from Canada to Ireland and Norway, were still politically dependent on their metropolis. Why, then, do critics continue to underplay Spanish America's experience of modernity in the nineteenth century? When studying modernismo, a movement that so thoroughly theorized and textualized nineteenth-century modernity and that spread across both the American continent and the Atlantic in this period of deep transformation, why have scholars insisted on downplaying, qualifying, or simply denying the existence of such an experience?

Modernity's Otherness to Itself

The perpetual state of critical questioning and contestation of Spanish American modernization in the nineteenth century may be a result of our positionality and, as I have suggested, the benefit of hindsight. In *A Singular Modernity*, Fredric Jameson reflects on how perceptions of modernity have shifted:

> It is worth remembering those states that, at their moment in the past, were universally considered to be the most modern: Frederick the Great's Prussia, Lenin's system of the soviets, and a little later, the party-cum-dictator system of Mussolini's fascism. . . . If we no longer think of them as modern in this way (with the possible exception of the first named), it is because, woefully, they turned out not to match the degree of efficiency also promised somewhere in the stereotype of modernity. But the United States today is not very efficient either. (211)[32]

A similar case can be made about Latin America, whose "modernity" is now questioned because it did not yield the same results in the twentieth century as in other regions of the West. Seen from this perspective, Latin America was eventually expelled from the West and placed in the category of "third world," a term that, despite its origins, has become a way for "successful" modernities to lump together the largest portion of the world, erasing the richness, complexity, and diversity of their histories and modernities, now defined exclusively by what they "lack." This is the mirage built into the concept of modernization itself. In this light, the conclusion of Jameson's thought is extremely appealing and productive: "What is more significant in all these cases is that the modernity of the states in question is a modernity for other peoples, an optical illusion nourished by envy and hope, by inferiority feelings and the need for emulation. Alongside all the other paradoxes built into this strange concept, this one is the most fatal: that modernity is always a concept of otherness" (211).

Thus, modernity is indeed always "somewhere else." I have alluded to the risks of assuming one manifestation of liberalism, the British and Anglo American model, as the norm from which all others are considered deviations. I have suggested that a more fruitful way to understand liberalism is as a theoretical construct whose manifestations were always diverse, none matching the ideal. Likewise, we may yet discover that all modernities are peripheral to the concept of modernity itself.

However, a question remains regarding the definition of that concept and its implications, about what Jameson calls "the stereotype of modernity": Whose stereotype is it and how was it formed? According to whose measure can we say with Jameson that this or that modernity did not achieve a certain level of efficiency? The answer can be glimpsed in Jameson's own comment that "the United States today is not very efficient either," because, while the United States may not be efficient, no one would ever say that it is not "modern." In fact, the United States and Britain are the only countries in which the idea that modernization is taking place "somewhere else" never seemed to be at work.[33] As we saw with the case of liberalism, British and Anglo American modernization are the parameter by which the level of efficiency of other nations is measured even when the former does not measure up to that very standard. In this light, the prevalent current use of the term "Western modernity" illuminates as much as it obscures: it designates a wide array of processes in Europe, North, and South America (as well as the African and other diasporas), but its narrative, the telling of the modern story, has been not Western at all, but Northwestern, and more specifically British and Anglo American. Thus, not only Latin America but also much of Europe itself was excluded from that narrative in the nineteenth century. The entire South Atlantic, the birthplace of modernity in 1492, was written out of a new "stereotype of modernity."

North by Northwest: The Rerouting of Modern History

A number of factors drastically changed power balances in Europe, across the Atlantic, and indeed around the world in the nineteenth century. This process began with the independence of most of the American continent and ended with the rapid expansion of colonial enterprises in Africa and Asia by some European nations and the rise of the United States as a new kind of empire that would outlast all others. These changes transformed the political map of the world. A new ideological framework developed that would shift power relations across the Atlantic from East-West (Imperial Europe–American colonies) to North-South (northern Europe/America–southern Europe/America) and would transform the meaning of modernity. More often than not, this fundamental shift is left unaddressed in the critical discourse on Latin America, where the term "metropolitan center" denotes the Iberian peninsula before 1810, then flows seamlessly into denoting the North Sea after independence, without inquiry into the profound implications of that move. These implications are important not only for both North and South America but also for Europe, a region from which Spain and Portugal are, as a result of this very shift, virtually erased in critical discourse. In this sense, scholars keep reproducing the ideological maneuver on which the north European discourse of modernity has rested and keep ironing over a complex web of power relations and cultural narratives.

From Catholic to Protestant Modernity: The Shrinking of Europe

The modern has always been driven by master narratives of power and colonialism. The birth of the modern took place when theological time gave way to linear time in the humanism of Renaissance Europe (Călinescu 15–35), and its foundational instance was the violence exerted on Europe's other in the Americas (Dussel, *Invention*). Thus, in 1492 Christianity became "the first global design of the modern/colonial world system and, consequently, the anchor of Occidentalism and the coloniality of power drawing the external borders as the colonial difference" (Mignolo, *Local* 21). Europe defined modernity not only in time but also in space and inseparably linked the two: it placed itself at the center and in the present/future while locating its others at the margins and in the past. Christianity, although fragmenting inside Europe, was still clearly the "anchor" of its "external borders" and remained a decisive tool in sustaining those borders, not only in relation to colonial difference in the Americas, but also against the Islamic power of the Ottoman Empire to the southeast. But the Christian wars in Europe proved a powerful factor of change. After the Peace of Westphalia in the mid-1600s, the slow decline of the

Catholic Spanish empire marked the rise of north European Protestant hegemony. Thus, as the Enlightenment and the Industrial Revolution expanded the path modernity had opened since the fifteenth century (Dussel, "Europe" 470) and revolutions swept across the Americas and Europe, the "external borders" of old were redrawn or, better, resemantized. That is, the division between a Catholic South and a Protestant North remained the same but its meaning was radically altered. As Dussel explains: "Beginning in the nineteenth century, this modern Europe, which since 1492 occupied the center of world history, defined all other cultures as its periphery for the first time in history." When Dussel says "modern Europe," he means *northern* Europe, since "in the usual interpretation of modernity, both Spain and Portugal are left to one side, and along with them the Spanish American sixteenth century" (471). In other words, the shift in the meaning of modernity meant a simultaneous shift in the meaning of "Europe" itself: the old North-South religious division was resemantized not just as modern versus premodern, but also as Europe versus non-Europe. Thus, the Spanish empire, which had occupied the center of world history since 1492, had become by the nineteenth century part of its periphery, part of those "other cultures" outside Europe.

The implications of this shift cannot be overstated because they still resonate today. Although neither Dussel nor Mignolo places much emphasis on religion, religion was nonetheless an integral part of this shift, as modernity and Protestantism became profoundly identified with one another. In fact, it could be argued that Mignolo's categorization of successive global designs as "the Christian mission of the early modern (Renaissance) colonialism, the civilizing mission of the secularized modernity, and the development and modernization projects after World War II" (*Local* 21–22) is itself caught up in the narrative of the second modernity. Christianity has been a central element of all three global designs in a different form: Catholic, Protestant, and finally simply Christian. The semantic shifts that turned modernity, northern Europe, and Protestantism into synonyms was radical because it implied an important variation on the conception of history as moving from East to West and the related concept of *translatio imperii*. Indeed, for Hegel, one of the most important ideologues of the new concept of modernity, history moved not just from East to West, but from East to Northwest by the hand of Protestant ideology.[34]

From Imperial Center to Peripheral Other

Enrique Dussel has offered an insightful critique of the profound impact of Hegel's philosophy of history for the understanding of European modernity. According to Hegel's vision, Asia was the beginning and Europe the end of history, while Africa simply remained outside world history (and America, notably, was the land of the future). Hegel divided Europe along a north-south axis; southern Europe, despite its past importance, no longer had an active role to play and was now to follow the lead of the North: "Germany, France, Denmark, the Scandinavian countries are the heart of Europe" (qtd. in Dussel, *Invention* 23). Furthermore, for Hegel, "the land south of the Pyrenees" is not European at all, but African: "When one is in Spain one is already in Africa. This part of the world ... forms a niche which is limited to sharing the destiny of the great ones, a destiny which is decided in other parts. It is not called upon to acquire its own proper figure" (26). On the fringes of Europe, the Iberian peninsula fares only slightly better than the continent to its south: although perhaps not entirely erased from history (as Africa is from Hegel's text), the Iberian peninsula is written out of modernity.

Dussel interprets Hegel's influential view of history as the best example of Eurocentrism because he reads the South in Hegel's text as "the periphery, the old colonial, dependent world" (*Invention* 25). Dussel's assessment, however, misses a crucial element: this new South does not include only the "old" colonial world (reduced by Dussel to Latin America) but the "old" imperial world as well (i.e., Spain and Portugal).[35] By failing to pursue the full implications of this shift, Dussel ultimately reverts to the very myth of Europe that he so insightfully identified. To be fair, Dussel and other scholars, such as Mignolo, have recognized the operation of exclusion of the Iberian Peninsula from the second concept of modernity. This erasure of Spain and Portugal is, however, subsequently ignored in their analysis, which focuses on Latin America, and they continue to refer to nineteenth-century modernity as "European."

The problem with this move is twofold. On the one hand, it perpetuates the myth of a single Europe, already shown to be false, while on the other, it recuperates the full scope of modernity and the foundational place of the Americas *only* in its first stage. Yet, according to Dussel's own argument, modernity begins in 1492 with the conquest of America by Spain, "the first modern nation" ("Europe" 471); for him, "the seventeenth century (as exemplified in the work of Descartes and Bacon) must then be seen as the result of one-and-a-half centuries of modernity: it is a consequence rather than a starting point. Holland (which gained emancipation from Spain in 1610), England, and France would expand the path opened by Spain" (470). If the second modernity is a continuation of the first, Latin America and the Iberian Peninsula cannot but remain an integral part of that later stage (just as, by the same token, it would be absurd to say that England and its American colonies or France or Holland were *not* modern prior to the eighteenth century). Dussel does not seem to pursue his own line of thought to this conclusion and seems, instead, to exclude Latin America (and the Iberian Peninsula) from the second modernity.

Following Dussel, Mignolo also regards the second (stage of) modernity as "foreign" to Latin America. In a manner reminiscent of Paz, Mignolo goes as far as to say that "the second phase of modernity ... was derivative in the history of

Latin America and entered in the nineteenth century as an exteriority that needed to be incorporated" (*Local* 19).[36] It is unclear why liberal and republican ideas were more "foreign" than the Christian ideas that Mignolo sees as the first "global design" or civilizing mission behind the conquest of America begun in 1492 (21–22). The only difference between the stages cannot possibly be one of foreignness but one of exclusion. The problem with the turn of Dussel's and Mignolo's arguments is that they fall back on the Hegelian vision of history whose fallacies Dussel so well exposed. If Latin America and the Iberian Peninsula were ever an integral part of modernity, they could not have stepped out of it in the nineteenth century. On the contrary, they were excluded from its narrative, "their destiny," as Hegel himself put it, "decided in other parts."

In the sixteenth and seventeenth centuries, Europeans considered Inca, Aztec, and all indigenous peoples of the Americas, as well as Africans, barbaric, the other of the modern civilizing mission of European Christianity. In the nineteenth century, it was Latin America *and* Spain and Portugal, the imperial powers of yesteryear, that were relegated by the Protestant North to the realm of the barbaric, uncivilized, nonmodern.[37]

In this way, the nineteenth century moves forward; new lines are drawn that cut across both Europe and the Americas, excluding the South of each from this new conceptualization of modernity. The essential point that is either missed or dismissed is not only that there was a fundamental and progressive shift in how "modernity" was defined, but also that the redefinition excluded both the old colonial *and* the old imperial world. Spain, Portugal, and Latin America were written out of modernity. To ignore this process and subsume the Atlantic under a monolithic view of "modern Europe/United States" as a metropolitan center opposed to a Latin American periphery perpetually excluded from that modernity obscures more than clarifies and prevents us from understanding the processes taking place, the complexities of the period, and the repercussions of both today.

Atlantic Challenges to the Neocolonial and Postcolonial

Spanish American postcolonial history has been written, to a fault, under the rubric of "neocolonialism." Should the same concept be used to explain the history of its former metropolis during the last two centuries? Spanish America and Spain were both excluded from a redefinition of the very modernity that they had set in motion more than three centuries earlier. As Spanish America geared up for its revolutionary wars, Spain was fighting its own "war of independence" from Napoleonic France—ironically, conflicts on both sides of the Atlantic were supported by Britain in a successful attempt to get both the old Spanish and the new French empires out of its way. Much like Mexico some years later, Spain would be invaded at least once more, in 1823, by French troops with the sanction of the European Holy Alliance, an invasion that, unlike that of Mexico, put an end to constitutional liberalism.[38] Moreover, Spain's development and role in the world market was, as shown earlier, similar to those of Spanish American countries (export of primary materials, import of manufactured goods, and an economy dictated, to an extent, by foreign investments). Could this trajectory mean that Spain had also entered a "neocolonial" period (or should it be simply "colonial," since "neo" implies a variant of a previous colonial relation)?

Let's consider for a moment the following depiction of nineteenth-century Spain:

> The liberals of the mid-century, it is argued, not only handed over the railways to foreign concerns: the laws of 1868, a direct result of the difficulties of the Treasury, opened up Spanish mines to foreign investment. Certainly foreign investment produced dramatic results where Spanish capital had not developed resources: in ten years foreign capitals and British engineers quadrupled the output of the Rio Tinto mines, making Spain the greatest copper producer in Europe and employing 9,000 workers by 1889. This created a series of foreign enclaves where foreign concerns behaved as quasi-sovereign states, *exploiting Spain as a colony*, and where decisions were made in Cardiff or Glasgow whither the profits flowed back. At the Tharsis mines, "in their sun helmets and white jackets, mounted upon horses in which they took great pride, these Scotsmen in their hill empire evoked the idea of a Raj not very different from that of India." Like Latin American nations, Spain had become an export economy supplying raw materials to the developed West; only one-tenth of Vizcayan ore went to local blast furnaces. (Carr 27; my emphasis)

This description by historian Raymond Carr (which includes a quote from S. G. Checkland's *The Mines of Tharsis: Roman, French, and British Enterprise in Spain*) cannot possibly show any more clearly the way the nineteenth century redefined center and periphery in a global scale that included Europe. Under the British gaze of the Scots from their "hill empire" (and of Carr himself), Latin America, Spain, and India occupy the same subaltern role in this narrative: the neocolonial, the ex-imperial, and the still-colonial. Why, then, do we never think of Spain as a postcolonial society but have no qualms in joining such different experiences as those of Latin America and India under postcoloniality, even though the Latin American experience was arguably closer to that of Spain? Why, when discussing Spain, does Carr allow for the implied existence of an "undeveloped" West, while most scholars of Latin America favor an unqualified "West" to which Latin America does not belong, but on which it always depends? And when exactly did Latin America stop belonging to the West and why, while the United States and Canada remained very much part of it despite the continents' common history of coloniality and diverse population?

The excerpt from Carr and the questions it raises demand that we scholars revisit our understanding of neocolonial relations in the nineteenth century and allow for a more complex reading of both transatlantic and intraeuropean dynamics. With Carr's picture in mind, the critical habit of speaking about postindependence Spanish America in a virtually unchanged colonial relationship to Europe (or "the West"), constructed as a homogenous imperial "center," gives us a skewed vision of historical events, power relations, and their implications. The fact is that the nineteenth century witnessed a succession of unprecedented events: the emergence of the Americas as politically independent entities, the collapse of an empire (the Spanish) that, in turn, became an economic colony (or neocolony?) of other empires (British), and last but most certainly not least the conversion of a postcolonial society into a new empire that would eventually become the only world superpower (the United States). In this light, the opposition Europe/Spanish America almost seems an empty critical gesture, and certainly a framework that needs to be revisited. The thick net of cultural discourses and power struggles, uneven modernization processes, and varied experiences of modernity is such that paradigms of center and periphery become ineffective frameworks for critical analysis and often perpetuate, rather than undo, the very power forces under critique. The importance of the nineteenth-century remapping of the West cannot be overemphasized and is worth exploring further, as it sheds new light on Spanish America's place on this map, on our own understanding of its experience of modernity, and on the project of Spanish American modernismo.

The Racial Discourse of Modernity

A Matter of National Characters

Hegel believed that "Spirit" did not continue its path to freedom in Catholic Europe not only for religious reasons but also for what he saw as the "fundamental character of these nations" (*Philosophy* 420). For Hegel, the "Romanic Nations" are a hybrid of German and Roman blood and thus heterogeneous and disharmonious (421); moreover they are "sensuous," and prone to superstition and "slavish deference to Authority" (413). Hegel was not the first to essentialize a particular character of southern cultures. Since the eighteenth century, intellectuals such as Montesquieu had been formulating the idea that history was moving north, and putting forth arguments about the influence of the environment and climate on alleged national character. In *The Spirit of the Law* (1748), Montesquieu claims that "men are more vigorous in cold climates. . . . This greater strength produces many effects: for example, more confidence in oneself, that is, more courage; better knowledge of one's superiority" (qtd. in Iarocci 16). Different national characters translate into different moralities, so that northerners "have a few vices, enough virtues, and much sincerity and frankness. As you move toward the countries of the South [*les pays du midi*], you will believe you have moved away from morality itself; the liveliest passions will increase crime; each will seek to take from others all the advantages that can favor these same passions" (qtd. in Dainotto 382). As Hegel would a few decades later, Montesquieu established a direct link between character and religion, and thus the division of the Christian church into southern Catholic and northern Protestant took place "because the people of the north have and will always have a spirit of independence and liberty that the people of the south do not, and because a religion that has no visible leader is better suited to the independence fostered by the climate than is the religion that has one" (qtd. in Iarocci 17).[39]

Southern intellectuals were already questioning this line of thought based on the very principle of the Enlightenment, that is, the universality of reason. Spanish thinker Benito Jerónimo Feijoo, for instance, had devoted one of the *discursos* of his *Teatro Crítico Universal* (1726–1740) [Universal Theater of Criticism] to undoing the climate fallacy. Although Feijoo agrees that climates may affect plants, animals, and humans differently in bodily constitution and customs, nonetheless, he explains:

> Estoy en esta parte tan distante de la común opinión, que por lo que mira a lo substancial, tengo por casi imperceptible la desigualdad que hay de unas Naciones a otras en orden al uso del discurso. Lo cual no de otro modo puedo justificar mejor que mostrando que aquellas Naciones, que comúnmente están reputadas por rudas, o bárbaras, no ceden en ingenio, y algunas acaso exceden a las que se juzgan más cultas. (300–301)
>
> [In this matter, I am so far apart from the common opinion that, in any thing of substance, I regard inequality in reason imperceptible between Nations. I cannot justify my belief in any better way than by showing that those Nations that are commonly considered uncivilized or barbarian, do not have any less ingenuity, and some might even have more, than those that consider themselves more civilized.]

Feijoo's argument is indeed as universal as it got at the time: He begins with the Europeans and continues with the Asians, the Chinese in particular, remarking that "por más que se han esforzado los Europeos, no han podido igualarlos, ni aún imitarlos" (309) [as much as Europeans have tried, they have not been able to match them nor even imitate them]. He then refers to North Africans (Feijoo betrays perhaps his own limitations and prejudices by not explicitly mentioning most of subsaharan Africa), and ends with the Native Americans in the best tradition of Las Casas, concluding: "Apenas, pues, hay gente alguna que examinado su fondo, pueda con justicia ser capitulada de bárbara" (317). [There is hardly any people who, upon close examination, may be called barbarian with any justice.] The shift in the power balance in Europe ultimately rendered voices like Feijoo's mute. Like the entire Hispanic intellectual tradition of the sixteenth, seventeenth, and eighteenth centuries, Feijoo was expelled from the nineteenth-century northern modern archive.[40] In the nineteenth century the issue of "character" was transformed, and the new division between North and South, Protestant and Catholic, modern and barbaric, found justification in the objective truth of the natural sciences and one of the most powerful and devastating discourses produced in the nineteenth century, that of race.

From National Character to Racial Difference

As Kwame Anthony Appiah succinctly puts it: "While the Christian tradition insisted on the common ancestry of all human beings, and the Enlightenment . . . emphasized the universality of reason, by the middle of the nineteenth century the notion that all races were equal in their capacities was a distinctly minority view" ("Race" 280). Indeed, as happened in other areas of human diversity and experience, nineteenth-century scientific discourse provided the justification for the redefinition of modernity in northern Europe and the imperial policies it generated. Much as Christianity provided the narrative that the Iberian modern expansion needed to justify itself in America and elsewhere, biology became the narrative that nineteenth-century modernity and its exclusionary practices necessitated. As Hobsbawm states: "In the form of racism, whose central role in the nineteenth century cannot be overemphasized, biology was essential to a theoretically egalitarian bourgeois ideology, since it passed the blame for visible human inequalities from society to nature" (*Empire* 252). Biological racism, then, became the engine behind the inequality-making machine of northern European modernity, for, sustained by the power of scientific discourse, it held as a "universal" and "objective" truth "that nonwhite people lacked either the intelligence or the vigor of the white races: among which the highest, it was widely agreed, was the Indo-European stock from which the Germanic peoples emerged. In England and North America, there was a further narrowing of focus: the Anglo-Saxons were the favored offshoot of the Germanic stock" (Appiah, "Race" 280). As modernity was rewritten on its way to northern Europe, the Enlightenment's concept of the universality of reason, allegedly one of its central elements, was transformed into the superior reason of some—the Northern folk. Indeed, Habermas explains how the concept of rationality of the eighteenth-century philosophy of history was transformed in the nineteenth by evolutionary theories of society:

> It is at this point that the developmental theories of the nineteenth century, culminating in Spencer, undertook a decisive revision of the rationalization thematic: they interpreted advances in civilization in a Darwinian manner, as the development of quasi-organic systems. The paradigm for the interpretation of cumulative changes was no longer the theoretical progress of science but the natural evolution of the species. With this, the thematic of rationalization was transformed into that of social evolution. (*Theory* 151)

It is in this context that the category of race soon became the framework from which to reinterpret both historical and contemporary events and a justification and explanation for "progress" and "development," that is, for "modernity" and its accompanying imperialist ventures.

The study of race as a constructed category, of the role of science in its construction, and of the devastating effects that it has had—and continues to have—across the globe has already generated a large and powerful body of critical work and has helped sustain an important amount of social and political change. What I want to emphasize, however, is that we must take care when using current notions of race to think through the complexities of the nineteenth century. More specifically, in the nineteenth century, the "white" race was a slippery category that contained what were considered different races, some of which—most notably the Anglo-Saxon, a subset of the Germanic or Teutonic race—were thought "whiter" than others, particularly the Iberian or Spanish race, itself a subset of the Latin race. These categories that today belong to the realm of ethnicity were thought of as racial in the nineteenth century and became a decisive force behind the remapping of modernity and power within Europe and the Americas, dividing them into two distinctly separate regions: a "superior" (modern) Protestant Anglo-Germanic North, which took over the names of "Europe" and "America" proper, and an "inferior" (un-modern) Catholic Latin South, whose geopolitical affiliations had to be qualified as "southern" Europe and "Latin" America.[41]

The Racialization of the Black Legend

The notorious discourse against the Spanish empire (known today as "the Black Legend"), produced in the Protestant North since the sixteenth century and based in part on critiques of the colonial enterprise by Spaniards themselves like Bartolomé de las Casas, was rewritten in the nineteenth century in racially "objective" terms and therefore free from any indictment of bias because of political motivations or historical grievances. As Álvarez Junco and Shubert state regarding the way Spanish history has been written: "These negative portrayals [of the Black Legend] became associated not only with Spanish policies but also with Spanish character and with the 'race' itself. The image of Spain as the epitome of absolutism and intolerance would remain fixed in the European collective mind for centuries" (2–3). Well-known is the simultaneous process of demonization and romanticization that Spain underwent in the nineteenth-century northern European imaginary, rendering it a backward and primitive country that was also "a paradise outside of history, untouched by industrialization, urbanization and capitalism" (5), a pattern that, as we saw earlier in this chapter, still haunts much of the way Latin American history is usually understood.[42] The pervasiveness of nineteenth-century racial categories and their strong association with the new concept of modernity have deeply marked the way the history of the Hispanic Atlantic has been written (notably in British and U.S. historiography) and internalized by Spaniards and Spanish Americans alike, so that what Álvarez Junco and Shubert say regarding Spain can easily be applied to Spanish America as well: "Such views have not been limited to the English-speaking world, but they have been unusually strong and persistent there. Moreover, with history written at the summit of the world-system of power, people at the lower levels often internalize such views and become obsessed with understanding what they are lacking. Both Spain and the Spaniards have long had to bear this burden of the stereotype" (1). This stereotype, we may add, is but the negative of the "stereotype of modernity" mentioned by Jameson, a negative necessary to the very existence of that stereotype.

At the beginning of his seminal book on Jewish self-hatred, Sander Gilman offers an anecdotal example that is telling in this regard. After bringing up Franz Fanon's description of the myriad of European negative associations to blackness, Gilman explains: "That blacks are black, that they are the antithesis of the mirage of whiteness, the ideal of European aesthetic values, strikes the reader as an extension of some 'real,' perceived difference to which the qualities of 'good' and 'bad' have been erroneously applied. But the very concept of color is a quality of Otherness, not a reality. For not only blacks are black in this amorphous world of projection, so too, are Jews" (6). Although Gilman's study is mostly concerned with nineteenth- and twentieth-century northern Europe (mainly Germany and Austria), he chooses to illustrate his point about the projection of blackness with a very brief analysis of Prosper Mérimée's *Carmen* (1845):

> Carmen is the quintessential Other—female, a gypsy possessing all languages and yet native only in her hidden tongue, proletarian, and black. For as Mérimée notes later in the tale, the gypsies are "the black ones." But when Carmen is first introduced to the reader, it is not at all clear who she is. The narrator hazards a guess

> that she "might be Moorish or . . . (I stopped short, not daring to say Jewish)." It is Carmen's appearance that leads the narrator astray. But his overlapping of images of Otherness—the Moor, the Jew, the Gypsy—is possible only from the perspective of the French narrator, for whom Otherness in Spain is an amalgam of all these projections. (6; ellipses in original)

Gilman ultimately dismisses the importance of *Carmen* for his discussion and moves on to analyze the racialization of the Jew as black in nineteenth-century German scientific texts. For my discussion, however, Mérimée's novel is important, for if Carmen was the "quintessential Other," as Gilman shows, so was the Spain which Carmen soon came to symbolize. Gilman's comment reveals the degree to which "Spanishness" was perceived as "black." Since Spain and Spanishness are outside the scope of Gilman's study, he naturally thinks that Mérimée's construction is of little significance outside fiction:

> Mérimée's . . . confusion of Others is quite blatant and has little polemical value outside the world of the fiction in his tale of Carmen. There is a considerable shift in the implications of the coalescing of structures or codes of Otherness when one moves to a later text in a quite different cultural context. Within the late-nineteenth-century racist tractates published in Germany, the image of the black Jew appears with specific political implications. (6–7)

What I am arguing here is not only that the logic behind Mérimée's *Carmen* had specific political implications for Spain *and* Spanish America, but also that Mérimée's work cannot be separated from those later images of "blackness" in racist scientific tractates, that they all exist on a continuum in the racial construction of post-eighteenth-century modernity. When the Comte de Gobineau published his influential *Essay on the Inequality of Human Races* in the mid 1850s, the stage had already been set and scientific studies proliferated, so his ideas about the superiority of the Aryan race and the dangers of miscegenation generated a widespread following, particularly, and not surprisingly, in Germany, England, and the United States. But not only there. As Spanish America was finishing its revolutionary wars of independence and embarking on the new enterprise of nation building, writing its own "narrative of futurity," as Alonso puts it, the pervasiveness of the racial scientific discourse was already at work. It soon became internalized, as modern discourses have successfully done in almost every realm, by its victims. I certainly do not mean to imply that the "racialization" of modernity had the same effect for southern Europeans and Spanish American Creoles as for the victims of the Holocaust or for those of the colonial enterprises worldwide, including those under Creole hegemony in the Americas, nor even that self-hatred took the same form or had the same effects for Spaniards as for Spanish American Creoles. My point is to stress that the similar symbolic operations at work were part of a continuum. Even if to a lesser degree than in other contexts, they did have serious consequences for Spaniards and Spanish Americans, including, by a domino effect of sorts, those in subaltern positions within Hispanic societies (blacks, Indians, mestizos, gypsies, etc.), who found themselves twice removed from power as subalterns of subalterns. They often became the scapegoats of Spain's and Spanish America's conflicted new positionality with respect to modernity, a modernity that increasingly in the nineteenth century became associated with the "Anglo-Saxon race."[43] Thus, British and Anglo American modernization became *the* measure of modernization, Jameson's "stereotype of modernity." In fact, as we shall see in Chapter 4, Spain and Spanish America, and the very concept of "Hispanicness," were central to the Anglo American construction of the new imaginary of modernity and its erasure of what Dussel calls its "first stage." For this reason, "Hispanicness" would also be central to Spanish American modernismo's discursive rebuttal of that construction.

The history of confrontation between the Anglo-Saxon and Iberian/Latin races is one of the most central elements of the transatlantic nineteenth century, yet it remains one of the least studied, still distorted and generally frowned upon in scholarship. The majority of scholars have followed a similar pattern: they either ignore the powerful force of nineteenth- and early twentieth-century Anglo racial discourse entirely or disguise it under the broader categories of "Western" supremacist attitudes and the "white" race (the category Anglo seems to matter only in reference to the early internal racial history of the United States). As a result, the Hispanic/Latin racial discourse is generally considered on its own, left standing in opposition to nothing real, and thus belittled and dismissed as further proof of the hopelessly colonized (and racist) mind of Spanish American Creoles who cannot think beyond European categories.

The profound impact of this racial divide in nineteenth- and early twentieth-century Europe has been now all but forgotten as the European Union has progressively erased and healed its wounds, and immigrants from a new global South occupy that symbolic—and real—space of otherness. Yet it determined much of Europe's past and its history of inclusions and exclusions; it determined the way European history has been written and erased, and it determines today (although perhaps increasingly less) what "Europe" still means in the global imaginary (i.e., northern Europe). In the Americas, on the other hand, this racial divide not only determined much of the continent's history, but it survives in the very name and identity of the southern half of the continent and in the ethnoracial categories still at work in the northern half. While Spain has recently been reintegrated successfully into the category "West" like a prodigal son or, rather, like a child who has finally reached maturity, Spanish America has been expelled finally and completely from that category.

The Symbolic Capital of Anglo-Saxon Modernity

Modernization and the Anglo-Saxon race became profoundly intertwined concepts in the nineteenth century. When José Martí spoke with urgency in "Nuestra América" (Our America) about a developing war of ideas, he was not stretching a metaphor but referring to a pressing reality with real consequences, as racial discourses fueled both domestic and foreign policies.[44] Eugenics programs became common at the turn of the century, and the conceptualization of race was a decisive force behind nineteenth-century political alliances and imperialism, "which saw the relations between states as a perpetual struggle for survival in which some races were regarded as 'superior' to others in an evolutionary process in which the strongest had constantly to assert themselves" (Joll 102). In the 1890s, Joseph Chamberlain, then British colonial secretary, called for an alliance with Germany by appealing to the discourse of race: "We find our system of justice, we find our literature, we find the very base and foundation on which our language is established, the same in the two countries, and if the union between England and America is a powerful factor in the cause for peace, a new Triple Alliance between the Teutonic race and the two great branches of the Anglo-Saxon race would be a still more potent influence in the future of the world" (qtd. in Joll 97).

Language, literature, culture—all were at the time part of the concept of race and thus essential components of discourses on racial superiority and inferiority, used to justify political action and civilizing missions. In this context, insistence on cultural independence, on the value of one's own literary history and traditions, the capacity to affect others in the cultural and literary realm, were not rhetorical issues or empty gestures, but acts of political consequence and, in the case of Spanish America, as we see in Martí's "Nuestra América," active resistance to the Anglo American "potent influence on the future of the world," as Chamberlain put it.

I propose thinking of culture and power at the turn of the century in terms close to those of Pierre Bourdieu's concepts of "symbolic capital" and "distinction." For Bourdieu, "the struggle for social distinction, whatever its symbolic form, is . . . a fundamental dimension of all social life" (Swartz 6). The association of modernization with the northern "races," and particularly the Anglo-Saxon, meant that to be Anglo-Saxon carried the ultimate mark of distinction or prestige. As in other instances of social life, those who did not possess that distinction wanted to, and looked for ways to, be like the northerners or else became, to use the words of Álvarez and Shubert, "obsessed with understanding what they [were] lacking" (1). Of course, this was not an overtly conscious operation. Indeed, for Bourdieu, "symbolic capital is a form of power that is not perceived as power but as legitimate demands for recognition, deference, obedience, or the services of others" (Swartz 90). The second half of the nineteenth century witnessed an international struggle for racial symbolic capital across the Atlantic with profound implications for our understanding of modernity (and its myths), a struggle particularly between the Anglo-Saxon and Iberian races. In the battle of racial discourses, the Iberian-American countries were considered backward, lacking in material resources and economic development; as we will see, Spanish American modernistas retorted by writing of their northern neighbors as overtly materialistic, a culture of consumers rather than thinkers, and ultimately the antithesis of the true modern spirit. The case of France is particularly important because it managed to belong to both camps—a middlebrow of sorts that could praise the superiority of the Germanic races (to which the Franks belonged) while also championing the Latin cause when necessary. France gained the highest level of cultural distinction while still managing to be associated by many with modernization, despite being a largely rural nation. Regardless of the country's economic power, French literature and culture were, from the second half of the nineteenth century to World War II, in a position of unrivaled power in the international field of symbolic goods. At a time when language, literature, race, and politics were intimately connected and new technologies were making possible the faster distribution of cultural and symbolic goods across the globe, the struggle for recognition and authority within a transnational cultural field was perceived as a matter of cultural survival and political relevance. It is within this context that we must read Spanish American modernismo and Hispanic modernities at large. For this reason and to understand more deeply the important links between nineteenth-century racial discourse and redefinitions of modernity, we must first explore the place of modernismo and Spanish American letters in the transnational/transatlantic cultural field.

CHAPTER 2

The Transatlantic Literary Field and the Rise of Modernismo

The burden is necessarily greater for an American—for he *must* deal more or less, if only by implication, with Europe; whereas no European is obliged to deal in the least with America. No one dreams of calling him less complete for not doing so.

—Henry James, *The Notebooks of Henry James*

It is surprising to compare the publication dates of various Latin American texts and others that are considered their model because in most cases they were contemporaneous; but at the time it seemed impossible to see the "originality" of Latin Americans.

—Graciela Montaldo, *La sensibilidad amenazada*

As the twenty-first century began, Jesús Martín Barbero, Néstor García Canclini, and other prominent Latin American intellectuals stated their belief that rather than geopolitics or geoeconomics, the world in the twenty-first century will revolve around geocultural circuits; it will be divided among different cultural spaces, one of which, they propose, must be Latin America: "Las luchas políticas, cada vez más, serán de disputa por el modelo cultural de la sociedad, es decir, por modelos y sentidos de vida individual y colectivo, por modelos de modernidad" (Garretón 34). [Political struggles will increasingly be over the cultural model of society, that is, over models and understandings of individual and collective life, over models of modernity.][1] Neither the diagnostic about the relevance of culture and definitions of modernity in the global scene nor the proposal about the Latin American cultural space may be particularly new. Well over a century earlier, Spanish American modernistas would have agreed with both as they set out to make the Latin American geocultural space count in the larger global cultural space. In 1891, José Martí published his most influential essay, warning about shifting conditions in the location, distribution, and manifestations of power, identifying the emergence of new geocultural networks and models of modernity, and stressing the need for Latin American culture to be a relevant part of what he diagnosed as a new universal order. He famously called this Latin American geocultural space "our America." Like intellectuals today, Martí believed that the times were over when people thought of culture as geographically limited, as something local and homogeneous. Martí, as would Darío, Rodó, and many others, identified a struggle over the symbolic, over the meanings of culture and modernity as individual and collective experiences, and their implications for a global politics of inclusion and exclusion, of domination and subordination.

Following the model of cultural fields developed by sociologist Pierre Bourdieu as a mediating concept between culture and power, between literature and society, in this chapter I read the constitution of modernismo in the context of the geocultural and geopolitical spaces that were emerging at the time and within which Spanish American modernismo must be understood.[2] I study what, adapting Bourdieu's concept, I call the transatlantic literary field, the European and American transnational field. This is a field of fields, a complex space marked by struggles over symbolic capital at a time when geocultural spaces were in the process of redefinition along sometimes overlapping, sometimes competing, and always shifting lines. I then analyze how those struggles affected the Spanish American literary field—a transnational field itself—and discuss some of the principle ways by which modernismo staked its claim within this field and accomplished what Bourdieu calls a "literary revolution," transforming the way literature was written in Spanish. In doing so, modernista writers constructed a Spanish American cultural space from which to think about Spanish America *and* Spain, and engage in the new cultural battles of modernity.

Bourdieu's Literary Field and the Limits of the National Model

The Field as a Space of Struggle for Symbolic Capital

The field of cultural production is a theoretical model developed by sociologist Pierre Bourdieu in order to break away from both the Marxist understanding of superstructure and the idea that culture is moved by " 'great individuals,' unique creators irreducible to any condition or conditioning" (*Field* 29).[3] Instead, Bourdieu's model functions as a mediator between cultural practice and social structures, a structural system of both symbolic and social relations. This system or "field" is relatively autonomous, that is, governed by its own rules and not directly by those of politics or economics or religion. Although the cultural field, like all other fields, is contained by the larger field of power, it is only indirectly affected by it (40), as the field itself, the relational structure of positions and position takings, mediates between external factors and a work of art. According to Bourdieu, society is divided into a large group of separate but homologous fields (the literary, the artistic, the scientific, the journalistic, the economic, and so on). Although separate, the fields are affected by each other through what Bourdieu calls "homology," a concept central to his theory: advances in one field may benefit other fields.[4]

The structure of any given field depends on the positions its agents occupy within that field, and it is always a dynamic structure as positions change within it. This is an essential element of Bourdieu's model, since for him "the literary or artistic field is a *field of forces*, but it is also a *field of struggles* tending to transform or conserve this field of forces" (*Field* 30). The literary field, therefore, is composed of two inseparable spaces. One space is that of literary position takings, "i.e., the structured set of the manifestations of the social agents involved in the field—literary or artistic works, of course, but also political acts or pronouncements, manifestos or polemics, etc." The second is that of literary positions, "defined by possession of a determinate quantity of specific capital (recognition) and, at the same time, by occupation of a determinate position in the structure of the distribution of this specific capital" (30). Rather than a consensual system, the literary field is thus defined by conflict: "The generative, unifying principle of this 'system' is the struggle, with all the contradiction it engenders" (34).[5] The struggle in the field is largely over capital, which Bourdieu's theory extends beyond the realm of material goods to encompass what he terms "symbolic goods" or "cultural capital," which functions much like in economics: the more cultural capital obtained, the more power, that is, the stronger the position in the field. An important concept developed by Bourdieu is that of "habitus," or system of dispositions (*Rules* 265), which is the result of early socialization of the agents in relation to factors like class, geographical origin, and so on.[6] Agents bring their habitus into the field, with which it interacts, and specific actions result from that intersection.[7]

The Shifting Meanings of Literary Autonomy

I have mentioned that for Bourdieu the cultural field is relatively autonomous and, indeed, autonomy is a central concept in Bourdieu's theory. Allegedly one of the pillars of literary modernity, autonomy is also a central concept for the study of modernismo. It is, however, a concept difficult to pin down because of its sometimes contradictory meanings. A first meaning of autonomy can be traced back to Kant and Weber and is related to the claim that literature must be judged exclusively according to literature's own rules. In other words, literature does not find its justification outside itself. Exemplary is the idea of "art for art's sake." For Bourdieu, the ultimate consequence of this concept of autonomy is the creation of modern artists/writers, masters of their own work and free from the political and/or religious demands that supported and constrained art in the past.[8] As Bourdieu explains it: "The ending of dependence on a patron or collector and, more generally, the ending of dependence upon direct commissions, with the development of an impersonal market, tends to increase the liberty of writers and artists." A condition of possibility for this notion of autonomy then clearly is the existence of a literary market. On the other hand, Bourdieu's description of the field as polarized by the opposition between autonomous and heteronomous forces is based on the realization by writers and artists that their "liberty is purely formal; it constitutes no more than the condition of their submission to the laws of the market of symbolic goods, that is, to a form of demand which necessarily lags behind the supply of the commodity, in this case, the work of art" (*Field* 114). In other words, one master is exchanged for another. In this context, however, Bourdieu defines autonomy in terms that almost contradict his earlier definition and in opposition to heteronomy, defined, in turn, by the dependency of literature on market demands.[9]

By what Bourdieu calls "the economic world reversed," rejection by the market and lack of sales become elements of prestige and distinction in the field and signs of autonomy, while producing works for the masses ("field of large scale production") is a sign of heteronomy and hence lacks prestige.[10] In other words, the more authors sell, the less autonomous they are, as their work is not fully free from external demand but subject to the public's taste. For Bourdieu, this second type of autonomy comes at a price. Not having readers creates what he calls the "logic of resentment, which makes a virtue of necessity" (50) by converting privation into refusal, to the point that it is difficult to tell which comes first. In other words, poets complain about the lack of a reading public while simultaneously rejecting the notion of writing for that reading public. Instead, nineteenth-century poets wrote for their peers, other literary producers like themselves, in what constitutes for Bourdieu a "field of restricted production." Money is thus directly linked to the issue of autonomy in both instances, albeit in opposite ways. Inasmuch as the first concept of autonomy as literature's authority over itself depends on the existence of a market that frees writers from external demands (by patrons, the state, the church), the market allows writers to earn money, make a living by their work, and become professionals. The second meaning of autonomy works the other way, since it implies that to depend on the market is to lose autonomy. In this instance, writers wanting to be masters of their own work must look for alternative ways to make a living or, as was often the case in the nineteenth and early twentieth centuries, live off inherited money. As Théophile Gautier put it: "Flaubert was smarter than us . . . He had the wit to come into the world with money, something that is indispensable for anyone who wants to get anywhere in art" (qtd. in Bourdieu, *Field* 68; ellipses in original). Regarding Gautier's comment, Bourdieu explains that in the case of the French Parnassians, for instance, there was a marked difference between those who had family money and "the advantage of not having to devote time and energy to secondary 'bread-and-butter' activities" and those who did not, many of whom "devoted part of their time to complementary activities," resigning themselves "more readily to 'industrial literature,' in which writing becomes a job like any other" (68). For Bourdieu, this issue goes to the core of the concept of professionalization: "The 'profession' of writer or artist is one of the least professionalized there is, despite all the efforts of 'writers' associations,' 'Pen Clubs' etc. This is shown clearly by (*inter alia*) the problems which arise in classifying these agents, who are able to exercise what they regard as their main occupation only on condition that they have a secondary occupation which provides their main income" (43). This is so not only because even successful authors are usually only so after a long time of publishing their work and obtaining recognition or public attention, but also because for every successful writer there are hundreds who do not succeed (at least in their lifetime).

In sum, autonomy in Bourdieu's work comes to mean at least two things. On the one hand, autonomy is the capacity of art to define its own rules and find justification in itself. In this sense, autonomy is to a large degree related to the constitution of a reading public and a literary market that frees literature from patronage. On the other hand, autonomy means freedom from the demands of that very market and the inversion of economic terms: the fewer sales, the more autonomy and symbolic capital.[11] As we shall see, the matter of literary autonomy has often been in dispute when dealing with Spanish American nineteenth-century literature and modernismo.

Crossing National Borders: The Transnational Literary Field

In studying the Spanish American literary field at the turn of the century, perhaps the first and most obvious issue that arises is that, strictly speaking, the Spanish American field is one and many at the same time. Bourdieu's model is a national one; his theory finds its horizon in the context of nation and hardly ever is he concerned with the relationship between national fields and the permeability of borders. The transnational dimension of cultural production and capital remains, thus, a noticeable gap in Bourdieu's work.[12] Any study of Spanish American modernismo from Bourdieu's model requires the expansion of the model, since modernismo crosses national boundaries. For historical, cultural, political, and linguistic reasons, Bourdieu could keep his theoretical model restricted to the French national frame at the turn of the century with relative ease, and certainly the case can be made that nation is an important force to consider when transferring Bourdieu's model to other contexts, especially in the nineteenth century, a period of nation-building projects and the writing of national literary histories across the West.

Nonetheless, because of the nature of cultural production, but also for historical, cultural, political, and linguistic reasons, any national field is bound to be affected to a greater or lesser degree by other national fields at any given time.[13] This is particularly so since the nineteenth century for a variety of reasons: the speed with which information became available, the way literature was invested with nationalist and culturalist concerns, and the consolidation of new political entities in the Americas that, although independent, were still largely connected culturally to their previous political metropolis. As literature was considered the highest expression of a linguistic community, these political changes radically transformed two European fields into two distinctly transnational literary, cultural, and linguistic spaces across the Atlantic: English in the North and Spanish in the South. The circulation of literature, symbolic capital, and power across the West was indeed reconfigured in the nineteenth century, and it is within this reconfiguration that I study the emergence of modernismo in Spanish America and its eventual displacement of Spanish peninsular cultural authority.

The Burden of "Europe"

The Spanish American Transnational Field

The Spanish American case could be the emblem of the notion of a transnational literary field, since in addition to specific literary, intellectual, and ideological debates in each national context, there also existed in Spanish America a sense of belonging to a larger entity with common cultural traditions and concerns, where writers and intellectuals shared a language and a sense of identity and competed for cultural and literary authority and prestige. The famous debate early in the century between Chilean José Victorino Lastarria, Venezuelan Andrés Bello, and Argentine D. F. Sarmiento on the nature of Spanish American language and identity serves as a paradigmatic instance of agents struggling for authority in the "Spanish American," rather than the specifically national, cultural field. Another paradigmatic example, if unfortunately less canonical, is the transnational dimension of nineteenth-century women's literary circles, such as the fruitful relationships between Argentine, Peruvian, and Bolivian writers.[14] Fueled by a sense of continental identity, this transnational literary space had been a reality at least since independence, but modernismo would consolidate it and invest it with new meaning at the end of the century.

Spanish America as a transnational cultural space is not an exceptional case. An important aspect of the geopolitical entity called Europe (even if that entity is an invention, as Dussel claims) was the construction of a common history. What makes the Spanish American literary field different from the European but similar to that of the United States is that it shared a literary language, Spanish, not only within its continental borders, but also with its European former metropolis. The European case, nonetheless, should also be thought of in transnational terms, a dynamic space of forces and struggles within geocultural borders that also held, as a whole, a dominant position within the transatlantic and, indeed, the global fields.

The European Transnational Field

Bourdieu could get away with ignoring the transnational element of all literary and cultural production, mostly because France was, at the turn of the century, *the* exceptional national case. Endowed with unequalled cultural prestige, France, and particularly its capital city, could afford to remain largely oblivious to literary and cultural developments outside its national borders, that is, to ignore them or simply not afford them sufficient symbolic capital. In other words, for a variety of reasons and in the hypothetical space of a transnational literary field, no other national or regional group of agents within or outside Europe managed to debunk the consolidated status and dominant position of the French in the second half of the nineteenth century.

A cursory look at other European countries, however, reveals national fields whose internal dynamics (the objective relations between positions and position takings) are profoundly marked by agents from other national fields, mainly the French. For instance, between 1851 and 1939 English literature, as Starkie notes, "obtain[ed] from France ... more than from any other country.... In the second half of the nineteenth century, the influence of France gradually ousted that of Germany, and ... French influence and prestige stood supreme during the twenty years which separate the two world wars" (11). The case of Italy is perhaps more striking as an even clearer example of how international agents exert change in national fields. I am referring to the role of French author Madame de Staël in sparking the literary debate that would bring about romanticism in Italy when she openly called on Italians to translate French and northern European literatures.[15] The same can be said about the relevance of the French literary field in the case of Germany, to the point that, as Casanova has argued, "a study of the formation of the German literary space from the end of the eighteenth century that overlooked its intensely competitive relationship with France would run the risk of completely misunderstanding its structuring engagements" (79). In Spain, where the first half of the nineteenth century was marked by the Napoleonic invasion, the war of independence, and the exile of the liberals, English and mostly French literatures had a decisive role in the Spanish literary field throughout the century.[16] In its last third, Zola's naturalism swept the continent from its French epicenter, generating waves of discussion and literary power struggles across the board, from Germany to Spain and Italy to England.[17] Finally, it is important to note that the permeability of national literary fields is not limited to the strictly aesthetic, but to most areas of literary production, including publishing trends (the *folletín*, for instance), translation practices, types of literary journals, book trade, and so on.[18]

Considered in this context, the scholarly insistence on highlighting the dependence of Spanish American modernismo on European literature is quite misleading in its broad generalization and ultimate simplification of a complex transnational dynamic, in which economic power and literary power seemed to not always go hand in hand. Between 1850 and 1918 (at the very least) virtually *all* European and American literatures were significantly "dependent" on the French. Furthermore, as Fernand Braudel points out, at the turn of the century, "France, though lagging behind the rest of Europe economically, was the undisputed centre of Western painting and literature" (qtd. in Casanova 11). Ignoring this larger context risks oversimplification and the reduction of Spanish American literature to the realm of the incommensurably different, as if Spanish America, because of its "neocolonial" condition, was the only region being influenced by French literature (or worse yet by an ill-defined "European" literature), or as if it is permissible for a German, Spanish, or Italian writer, but not for a Spanish American writer, to be receptive to French trends.[19] This is not to say that we should dismiss the idea of uneven relations between Spanish America and Europe entirely. However used and abused the idea of Spanish American literary dependency has been, and however much it may have blinded us to the complexities and inequalities of the European construct itself, it is still very much a valid perspective inasmuch as it forces us to consider two important elements that I now take up: the historical force of the concept of Europe and the postcolonial condition of the Americas.

Fields and Imagined Communities

In nineteenth-century Europe, debates on national literatures often were mediated by agents from foreign literatures—books or pieces in translation in literary journals, for instance, or as in the case of Madame de Staël in Italy, the direct intervention of foreign intellectuals. However, although a composite of multiple fields with vastly different amounts of power, the literatures of Europe can also be thought of as constituting one large transnational field where national subfields struggled for recognition and prestige. Like any nation or other supranational entity (such as Latin America), Europe is an "imagined community" in Benedict Anderson's terms, joined by constructed narratives of belonging and common history even if composed of groups with varying degrees of power. The result is a pan-European sentiment that, like all nationalisms, is fueled and maintained by opposition to its others, in this case, the non-European literary fields. Moreover, unlike individual writers, whose life span is finite, nations conceive of themselves as eternal; in the struggles for literary and cultural authority, losing power in the field thus can be considered a temporary condition susceptible to being reversed. For example, while French literature reigned supreme in the second half of the nineteenth century, so had British and German in the first half, and Spanish and Italian before the 1700s. It was then possible to imagine that, say, Spanish literature might with time regain a position of power in the European literary field. This geocultural space, of which literature was a central part in the nineteenth century, thus was strongly associated with Europe's self-construction, colonial enterprises, and self-appointed civilizing missions.

Postcoloniality and the American Literary Fields

At the same time and as a consequence, Creole Americans from both North and South, who although politically independent saw themselves as culturally European, perceived European literature as dominant: the wealth of European symbolic capital and its prestige might have changed national locations, but it had remained within Europe.[20] Thus, the authority of "European" culture was established and accepted both in Europe and in its Western ex-colonies, regardless of American Creoles' actual estimation of the specifics of European politics, societies, economies, and general political power. As Jean-Philippe Mathy comments: "Even Walt Whitman, for all his buoyant enthusiasm for his country's democratic vistas, was not immune to what Melvin Lasky has called 'the temptation of Europe' " (24). Since their constitution, then, all American literary fields were dealing with a position of subalternity in the Western transnational cultural field, a position that was ambivalent and contradictory, simultaneously recognized and challenged, and marked by continuous struggles for authority. Andrés Bello called on poetry to leave Old Europe and come to America where new materials were plentiful, yet he defended the unity of the Castilian language against its disintegration in America. An iconic figure of U.S. literature and a critic of European politics, James Fenimore Cooper lamented exactly the opposite, that is, the lack of materials that America offered the writer in contrast to Europe, a sentiment "echoed throughout [U.S.] literature from Hawthorne to Henry James" (Lasky 72). From Sarmiento in the South to Cooper in the North, the burden of European culture seemed ever present in the American literary fields, where literary and cultural distinction depended on the apparent paradox of being well up on the latest from Europe and simultaneously creating a uniquely "American" literature.[21]

While in Latin American literary studies there seems to be an assumption that this relationship with European culture was a particularity of the region's neocolonial condition, the situation in the United States was not very different. Indeed, as Leonard Tennenhouse explains, from the mid-eighteenth century to the 1850s, "[U.S.] authors and readers were more interested in producing and consuming English literature than in creating, in the words of Elaine Showalter, 'a literature of their own' " (1). Even at the end of the nineteenth century, Henry James could still write, "The burden is necessarily greater for an American—for he *must* deal more or less, if only by implication, with Europe; whereas no European is obliged to deal in the least with America. No one dreams of calling him less complete for not doing so" (524–25). T. S. Eliot's remarks about James make explicit the extent to which American intellectuals internalized metropolitan constructs and aimed to reproduce them, changing them in the process: "It is the final perfection, the consummation of an American to become, not an Englishman, but a European—something which no born European, no person of any European nationality can become" (qtd. in Lasky 75).[22] This troubled relationship with European culture, then, was common to both hemispheres of the American continent, as were the struggles generated over literary authority in each national and regional field.

In addition to pointing out the importance of this "burden" for American writers and the American literary field, my aim here is both to show the relevance of the critical attention to the power inequalities between Spanish American and European literary discourses *and* to argue for the need to see them in their context, to place them in the general and complex network of power inequalities across the Atlantic. Despite the increasing differential in economic, political, and military power between North and South in the Americas as the nineteenth century progressed, and although both were independent, each maintained an ambivalent relationship with European literature and culture—a relationship for which dependency theories exclusively based on economic models cannot account. Reproducing the United States and Europe as a perpetual imperial pair overlooks the cultural power differential between the regions at the time, which placed the United States closer to Spanish America than to Europe. Lawrence Buell has argued that compared to the U.S. political sphere after the War of 1812, in the U.S. literary-cultural sphere "the specter of neocolonialism loomed much larger both as a market reality for the publishing industry and at the level of internalized tastes and templates. Although an antebellum American merchant or military officer would have been nettled by the assumption of British cultural superiority without feeling greatly threatened by it, an aspiring writer—especially if this person were a moderately well-educated white male—might have felt himself dismissed as little better than a Caliban" (203).[23]

Referring explicitly to commonalities between North and South America, Gerard Aching's critique of the way Benedict Anderson sees Latin American nationalism as failed is relevant here as well: "Anderson's comparative look at the Americas leaves no room to consider the fact that at the time of their respective independence from former colonizers the political elite both in the United States and Latin America maintained strong cultural and flourishing economic ties with Europe" (*Politics* 123). As with Spanish American modernity, there is a danger in reading history backward, that is, projecting into the past what we now know were the outcomes of processes begun in the nineteenth century. The unique trajectory of the United States from colonial society to imperial power often makes scholars forget the parallels Aching points out.

Another central aspect of nineteenth-century cultural relations in the Americas is their particular relationship with their former metropolises. While French culture and literature had an unequalled pull on the rest of Europe and across the Atlantic, the cultural ties of the American ex-colonies with their respective ex-metropolis added another layer to the way cultural forces were distributed across the transnational field. Thus, the cultural legacy of the U.S. colonial situation was that the United States "continued to import both its literature and the terms by which it judged its literature from England long after it had achieved its political independence" (Brodhead 467–68). Henry Tuckerman, who in 1864 argued the existence of U.S. cultural "autonomy," did so by affirming that "Shakespeare and Milton, Bacon and Wordsworth, Byron and Scott have been and are more generally known, appreciated, and loved, and have entered more deeply into the average intellectual life, on this than on the other side of the Atlantic," thus confirming British literary authority (qtd. in Buell 200). As late as 1876, for every book by a U.S. author exported to Britain, ten British-authored books were imported to the United States.

In the case of Spanish America, the well-known strong reaction of liberals against Spain—stronger in some areas like the Rio de la Plata (where Sarmiento is the most canonical example of *antiespañolismo*) than in others like Colombia or Mexico—did not mean that Spanish literature and culture stopped exerting influence and having a significant presence in the literary field of the region. The importance as granters of literary prestige that Juan Valera and other Spanish writers and critics still had in the 1880s (which Spanish American modernismo would challenge) speaks to the weight that Spain still carried across the Atlantic. Although for most of the century this influence was linked to mainly conservative Catholic sectors of postindependence society (C. Rama 103–14), Spanish American liberals had their own ties with Spain: Spanish liberal writers who were critical of Spain themselves were read and admired by their American peers, brothers of sorts in a common cause (Shumway 128, 139). This was most notably the case of Spanish writer and journalist Mariano José de Larra, the most cited Spanish author in the first part of the century, according to Carlos Rama (145). Even the most anti-Spanish intellectuals of postindependence Argentina such as Juan Bautista Alberdi and Sarmiento professed their admiration for the Spanish journalist. Alberdi wrote articles under the pseudonym "Figarillo" (after Larra's pen name "Fígaro") and openly acknowledged his intellectual debt to the Spaniard: "I call myself Figarillo . . . because I am the son of Fígaro, . . . his product, and his imitation to such a degree that if there had been no Fígaro, there would be no Figarillo. [I am] the posthumous work of Larra" (qtd. in Shumway 139; ellipses in original). Even Sarmiento considered Larra "the Cervantes of the regenerated Spain" (139). In the midst of these conflicting views on Spain, many Spanish writers published their work in Spanish America in both book and serial form throughout the century, and many of them were widely read.

While U.S. literary culture was mostly modeled after England's for much of the nineteenth century, Spanish America seemed to have a much more complex relationship with Spain, largely due to the new place of Spanish culture and the Spanish "race" in the second stage of modernity. This ambivalence would be quite important for modernismo, which would manage eventually to marry liberal and conservative views by building on the liberal tradition of portraying Spain as a backward nation, while strategically defending the importance of the Spanish cultural tradition so dear to conservative Creoles. In so doing, modernism would accomplish what neither liberals nor conservatives had: enter the Spanish field and take away any remnant of its cultural authority over the Atlantic.

The Impact of European Literature: Symbolic Capital, Prestige, and the Literary Market

European Agents in the Spanish American Field

When assessing the effect of transnational agents in the Spanish American literary field, it is important to note, especially when trying to understand modernismo, that the presence of European literature in the Americas had significant implications for the American market of symbolic goods. European literature affected not only what Bourdieu calls the field of restricted production, in this case, American writers reading European writers, but also the field of large-scale production: sales and general readership. A considerable number of the books published in the Americas were by European writers. This is one of those instances that Bourdieu overlooks in his study of the French literary field that needs to be incorporated into his theory not only in a transnational context but also in most national contexts. For most national fields in most time periods, foreign literature certainly has an impact on both the field of restricted production (such as that of poetry) and the field of large-scale production (the serial or popular novel, for instance). Although not strictly national, these agents (texts, authors, etc.) occupy specific positions in the national field, and hence they are an integral part of the struggles for symbolic capital that define that field. Additionally, since they are competing for the same reading public, they are also bound to have an impact on the degree of autonomy and heteronomy of certain positions within the field at any given time, as well as on the level of autonomy of the field as a whole.[24]

When looking at a particular national literary field, in other words, we must pay attention to the competing positions not only of national agents but also of international ones, especially in contexts where readers often endow foreign texts with added value merely because they *are* foreign (for instance, at the peak of French cultural prestige in the nineteenth century, French literature was probably as fashionable to read as French fashion was to wear). Foreign literature then is relevant not only at the level of producers, that is, of writers themselves, where it has been mostly studied in the form of literary influences, but also at the level of reception, affecting what people read and demanded.[25]

According to a survey by an Argentine library in 1884, 87 percent of borrowers read primarily novels. The most-read authors were, in descending order of preference, Alexandre Dumas, Xavier de Montepin, Enrique Pérez Escrich, Manuel Fernández y González, Charles Paul de Kock, Jules Verne, Honoré de Balzac, María del Pilar Sinués, Pierre Alexis Ponson du Terrail, Émile Gaborieau, Eugène Sue, Adolphe Belot, Pedro Antonio de Alarcón, Benito Pérez Galdós, Victor Hugo, José Selgás, Georges Ohnet, Edmundo De Amicis, Jules Claretie, and Charles Dickens (Prieto 47). As this survey shows, the preferred authors were European, mainly French and Spanish; no Spanish American novelist was among the most read by the Argentine public. There clearly was a growing readership, enough to grant translations of foreign writers not from Spain. This had been the case, albeit in smaller numbers, since Independence.[26] According to William Moseley, English and Spanish romantic historical novels were known, read, and reedited in Chile in the 1830s and early 1840s. By 1845, the publication of *folletines*, or serial novels, in newspapers was well established (Subercaseaux 60).[27] Most of them were translations from the French and were subsequently published in book form, so that in the ten years between 1844 and 1854 "there appeared at least twenty-one editions of translations of Dumas and eight of Sue" (Moseley 276).[28] Historian Diego Barros Arana says of Sue and Dumas: "Se les leía en todas partes; y en los salones más encumbrados, así como en los círculos más modestos, se hablaba de ellos, tributándoles un ardoroso aplauso" (qtd. in Moseley 276). [They were read everywhere; everyone talked about and applauded them, both in the highest salons and in the most modest circles.][29] Then tastes seemed to shift, so that between 1854 and 1858 it was Spanish American writers who were most published. After 1858, however, the Spaniards took center stage: Antonio de Trueba, Perez Escrich, and Fernández y González, who in turn "had a great influence on the Chilean novelists Ramón Pacheco, Liborio Brieba, and others" (Moseley 275). At the other end of the region, in México, where European serial novels also appeared regularly in periodicals and as books, Spanish novelist Pérez Galdós was, according to John H. Sinnigen, the most published foreign author of the nineteenth century.

The publication of European serialized novels in Spanish America was such a central element of its literary field that it made Sarmiento, who supported their publication, exclaim that "Soulié, Dumas, Balzac, han estado enseñando a leer a la América del Sur, que para leer sus novelas-folletines se han convertido en una vasta escuela" (qtd. in Subercaseaux 60) [Soulié, Dumas, Balzac have been teaching South America how to read; it has transformed into a vast school in order to read their serial novels]. Contemporary complaints about the lack of national authors must be understood within this context. In an article from *La Nación*, for example, an anonymous critic lamented:

> Claro que tendremos que referirnos casi exclusivamente a los libros extranjeros, pues de los argentinos poco o nada puede decirse, como que son escasos, siéndolo aún más sus lectores. Sólo de vez en cuando aparece uno, como a tentar fortuna, hace un poco de ruido, obtiene artículos o sueltos de los diarios, y luego cae en el silencio, queda uno que otro ejemplar en la biblioteca de algún aficionado y el resto en los depósitos de las librerías. (qtd. in Prieto 49)
>
> [Of course we have to refer almost exclusively to foreign books, since nothing can be said about the Argentine: they are scarce and their readers even more so. Only once in a while one appears, like trying its luck, it makes a bit of noise, it gets some reviews or some small reference in the paper, and then it falls into silence, with a few copies remaining in the libraries of some fans, and the rest in the stockrooms of bookstores.]

This gap between national and foreign authors is evidence of how much the circulation of symbolic goods in the transnational literary field affected national literary markets. The tremendous impact that French literature had on the rest of the Western fields on the one hand, and on the other hand the impact that European literary agents (authors, texts, prestige) had on the other side of the Atlantic in the nineteenth century, must be taken into account when assessing Spanish American and other literatures, and this assessment should go beyond a traditional understanding of literary influences. The power of European literature affected production and reception, writers' attitudes, readers' tastes, and publishing trends, as well as struggles and competitions for symbolic capital, for literary authority, and for the market. International authors, translations, publications, and reviews were, as they still are, important forces to consider.

Position Takings and the Spanish American Challenge to European Symbolic Capital

As an emergent player in the last third of the nineteenth century when continental readership and book markets were growing, Spanish American modernismo had to contend with European literature in the field. Referring to the radical change in the relationship between form and culture carried out by the modernistas, Montaldo has persuasively argued: "Lo que el Modernismo cambió radicalmente en la cultura latinoamericana fue la relación con la *autoridad* cultural de los países centrales, pues se metieron abruptamente en su historia y en sus textos comenzaron un lento proceso de disolución de las jerarquías intelectuales, las ideas de modelo" (61). [What modernismo changed radically in Latin American culture was its relationship with the cultural *authority* of the central nations, as the modernistas abruptly entered the history of the latter and began a slow process of dissolving intellectual hierarchies and the idea of models.] Although I expand on the issue of modernismo and European authority in the next chapter, here I want to place Montaldo's idea of the modernistas' dismantling of intellectual hierarchies in the context of the Spanish American literary field: the presence of European literature in the market of symbolic goods put national authors at a disadvantage; foreign writers enjoyed a level of distinction and literary prestige that Spanish American authors now had to attain for themselves.

Literature had been consecrated since romanticism as one of the foremost indicators of the character and value of a people. In a time of nation building, both in Spanish America and elsewhere in the West, the matter of creating a "national literature" was a priority. As we have seen, it was mainly with the European literary tradition and its cultural authority that writers had to contend in the Americas. In an increasingly autonomous field, this struggle was ever more tied to the wishes of the reading public and the capacity to attract readers. Spanish American authors were trying to create national literary traditions that would be recognized as such not only in the field of restricted production, that is, by the institutions of consecration internal to the field itself (other authors and critics, literary historians, etc.), but also in the field of large-scale production. In other words, Spanish American writers (much like their counterparts in the United States) needed to build a readership that would grant prestige to national production and, hence, consume it.

One highly successful example of this effort is the novel *María* by Colombian author Jorge Isaacs. Efrain and María, the main characters whose romance moves the plot, are avid readers of Chateaubriand's *Atala*. This is unsurprising since this novel had been translated into Spanish only a few months after it was first published in French, and it had seen many editions since (Haberly 392). *Atala*'s intertextuality with Isaacs's novel has been well documented. I suggest, however, looking at the consequences that the publication of novels like *María* had for the Spanish American literary field and the position of European texts in it. *María* managed to occupy the position previously held by texts like *Atala*, so whereas María and Efrain had to read Chateaubriand's novel, subsequent generations of Spanish American readers now had *María* available to them. To the extent that it became a national novel, a foundational romance (according to Doris Sommer), *and* a tremendously successful text beyond Colombia, serialized in newspapers from

Mexico to Argentina and seeing more than fifty editions in thirty years (McGrady 13), *María* was a success.

Furthermore, to the extent that *María* became a reference for later Spanish American romances, the novel brought about a significant change in the Spanish American field.[30] Other texts attained a prominent position in the field not by directly challenging successful European novels but by tapping the rich vein of local traditions and mimicking popular forms. The most striking example is José Hernández's *Martín Fierro* in Argentina, a highly successful text with legendary print runs. Spanish American texts like these, with varying levels of success, confronted the authority of European culture and its prestige in the market to a significant degree.

The nationalization of literature and literary markets occurred largely through the representation of national subjects. This process strengthened over time so that by the last quarter of the century, national literatures were consolidating (much like the nations themselves). By this time, the reading public was rapidly increasing and diversifying, and although the competition from European books was still strong, the field had become notably more complex: it now had a larger number of positions and the struggle for symbolic capital was more difficult. As modernismo began asserting its presence in the literary field, it had to compete with both foreign and national products.[31]

Revisiting Julio Ramos's "Divergent Modernities": The Literary Market and Journalism

I have been referring to the preferences of readers in the literary market and the competition for positions within the Spanish American literary field. However, scholarship has questioned the conditions of possibility of that market and, consequently, the professionalization of the writer and the existence of an autonomous literary field in Spanish America (i.e., literary modernization). As a result, the very idea of modernismo's literary authority has been challenged. How could modernismo succeed in removing literary and cultural authority from Spain (as I will argue that it did) when the authority of literary discourse was not even established in Spanish America in the first place? Here we encounter another important consequence in Spanish American literary studies of the myths of European modernity discussed in Chapter 1: the mirage of a "modern" and fully autonomous European literary field against which the Spanish American experience is bound to be understood as failed or incomplete.

The most influential study to argue Spanish America's imperfect literary modernization is Julio Ramos's classic *Desencuentros de la modernidad en América Latina: Literatura y política en el siglo XIX* (1989; published in English as *Diver-*

gent Modernities: Culture and Politics in Nineteenth-Century Latin America [2001]), which has marked the way Spanish American literature and modernity (literary and otherwise) have been understood for the last two decades. Through an insightful analysis of early nineteenth-century works by Bello and Sarmiento and of modernista journalistic writings, or *crónicas* (chronicles), mainly Martí's, in the last third of the century, Ramos constructs the persuasive but problematic argument that Spanish American literature never quite managed to fully legitimate itself, that is, to achieve complete autonomy and establish the authority of literary discourse.[32] Spanish American literature remains, according to Ramos, irreducibly heterogeneous, hybrid, torn between its will for autonomy and the pressures of external discourses that continually limit that autonomy.

Once again, Spanish America stands in sharp contrast to Europe and the United States, where, in Ramos's view, "el proceso de autonomización del arte y la profesionalización de los escritores bien podían ser procesos sociales primarios, distintivos de aquellas sociedades en el umbral del capitalismo avanzado" (*Desencuentros* 11–12) ["the autonomization of art and the professionalization of writers was a primary social process, distinctive of those societies on the threshold of advanced capitalism" (*Divergent* xl)]. While Ramos briefly contemplates the possibility that European literature might also be heterogeneous, that, in fact, full literary autonomy might not even be possible, he sets it aside and reiterates: "Aun así habría que insistir en la extrañeza irreductible de la literatura latinoamericana" (83). ["Nevertheless one must insist on the irreductible strangeness of Latin American literature" (79).][33] Assuming the homogeneity and evenness of modernization in Europe and the United States, Ramos views the heterogeneity of Spanish American literature as a direct result of Latin America's "uneven" modernization, which prevented the conditions of possibility for literary modernity, that is, for the institutionalization of literature. Hence, according to Ramos, literature in Latin America remained profoundly heterogeneous, neither fully autonomous (as he assumes was the case in Europe and the United States) nor fully serving a state function (as he argues was the case in Latin America in the first half of the nineteenth century). Instead, beginning with modernismo, Latin American literature has been marked by a tension, torn as it were between its will to autonomy and its incapacity to completely detach itself from the public sphere, thus keeping a large measure of political authority. Ramos does not consider this to be the case in Europe or in the United States.[34] The core of Ramos's argument rests in his belief that Latin American "uneven" modernization resulted in the lack of a reading public and of a literary market, thus limiting "la voluntad autonómica y promoviendo la dependencia de la literatura de otras instituciones" (84) ["the will to autonomy in literature and promoting the dependency of literature on other institutions" (80)], mainly the newspaper.

An Unresolved Paradox: Newspapers without Readers

There is an unresolved tension at the core of Ramos's argument. He claims that the reading public in Spanish America was too small to allow for the institutionalization of literature, forcing modernista writers to turn to journalism. This begs the question: If there was no readership, who read those journalistic pieces, and how could modernistas make a living writing them? In other words, who were the readers of those periodicals, most of which also published fiction and poetry in their pages? According to Adolfo Prieto, by the end of the nineteenth century there were approximately 200,000 daily print copies of newspapers in Argentina (not including weekly publications and magazines) for an estimated total of sixty million per year. By 1882, in fact, Argentina was the third country in the world in number of periodicals per capita (Legrás 20). In Colombia, "en 1836 era tal el furor periodístico que se pensó conveniente y rentable establecer una fábrica de papel periódico en Bogotá, una ciudad que tenía menos de 30.000 habitantes" (Melo) [in 1836, the rave over newspapers was such that building a paper factory in Bogota, a city of less than 30,000 inhabitants, was considered convenient and profitable]. By 1839, the factory was in operation. Even in Peru, where speakers of Quechua and Aymara made up a large portion of the population, a correspondent for Chile's *El Mercurio*, Pedro Félix Vicuña, noted in the 1840s:

> Lima is an odd, one might even say unique place; everyone here has a passion for writing . . . and whoever writes is certain to be read . . . Do not think that gentlemen are the only ones who read here; the people, artisans, and laborers of all types save their money in order to buy an issue of *El Comercio*, and those who are too poor to purchase their own copy borrow from others. Those who do not know how to read listen, comment and discuss with the rest. Even the women join in. (qtd. in Forment 218; ellipses in original)

Vicuña's description hardly matches Ramos's notion of an absent readership.[35] In addition to their publication in each Spanish American nation, a number of these periodicals were also published abroad (mainly in the United States and France) for a Spanish-speaking audience.[36] Serial novels published in newspapers were widely published and read across Spanish America as early as the mid-1840s, as we have seen.

While numbers like these clearly indicate that Ramos is right to highlight the importance of newspapers in Spanish America, they also show that a lack of readers as a factor for interpreting literary modernity there needs to be reconsidered. Ramos's argument rests on an unresolved paradox: insufficient readers forced the Spanish American writer to work for newspapers whose existence, however, depended on readers. Ramos himself acknowledges the importance of newspapers for building a reading public in Europe: "*Público*, en el sentido moderno (ligado al mercado), que a su vez fue inicialmente fomentado por la prensa y luego por una industria editorial, cuya creciente autonomía del periódico se cristaliza en el mercado del libro, en la segunda mitad del siglo XIX" (*Desencuentros* 84). ["*Public* in the modern sense, that is, tied to the market. This public was initially cultivated by the press and later by a publishing industry whose growing autonomy from the newspaper was consolidated in the book market in the second half of the nineteenth century" (*Divergent* 80).] The question that remains unanswered is why newspapers encouraged literary autonomy in Europe but allegedly prevented that autonomy in Spanish America.

The Book Market and the Ghostly Readers

Ramos's contention that a "modern" reading public that is tied to the market and believes in the authority of literary discourse can exist only if it is connected to the book market is also questionable. It is arguable that literary autonomy needs the book form, that somehow only through the actual format of pages bound in a book can literature assert its authority, among other things because it was not a format that could be exclusively identified with the category of literature as Ramos seems to define it. Sarmiento's *Facundo* (1845), which Ramos considers the embodiment of a literary practice still tied to the political sphere, was no more autonomous nor had it any more literary authority when it was published in book form in July 1845 than when it appeared in installments between May and June that year in the Chilean newspaper *El Progreso*. Conversely, the serial novels (both local and foreign) published in that same country in that same decade were no less literary because they appeared first in newspapers. Ultimately, the most common form of publication for most of the nineteenth century across the West was not books but periodicals. Martyn Lyons explains that as late as 1871, some decried in France "the 'desacralization' of the book . . . swamped by an ocean of triviality produced by the newspaper press" (2). Likewise, in the United States, the nineteenth was "a century in which most literary reading was done in magazines" (Brodhead 471). There is no evidence that the specificity of literary discourse and its authority could be attained only in book form.

This is not to say that the book was unimportant in the nineteenth century, of course. Regarding a book readership in Spanish America, I have mentioned the fifty editions that Isaacs's *María* (1867) saw by century's end. Other classic examples include Hernández's *Martín Fierro* (1872), which by 1894 had already seen fifteen editions and sold more than 64,000 copies. When Gutiérrez's *Juan Moreira* (1880) was originally published in serial form, according to Leon Benarós, "el público se agolpaba a las puertas del diario *La Patria Argentina* para seguir el folletín que Gutiérrez había escrito quizá la noche anterior o algunos días antes" (qtd.

in Rodríguez McGill) [the public would gather at the door of the newspaper *La Patria Argentina* for the next installment that Gutiérrez had written perhaps the night before or a few days earlier]. In book form, *Juan Moreira* sold more than 100,000 copies by the end of the century, and Gutiérrez's other novels also had respectable sales.[37] Scholars commonly qualify these numbers as "exceptional" for Latin America, but the fact remains that those books sold and people bought them.

There are indeed indications of book sales and profits since early in the century and for less widely popular literary texts. According to Jorge Rivera, by 1834 Esteban Echeverría's poetry collection *Los consuelos* (*Consolations*) had a considerable distribution, as did the thousand print-copies of his *Rimas* (*Rhymes*) in 1837 (13).[38] In the 1840s, both collections were reedited when Juan Manuel Rosas was in power and Echeverría in exile in Uruguay, a reedition that prompted outrage from a newspaper columnist in Montevideo: "La edición [ha sido] hecha sin consentimiento del autor, y en fraude de su *indudable derecho de propiedad en su obra* . . . se explota su nombre, se especula así con su capacidad, se aprovecha fraudulentamente de su trabajo, del fruto de su talento, *para ganar dinero*" (qtd. in Rivera 14–15; my emphasis). [The edition (has been) made without the author's permission and against *his undoubted property rights* for his work . . . ; they exploit his name, speculate with his abilities, fraudulently take advantage of his work, of the fruit of his talent, *in order to make money*.] As Rivera points out: "La edición de las obras de Echeverría no era precisamente un mal negocio" (11). [The edition of Echeverría's works was not exactly bad business.][39]

As scarce as it still is, the data about sales point to the existence of market forces and a growing readership in Spanish America since early in the century. In a recent study, Eugenia Roldán Vera shows how the "type of relation between booksellers and customers and between the public and private dimensions of book selling was to change gradually after independence. Books came to appear more accessible: they were advertised in periodicals, subscription agencies were formed, and they were more openly displayed in shops" (20). Moreover, "bookshops started to become public places, meeting points for conversation and reading [for] a variety of (male) visitors of different social status and professions," but "other practices of book selling outside the established bookshops also account for a certain kind of 'democratization' of reading." Finally, Roldán Vera offers an assessment that is far from the bleak picture often presented in discussions of nineteenth-century readership: "Not everybody could afford the same kind of books, but many people could find a book appropriate for their different ranks and occupations. . . . If it is not possible to say that print culture had become extensive to the majority of the population, it is clear that at least it was able to attract a wider and more diverse public than ever before" (21).

The consolidation of the book market in Europe and the United States was also a slow and uneven process. In an essay discussing the reading public in England, arguably the most developed in Europe, Paul Sturges shows that the book industry began to develop only after the 1850s, did so progressively, and did not become fully established until the end of the century:

> [After 1861] publishing became polarised. At one extreme there were houses supplying high priced new works, usually in fairly small editions, to a market dominated by the circulating libraries. At the other extreme there were houses publishing reprints, part-works, sensational novels and the like, in editions of thousands and tens of thousands, at prices which were brought down and down during the period. Not until the end of the century was the potential purchaser who wanted a good quality, but affordable, edition of a new or recent title, well catered for.

It is illuminating to compare Sturges's assessment of the English case to the marketing strategies and the numbers offered by an article in Buenos Aires's *La Nación* from the 1880s, precisely when, according to Ramos, Martí had to turn to journalism (for the same newspaper) because of a lack of book readers:

> Viene después [de los textos de enseñanza] la novela en general, que ha tomado incremento últimamente merced a la libre reproducción que en ediciones baratas e incorrectas se hace de las obras más propias para producir sensación—folletines dramáticopoliciales en su mayoría—entre los cuales no es raro ver resucitar de nuevo a *Rocambole* que Javier de Montepin suministra en abundancia, y que por casualidad o por capricho, se ven mitigadas con alguna u otra obra verdaderamente literaria, de Zola, de Daudet o de Tolstoi. . . . Puede calcularse la venta anual de estas obras en unos cincuenta mil volúmenes por lo menos. Los editores especialistas, en efecto, no hacen impresiones de menos de dos mil o tres mil ejemplares, y el tipo general es el de diez mil, que venden en tres o cuatro años: por eso no se limitan a un número reducido de obras, pues su variedad facilita el negocio. (qtd. in Prieto 49)[40]

> [Next (to textbooks) comes the novel, which has seen a recent increase thanks to the free reproduction made, in cheap editions full of mistakes, of those novels more likely to cause a sensation, mainly serialized detective dramas (among which it is not unusual to see the return of *Rocambole*, abundantly provided by Xavier de Montépin), which are mitigated by this or that true literary work by Zola, Daudet, or Tolstoi. . . . The annual sales of those works can be calculated to be around fifty thousand copies, at the very least. In fact, specialized publishers do not make print-runs of less than two thousand or three thousand copies, and the most common is of ten thousand, sold within three or four years: that is why they do not limit themselves to a small number of novels, since variety helps the business.]

These numbers clearly indicate a market for books in addition to the already established market for periodicals.[41] They indicate, moreover, the resourcefulness of the publishing industry as measured by diversity. They further point to a growing gap between "high" and "low," between popular literature and what the article deems "true literary work." Finally, they plainly show what critics have consistently failed to notice, that most of the books were by foreign authors. This tells us much about the international literary market indeed, but it does not change the fact that there *were* readers who bought all those copies and many more who read them, all of whom surely understood "literature" as a distinct activity.[42] By limiting their gaze to the national, literary scholars have been looking for readers—and not finding them—in all the wrong places. Readers did not appear out of thin air to buy *Juan Moreira* or *María*, only to vanish like ghosts afterward. Rather, scholarship has rendered them ghostly by failing to acknowledge what they read.

Writers' Complaints, or Who Counts as a Reader?

A problem when assessing readership in turn-of-the-century Spanish America is that caused by relying unquestioningly on comments about readers made by modernista writers. Ramos, for instance, cites the narrator of José Martí's *Amistad funesta* (Fatal Friendship; 1885), complaining that in Spanish America "las artes delicadas que nacen del cultivo del idioma no tienen el número suficiente, no ya de consumidores, de apreciadores siquiera, que recompensen con el precio justo de esos trabajos exquisitos, la labor intelectual de nuestros espíritus privilegiados" (*Desencuentros* 84) ["the delicate arts, which are born from the cultivation of the language, do not have the sufficient number of consumers, much less connoisseurs, who might compensate for the fair price of these exquisite undertakings, the intellectual labor of our privileged spirits" (*Divergent* 80)]. However, the very language of Martí's narrator, his word choices ("delicate arts," "cultivation of the language," "connoisseurs," "exquisite undertakings," and "privileged spirits"), should alert us to the fact that, in all probability, he was not thinking precisely of the adventures of Rocambole when talking about readers.[43] Moreover, in the prologue to the projected edition in book form (*Amistad funesta* was first published in serialized form in a newspaper under a female pseudonym), Martí stated that he disliked romances because of all the requirements established by market demands and explained that he wrote the book only *to make money*, which would hardly be the case if there were insufficient readers, as his narrator claims. The complaints of modernista writers about readers have to do, more often than not, with what the readers liked to read rather than with the nonexistence of readers.[44]

The character Lord Henry claims in Oscar Wilde's *Picture of Dorian Gray* (first published in serial form in 1890) that "there is no literary public in England for anything except newspapers, primers, and encyclopedias. Of all the people in the world the English have the least sense of beauty of literature" (45). Yet no one takes this to be a faithful description of insufficient readership and a lack of an autonomous literary field in England. If anything, the claim is viewed as a reflection of Wilde's own opinions about that public. Similarly, Rubén Darío cites the following comment about the English reading public by Arthur Symons—a British poet, critic, editor, and the author of *The Symbolist Movement in Literature* (1899), a text generally regarded as the introduction of French Symbolism in England and a landmark in the development of English poetic modernism: "El publico, en Inglaterra, me parece ser el menos artístico y el menos libre del mundo, pero quizá me parece eso porque yo soy inglés y porque conozco ese público mejor que cualquier otro." [It seems to me that the public in England is the least artistic and least free in the world, but perhaps it seems so to me because I am English and because I know this public better than any other.] To this, Darío remarks: "Hay artistas descontentos en todas partes, que aplican a sus países respectivos el pensar del escritor británico" (*Poesías* 694). [There are unhappy artists everywhere that apply the thoughts of this British writer to their respective countries.] As in most other instances of the myth of modernity, nineteenth-century literary modernity seemed to always be "somewhere else."

Journalism, Literature, and Politics: Beyond Spanish America's Exceptionality

Journalism was (and still is) one of the primary bread-and-butter activities that many authors and poets turned to in order to make a living, not only in Latin America, but elsewhere. As Rubén Darío put it regarding France: "Most writers communicate with their public, give their opinion and do their social work by means of the newspapers; . . . Zola had set the example. He made it quite clear: journalism only kills off the weak. In the journalistic profession an intellectual will find a fortifying gymnastics" (qtd. by Browitt 121). For Ramos, the journalistic chronicle, with its mix of the literary and the journalistic, the aesthetic and the political, is a peculiarity of the Spanish American "uneven" literary field and imperfect modernization. Yet, the journalistic chronicle also had a very important place in Europe, especially, as José Luis Martínez Albertos has shown, in Southern Europe: Spain, Italy, and France.

Focusing on the case of France and comparing French with British and U.S. journalism, Jean Chalaby explains that "traditionally, French literary figures and celebrities have always been very involved in journalism. . . . Not only literary values but also literary capital was of a tremendous importance in the world of the press. The highest honour for a French journalist was to be received by the French Academy" (313–14). In France, literary prestige also was an asset rather than a handicap for a career in journalism, and consequently "the journalistic practice most literary in character was the most prestigious. This honour was conferred upon the chronicle. . . . Thus, this genre was mastered by literary writers" (315). In the 1920s and 1930s, *Paris-Soir*, the newspaper with the largest circulation in Europe at the time, hired a large number of "confirmed literary writers," most of whom were employed as "reporters and special correspondents" (313). Likewise, in Spanish America, it was precisely the extent to which literature already enjoyed its own distinctive and autonomous authority as a discourse that is evinced by the fact that newspapers often hired authors and poets because they had *already* attained consecration in the literary field. Such was the case, for instance, of Rubén Darío, who was asked to be a foreign correspondent for *La Nación* in 1900, after he had attained a degree of fame as a poet.[45]

It is significant that Martínez Albertos, Chalaby, and Aníbal González all consider the chronicle and, more generally, Latin European/American journalism in opposition to the Anglo-Saxon journalistic model.[46] Modern journalism was—and is—perceived by many, including contemporary critics like Chalaby, to be an Anglo-Saxon invention: "A French observer of the American press declared in 1856 that the 'press is essentially an Anglo-Saxon institution' [while] another French journalist could echo, in 1903 that 'The United States is the holy land of journalism.'" Chalaby adopts this belief as his own when he affirms that "the concept and the practice of news, just as the rest of journalistic practices, were invented and developed in America and England. Towards the closing decades of the nineteenth century, these practices were imported and adapted in France, often by the Anglo-Saxons themselves." Much like the nineteenth-century concept of modernity to which it is linked, the Anglo-Saxon journalistic model (or at least an idea of it) became the norm; by comparison, all other models were (and are) considered "undeveloped," "too political," or "too literary." Coming from journalism rather than literature, Chalaby reaches the same conclusion as Ramos but in reverse: "Literary imposition on French journalists had the effect of preventing the development of journalistic discursive practices in this country" (317). This conclusion requires not only having a predetermined vision of what constitutes true and false journalism, but also overlooking the many instances where Anglo-Saxon journalism itself did not conform to that norm.[47]

As in other aspects of nineteenth-century modernity, rather than insisting on setting Spanish America apart from a hardly questioned and homogeneous European/U.S. center, a more fruitful line of inquiry would be to explore the relationship between literature and journalism, politics and aesthetics; that is, the shifting and always inconsistent possibilities of autonomy, and the formations of specific fields across different sets of geopolitical boundaries and cultural traditions in continuous interaction with each other.

The Difference of Modernismo I: Spanish Americanism, Cosmopolitanism, and Modernity

Regarding the modernista context of production, journalism, the issue of readers, and the possibilities of literature, Susana Rotker seems closer to an explanation of the Spanish American literary market when she contextualizes modernista complaints about the reading public as a matter of different manifestations of the literary: "Esta distancia entre escritores y público no es atribuible a una sociedad que no consumía literatura, puesto que la situación era muy otra para los autores que hicieron una apuesta de escritura más referencial" (78). [This distance between the writers and their public is not attributable to a society that did not consume literature, since the situation was quite different for authors who bet on a more referential type of literature.] Among those authors, as we have seen, some were foreign, so we must add to the positions of Spanish American literary texts in the literary field, mostly tied to the realm of the national rather than the continental, the more dominant positions of foreign texts. It was into this general field, into this struggle of forces, that modernismo would enter in the 1880s.

Although Rotker does not consider the role of translated texts or the matter of European authority in the field, she rightly reminds us of the importance of reading modernista texts in relation to contemporary literary production in Spanish America, dominated largely by novels (79). The new modernista writers were trying to establish themselves in what had become a complex literary field, one far more diverse than in the first half of the century. In Bourdieu's terms, the entrance of modernismo was bound to bring about a change in the structure of the field, as any newcomer would. To enter the field is to stake a claim, that is, to try "distinguishing themselves from what already exists, even if [agents] do not all go so far as the founders of the *Revue de métaphysique et de morale* and explicitly declare the aim of 'doing something different' " (*Field* 58–59). In fact, modernismo did go that far, making difference their motto and rejecting normativity. Famous are the lines of Rubén Darío in which he claimed that his literature was just his own, and Carlos Reyles declared his own novels "something different."[48] Likewise, according to Amado Nervo, the uniqueness of his first novel, *El bachiller*, published in Mexico a year earlier than Reyles's text, had a similar impact: "Por lo audaz e imprevisto de su forma y especialmente de su desenlace, ocasionó en América tal escándalo, que me sirvió grandemente para que me conocieran" (qtd. in Durán 69). [Because of the audacity of its form, never seen before, and especially because of its ending, it caused such a scandal in America that it really helped me become known.] These examples of modernista position takings in the Spanish American literary field are clear signs of the transformation taking place within it.

The Spanish American texts whose positions were dominant at the time of modernismo's ascent were mainly novels, as Rotker has shown (79). These novels shared at least two elements. One is the emphasis on representation: most are realist fictions of some sort. The other and perhaps more important element is that all of them find their representational horizon in the realm of the nation. After the continental impulse of Independence, nationalism dominated the literature of most of the nineteenth century. Despite a sense of belonging to a larger cultural space, literary production remained mainly determined by a nationalist urge and the constitution of national literatures, whose agents were in direct competition primarily with European texts. In fact, in the imagined community of Spanish American readers, it was those European texts that provided a shared experience of reading for most of the nineteenth century. If readers from Mexico, Colombia, Peru, and Argentina met, they were more likely to share their admiration for Chateaubriand's *Atala* or Sue's *Les mystères de Paris* than for novels by authors from their own countries.

Into this arena came modernismo, from its inception and as it entered the field of positions fundamentally a transnational movement, both in the sense of creating a continental literature and in the effort to make that literature an integral part of the global literary landscape. The modernistas created a literature that could compete with the prestige of European literary production, but that also asserted its own *difference*—that is, it "existed" in the field, in Bourdieu's terms—from dominant nationalist positions. They aimed to conquer the Spanish American market of symbolic goods with a Spanish American literature that readers across the continent would read and admire.[49] They did this largely by constructing their difference on the pillars of Spanish Americanism, cosmopolitanism, and modernity, making them fundamental components of modernista literature.

Spanish Americanism

Although modernistas did not quite create Spanish America as a geocultural space—for it was there even before Independence, albeit differently construed—they infused it with new life and new meanings, eventually making it the ultimate point of reference for all subsequent literary and cultural production in the continent to this day. While most of nineteenth-century literature had thought of itself in relation to the nation, modernismo introduced both Spanish Americanism and cosmopolitanism as elements of the cultural field, that is, as elements of distinction and as cultural capital.[50] This was accomplished not only through their literary works, but also through the creation of a massive net of transnational connections in journals and magazines, through articles published in newspapers across the continent, and through prologues, reviews, and so on.[51]

The strong sense of cultural commonality was enhanced by technological changes that brought about better and faster communication among countries and regions, not only through print distribution, but in the form of travel and direct contact between writers. These changes made it possible for modernista writers to read each other's work, as well as to establish important relationships and networks through meeting in person, which could now happen easily in Buenos Aires, Caracas, Havana, New York, Madrid, or Paris. Even when Spanish Americanism did not explicitly enter the realm of representation, it was an essential component of the modernista project from its beginnings: it was its battle cry, its banner, and its raison d'être in a new global context. From its literary language and aesthetics to its sense of community through travel and journals, modernismo always conceived of itself as Spanish American *and* cosmopolitan.

Cosmopolitanism

The modernista chronicle is an example of the extent to which modernismo redefined Spanish American writing, breaking away from the localism of representation that until then had defined it. Modernismo carved out its own space by claiming that the "Spanish Americanness" of literature resided in both its content and its form, and especially in its capacity to be not only the object but also the subject of writing. In other words, Spanish Americanism and cosmopolitanism were conflated in modernismo, establishing the idea that in an increasingly global order Spanish American writers should represent not only themselves, but also the world at large. Inasmuch as the transnational literary field is located within the transnational field of power, the act of writing, of naming the others, was (is) also always an act with political implications. At times, this naming was done in admiration of elements of European, North American, and other modernities, at times in critique and rejection of them. In any case, both admiration and critique resulted from imposing the Spanish American gaze onto the European, North American, Asian, and African objects.[52]

The thousands of chronicles written in this period are testimony to this effort by modernistas to represent themselves and others, be it nations who claimed to be at the vanguard of the modern or those whose modernities were in dispute.[53] In the humorous tone that characterizes many of his journalistic writings, Amado Nervo made very clear this power of discourse in his chronicle entitled "Nuestra insignificancia":

> Todos los días, a todas horas y en todos los tonos se repite que en Mexico no hay arte, que en México no hay literatura, que en México no hay nada. . . . ¿Qué somos sino un triste planeta que refleja luz prestada: la luz de esa Francia artística, de esa Francia intelectual, esa Francia única, cerebro de Europa y del mundo entero? . . . Aquí ni el derecho a pensar tenemos. Los pensamientos nos vienen de París, con brevete y embase elegante. . . . Me he preguntado muchas veces: "¿por qué los franceses valen tanto? ¿por qué nosotros no valemos nada?" . . . Los franceses valen

> infinitamente más que nosotros, porque a nosotros, a todos los latinos que no somos franceses, se nos ha ocurrido que valen mucho: porque hablan mucho, porque declaman mucho, porque dogmatizan mucho, pero con elegancia. (558–59)
>
> [Every day, at all times and in every tone, it is repeatedly said that there is no art in Mexico, that in Mexico there is no literature, that there is nothing in Mexico.... What are we but a sad planet that reflects borrowed light: that of artistic France, intellectual France, unique France, the brain of Europe and the whole world? ... Here we do not even have the right to think. The thoughts come from Paris, with a tag and elegant wrapping.... I have often wondered: How come the French are so worthy? How come we are worthless? ... The French are worth infinitely more than us because we (all Latin people who are not French) have decided that they are worth much: because they speak much, declaim much, dogmatize much, but with elegance.]

Here Nervo exposes the capacity of discourse to shape perceptions and thus to establish relations of power and cultural authority. The modernista claim to discursive authority and legitimacy aimed to undermine the self-appointed authority of European discourse, whose horizon of representation had never been limited to itself. The legitimacy of Spanish American literature to speak about anything and anyone, to define itself and define others, was an undeniable and remarkable accomplishment of modernismo that has not been sufficiently recognized.

Cosmopolitanism thus understood was a central component of modernismo's claim to "difference" or "existence" in the literary field. It was the source of struggles with the nationalism that still dominated in a field where the representation of European culture was almost exclusively left to European texts. With modernismo's advent, readers who wanted to know about France could certainly read French authors, but they could also now read Spanish American authors. Cosmopolitanism, then, did not contradict Spanish Americanism, but rather complemented it. In order for Spanish American literature and culture to make any sense at all, it had to be as part of a global literature and culture and in equal dialogue with others.

Rodó would make this clear when, discussing the modernista novel, he affirmed that the autochthonous and the cosmopolitan had to go hand in hand: "Pero al lado del tributario fiel de la región, al lado del hijo fiel de nuestra América, ... está en nosotros el ciudadano de la Cultura universal, ante el que se desvanecen las clasificaciones que no obedezcan a profundas disimilitudes morales.... Como el esclavo de Terencio, podemos reivindicar para nuestro ambiente espiritual 'todo lo que es del hombre' " (161). [But next to the faithful tributary of the region, next to the faithful child of our America, ... is also within us the citizen of universal Culture, before whom all classifications that are not due to profound moral differences vanish.... Like Terence's slave, we can vindicate for our spiritual environment "all that is human."] Rodó—ironically often called the anticosmopolitan face of modernismo, when not plainly labeled antimodernista—understood Spanish Americanism and cosmopolitanism as inseparable. Citing Terence's famous line, which Appiah has recently called "something like the golden rule of cosmopolitanism" (*Cosmopolitanism* 111), Rodó makes clear that Americans can claim as theirs the culture of all other peoples by virtue of human commonality; by the same token, other peoples can claim Spanish American culture as their own.

Modernity

In Rodó's reference to "nuestra América," as in Martí's famous essay a few years earlier, the balance between remaining grounded in Spanish America but committed to cosmopolitanism—what in contemporary terms we might call the relationship between the local and the global—is strongly connected to the changes brought about by modernization. Reyles ended the prologue to his *Academias*, which prompted Rodó's essay, with the image of a Spanish American army of young writers ready to conquer the world in the name of modernity; the image summarizes just how interconnected Americanism, cosmopolitanism, and modernity were in modernismo. Rodó's answer to Reyles's army was: "Y sea bienvenido en su nombre el esfuerzo de los que se adelantan para hacer colaborar al alma de América en esta inmensa labor renovadora" (50). [And let us welcome in its name the effort by those who go ahead to make the soul of America collaborate in this immense labor of renewal.] By the time Rodó wrote his essay on Reyles's new novel, modernity had been central to modernismo for more than a decade as the movement consolidated its position in the field. Martí wrote one of the best and earliest reflections on nineteenth-century modernity and the place of art and literature in a world of rapid modernization in another prologue, to Bonalde's "Poema del Niágara." Modernity was, of course, behind the very term with which Rubén Darío baptized the movement in 1890.

What is striking about Spanish American modernismo is both the extent to which these writers embraced the concept of the modern and made it their own, and their growing awareness of the importance of their new term, "modernismo," to describe something that reached beyond a simple school or trend. In this sense, modernismo was not just another literary "-ism." The statement, still often repeated, that modernismo was the Spanish American version of French Symbolism and Parnasianism completely misses the point; it is high time that we as scholars dismantle that inaccurate and misleading notion. Matei Călinescu may have been the first critic to make this clear when he pointed out the capacity of Spanish American modernismo to see beyond the specifics of schools to conceptualize an entire way of understanding literature: "They were able to penetrate beyond the mere appearances of difference to grasp the underlying spirit of radical innovation, which they promoted under the name modernismo. It is interesting to note here that French literary history itself, fascinated with the detail of late nineteenth-century aesthetic polemics, has been unable or unwilling to develop a historical-theoretical concept comparable to the Hispanic modernismo" (70).

The lucidity, ambition, and capacity of modernismo to capture the global zeitgeist was unmatched, for there was nothing remotely like it in scope in France or anywhere else in the West.[54] Spanish American modernistas were responsible for an early conceptualization of an entire period, of the new way in which literature was thinking about itself and establishing a different relationship with the changes brought about by modernization, not only in one's own backyard, but also across the globe. Thus, Spanish Americanism, cosmopolitanism, and modernity became the three inseparable pillars of modernismo.

The Difference of Modernismo II: Creating a New Spanish American Literature

Toward a Spanish American Literary Language

According to Bourdieu's model, we may remember, newcomers in any field must "get themselves known and recognized ('make a name for themselves'), by endeavoring to impose new modes of thought and expression" (*Field* 58). If Latin Americanism, cosmopolitanism, and modernity were modernismo's new modes of thought, they came accompanied by a radical change in literary expression. In a field dominated by either European or Spanish American texts that placed value on representation of the national, the modernista stress on form further set their literature apart and was one of the most debated elements of the movement in the struggles for symbolic capital. This focus struck a blow to the representational localism of the realist and naturalist language of the vast majority of the competition. Against the nationalist impulse of their contemporaries, modernista literary language crossed borders and became Spanish American.

While Matto de Turner was concerned with representing Peruvianess and Cambaceres, as Gabriela Nouzeilles has persuasively argued (*Ficciones*), focused on an Argentina that he saw sickened by European immigrants even in its language, modernistas from all corners of the continent created a literary language that knew nothing of national boundaries and that was open to change and cross-pollination, not enclosed in traditionalist claims to linguistic purity. Among these writers were Darío from Nicaragua, Martí and Julián del Casal from Cuba, Gutiérrez Nájera and Nervo from Mexico, Silva from Colombia, Rodó and Reyles from Uruguay, Ricardo Jaimes Freyre from Bolivia, Leopoldo Lugones from Argentina, Díaz Rodríguez from Venezuela, and many others. In the opening statement to their *Revista de América* in 1894, Darío and Jaimes Freyre explained their aim: "Mantener, al propio tiempo que el pensamiento de innovación, el respeto a las tradiciones y la gerarquía [*sic*] de los maestros; trabajar por el brillo de la lengua castellana en América, y, al par que por el tesoro de sus riquezas antiguas, por el engrandecimiento de esas mismas riquezas en vocabulario, rítmica, plasticidad y matiz" (45). [To maintain at once thoughts of innovation and respect for the traditions and hierarchies of the masters; to work for the brilliance of the Castilian language in America and for both its treasure of ancient riches and the expansion of those riches in vocabulary, rhythm, plasticity, and nuance.] Language for the modernistas was another central component of the balance between Spanish Americanism, cosmopolitanism, and modernization. By opening up the "ancient" Castilian language, modernismo aimed to both modernize it and make it Spanish America's own. The final border modernismo would cross in order to impose the authority of the new Spanish American language was Spain's, whose claim to Castilian was (and unfortunately still remains) too often encoded in imperialist terms. This would ultimately imply taking away Spain's authority over the Spanish language. Indeed, implicit in Darío and Freyre's quoted words, there is a reversal of colonial relations: if Spain used to mine the "riches" of America in colonial times, it is now America that is taking the raw materials of the Spanish linguistic treasure and transforming it into something new, into a value-added manufactured good, as it were, with which to participate in the world cultural market.

Modernismo created a transnational Spanish American cultural and literary field by managing to appeal to both the traditional conservative and the modernizing liberal sides of the Spanish American social and political spectrum, as we have seen. Language, so inextricably linked to identity, had to be at the core of their enterprise. As Baldomero Sanin Cano explained it in 1890 in "Literatura americana" (American Literature):

> Hay en América [quienes] miran de reojo las innovaciones y proscriben la introducción de voces y frases extranjeras. . . . Las exigencias comerciales y civilizadoras de Buenos Aires y México, la comunicación inmediata con países extranjeros y con inmigrantes, van modificando la lengua. Y entre estos dos extremos se halla la juventud literaria que, sin abandonar las tradiciones del idioma, se esfuerza en hacerlo más apto para servir los fines del arte moderno. (121)

> [There are in America [those who] look at innovations with suspicion and forbid the introduction of foreign words or phrases. . . . The commercial and civilizing demands of Buenos Aires and Mexico, the immediate communication with foreign countries and with immigrants, are modifying the language. And between these two poles we find the literary youth, who, without abandoning linguistic traditions, work hard to make the language more apt to serve the ends of modern art.]

By doing so, not only did modernistas stress and further the autonomy and authority of the literary field, but also they helped establish the autonomy, importance, and relevance of a specifically Spanish American literature in the transnational struggle for cultural capital and power. Furthermore, with competition from European texts curbing the emergence or success of local authors, a specifically Spanish American literary expression might tip the balance the other way, that is, to earn prestige and cultural capital, and compete in the international market of symbolic goods. To intervene in both continental and transnational literary culture and create a distinctively Spanish American discourse, modernismo had to begin with the most basic tool of the writing craft, making literary language itself its own.

Poetry in the Field of Positions

The renovation of literary expression in Spanish carried out by modernismo was not limited to the realm of poetry, something often assumed given the disproportionate critical attention modernista poetry has received. Most of the dominant texts in the Spanish American field as modernismo emerged were novels, as I have mentioned. Modernista poetry had little to no competition in the struggle for symbolic capital in a field where poetry had virtually ceased to be an important force. Indeed, it had been languishing since the height of romanticism and, with the exception of the popular (or, as in the notable case of *Martín Fierro*, texts mimicking the popular), poetry in Spanish had become, for the most part, stale and academicist in both Spanish America and Spain. In this context, it is understandable that modernismo rose to a dominant position in the literary field first in poetry, although it certainly was not an exclusively poetic movement, nor was its aesthetic project limited to that genre.

This poetic wasteland helps explain Darío's literary success and leadership in the field of restricted production. To an extent, Darío was able to capitalize on innovations and advances being made by writers like José Martí, Manuel Gutiérrez Nájera, Julián del Casal, and José Asunción Silva, among others, all of whose writings, in both prose and poetry, were already having an important impact in the field.[55] While prose, and especially fiction, had to contend with a more diverse and complex competitive field, poetry was experiencing a relative vacuum. Rubén Darío's talent and mastery of Spanish prosody and poetic form and language—the new language that was rapidly gaining literary prestige thanks to elder peers like Martí and Nájera and generational mates like Silva and Casal—coupled with his equally masterful use of networking, travel, and self promotion (all position takings) placed him at the forefront of the poetic movement. Additionally, by 1896, the year of *Prosas profanas* and Darío's own consolidation in the field, all of the peers just mentioned had died quite young, and up-and-coming poets like Amado Nervo and Leopoldo Lugones were just beginning to establish themselves.

These factors that move beyond the strictly literary and are crucial to position taking in the literary field should not be underestimated, as they give us a more nuanced understanding of the emergence of poetic modernismo in Spanish America and, as we shall see, in Spain; there, many received with anxiety the fact that the much-needed renovation of poetry came from Spanish America. Conversely, modernismo had a tougher struggle in fiction, particularly in the novel, since the competition in the field was stronger and the prestige of realism and naturalism, on the one hand, and the market success of serialized romantic novels, on the other, made emergence and consolidation more difficult. Modernismo did succeed, however, in the realm of the novel, which would eventually become dominant in the field, starting with the splash made by texts such as Nervo's *El bachiller* (1896) and continuing with the notable success of such novels as Díaz Rodríguez's *Ídolos rotos* (1901) and *Sangre patricia* (1902) and, especially, Enrique Larreta's *La gloria de don Ramiro* (1908).

Familiarization: Building a Transnational Modernista Public

This new literary language required new readers, that is, a new kind of public, and modernistas had to build it. As José Fernández, the protagonist of José Asunción Silva's 1896 *De sobremesa* (*After-Dinner Conversation* [2005]) tells his audience of friends: "Es que no yo quiero *decir* sino sugerir y para que la sugestión se produzca es preciso que el lector sea un artista. . . . Golpea con los dedos esa mesa, es claro que sólo sonarán unos golpes, pásalos por las teclas de marfil y producirán una sinfonía. Y el público es casi siempre mesa y no un piano que vibre como este" (43). [I do not want to *say* but to suggest, and in order for the suggestion to be produced it is necessary that the reader be an artist. . . . Hit a table with your fingers; it is clear that all that will sound are some knocks; run them over the ivory keys and they will produce a symphony. The public is almost always a table and not a piano that vibrates like this one.][56] Even the structure of Silva's novel (the act of reading a text to a group of friends after dinner) points to the modernista preoccupation with the creation of a new public. Early in the novel, one of the friends listening to the protagonist read from his diaries leaves, upset because he is unable to understand anything; the remaining three express at different points divergent opinions on José's writings. According to Peter Brooks, in realism there was "an apparent need for and confidence in the shaping order of plot, whatever its ultimate inconsistencies and limitations as an explanatory system" (237). In modernista writing, on the contrary, we find what Brooks has defined (regarding European modernism) as "an increasingly acute self consciousness about the status of narrative within art that is itself self-consciously 'modern,' . . . [an] intense awareness of the epistemological and linguistic problems posed by storytelling" (236).[57] What might seem aloofness on the part of the protagonist of *After-Dinner Conversation* about "table-readers" is ultimately betrayed by the novel itself in its intense preoccupation with the act of reading, specifically, with inviting its readers to become a new kind of reader, "piano-readers." In other words, Silva's novel, emblematic of modernista writing in this as in most other regards, is quite concerned with creating a new public.

Bourdieu explains that for a literary revolution to occur, that is, for a new set of producers to become dominant in the field, a new category of consumers is usually needed. He calls the process of creating that new category "familiarization." As he explains: "The most innovative works tend, with time, to produce their own audience by imposing their own structures, through the effect of familiarization, as categories of perception legitimate for any possible work" (*Rules* 253). I believe that was the case of modernismo as it imposed itself in the Spanish American (and in the Spanish) field. The kind of public demanded by Silva's protagonist and by fellow modernistas required a significant transformation of traditional reading practices, particularly in a field dominated by realism, and so it is not surprising that modernistas complained time and again about the lack of such a reading public. However, as Michael Warner has argued in another context: "No single text can create a public. Nor can a single voice, a single genre, even a single medium. All are insufficient to create the kind of reflexivity that we call a public, since a public is understood to be an ongoing space of encounter for discourse. No texts themselves create publics, but the concatenation of texts through time. Only when a previously existing discourse can be supposed, and when a responding discourse can be postulated, can a text address a public" (62). One of the achievements of modernismo was the creation of such a new public, a "new ongoing space of encounter for discourse," through the concatenation of many texts and many genres in many contexts.

From its entrance into the field, modernismo began engaging readers on many fronts. At a time of wider democratization of culture, of a "sensibilidad amenazada" (sensibility under threat), as Montaldo calls it, when the traditional values of lettered culture were being challenged by the many changes of modernization, modernistas engaged those changes by aiming to appeal to both their literary peers and a broader readership, that is, the fields of restricted and large-scale production, in Bourdieu's terms. Those who thought literature through a national lens they encouraged to appreciate a common Spanish American cultural and linguistic space and to think literature transnationally. Those who invested European literature with capital and prestige they encouraged to appreciate and recognize Spanish American literary production. Modernistas aimed to appeal to the high and the low, their fellow authors and poets and the general public. Martí is but one notable example of this endeavor: his broad appeal ranged from his sophisticated

Versos libres to the popular form of his *Versos sencillos*, from writings for children to translations of foreign texts. Translation was, in fact, one of the most prolific activities of Spanish American modernistas and, as noted, should be considered an integral part of their position taking in the literary field, an important way to establish modernista literary language. Although perhaps more active in the field of restricted production (translations of French symbolist poetry, for instance, or of Japanese haiku), modernistas also translated popular texts, such as Martí's translations of Helen Hunt Jackson's *Ramona* and Hugh Conway's *Called Back* (*Misterio*), for example. Besides bringing in money, translations were a way of exposing modernista literary language to a larger audience.[58]

The specificity of the modernista crónica and its importance to the movement is yet another example of familiarization, for through the crónica modernista writers built a reading public that would appreciate and keep demanding their work. They were developing a new transnational category of consumers (Bourdieu), a new reading public (Warner). In this sense, the aesthetic will that Ramos rightly identifies in the journalistic writing of the modernistas was part of a struggle for the recognition less of the authority of literary discourse than for the authority of *their* literary discourse. When Spanish novelist Juan Valera, a *cronista* himself, was told that journalism was killing literature because it stole the few existing readers in Spain, he replied that, on the contrary, it was because of newspapers that literature still had a chance, since they showcased literary products (through articles, book reviews, and crónicas) that could pique the curiosity of the readers, spark their interest, and make them buy books (*Obras* 3:461). In other words, newspapers had the potential to turn "periodical" readers into "book" readers. By this logic, it is not hard to imagine readers of *La nación* becoming familiar with the names José Martí and Amado Nervo, enjoying their crónicas, and seeking out their other work. Enrique Gómez Carrillo, for instance, gained his reputation first as a critic and cronista and then as a novelist. In this way, modernista journalistic writing could serve as a platform and get readers acquainted with and accustomed to the new product. In the literary market, advertising is an important position taking; to an extent, the crónica advertised the author. As Warner suggests, building a public does not happen with one text; it takes a concatenation of texts, the creation of an entire discursive space. The flourishing of the modernista crónica and the fact that it was sought out by many newspapers also indicate modernismo's success at creating that public.

Modernismo carried out a veritable revolution in the Spanish American literary field and in the process created a new language in which to represent Spanish America and its others. Aware of the implications of what Martí had called the battle of ideas in a new global order, modernismo strived to become a force to contend with in the transnational market of symbolic goods, to occupy a position in the transnational literary field, and to attain cultural authority, freeing Spanish America from what Henry James called "the burden of Europe." There is a sense of entitlement in modernista writing that is remarkable, a self-confidence and trust in the authority of Spanish American literary discourse to speak about anything and anyone that is striking. Neither had characterized postindependence literature and, arguably, they would be seen only sporadically after modernismo.

Yet the burden of Europe was heavy. To the extent that each America shared a language and literary tradition with its former metropolis, literary authority and an important part of the institutions of prestige and consecration were still largely located in those metropolitan centers. When modernismo was establishing itself in the Spanish American field, literary and linguistic authority remained, to a significant extent, in Spain, as Nervo suggests:

> Mientras Menéndez Pelayo que hace antologías, doña Emilia que escribe sobre Rusia y *Clarín* que mide el mérito de los versos por las palabras de castellano viejo que contienen, no escriben a un poeta americano una carta de plácemes, el tal no es poeta ni Cristo que lo entienda; mas una vez que puede mostrar cartas de aquellos 'ultramarinos' ilustres de literatura oliente a garbanzo, boca abajo todo el mundo. (446)

> [Unless Menéndez Pelayo, who writes anthologies, doña Emilia [Pardo Bazán], who writes about Russia, and [Leopoldo Alas] Clarín, who measures the merit of verses by the amount of Old Castilian words they contain, write an American poet a congratulatory letter, such poet is no poet no matter what; but once he can show letters from those illustrious writers of garbanzo-smelling literature from overseas, then everyone on bended knee.]

Even so, Nervo's text and particularly his sarcastic tone cancel the authority they describe as he mocks the consecrated literary popes of Spanish letters. One of modernismo's more lasting achievements was not only to question Spanish cultural and literary authority, but to take it away from the Peninsula. When in 1896 Reyles wrote a prologue that upset much of Spain's literary establishment, he referred to the existence of a new public in both Spanish America and Spain, demanding that the novel in Spanish keep up with the changes of modern life. By the time Rubén Darío made his second visit to Spain in 1900, the reversal of authority had already taken place, as modernismo had transformed the literary field of the ex-metropolis, whose readers were now following the lead marked by those on the other side of the Atlantic. Only then was the modernista literary revolution complete.

CHAPTER 3

The Conquest of the Metropolitan Literary Field

> It is important to say it because many pretend not to know it: that a kind of inverted conquest took place in which the new caravels, departing from the old colonies, set course for the coast of Spain. Militant critics from the Peninsula used to say that the books then recently arrived from America were, although quite well drafted, sick with modernist mania.
>
> —Manuel Díaz Rodríguez, *The Way of Perfection*

> To produce effects is already to exist in a field, even if these effects are mere reactions of resistance or exclusion. It follows that the dominants have trouble defending themselves against the threat contained in any redefinition of the right of entry, explicit or implicit, since they are granting existence, by fighting against them, to those they want to exclude.
>
> —Pierre Bourdieu, *The Rules of Art*

It is tempting to begin a discussion of the impact of Spanish American modernismo in Europe with the first transatlantic voyage made by Rubén Darío, since in 1892, four hundred years after Columbus's ships sailed in the other direction, Darío first landed on the shores of Spain. Indeed, modernismo found in Darío's trip both an impulse and a powerful symbol. As a fellow modernista would put it a few years later, Rubén Darío, leading an entire generation of American writers, carried out an "inverted conquest" (Díaz Rodríguez 61) of the former metropolis. Despite the appeal and importance of Darío's transatlantic crossing, however, the beginnings of the modernista "conquest" can be traced back to the complicated reception of Darío's book *Azul* in Spain. On 22 and 29 October 1888, Juan Valera, a well-established Spanish novelist who was writing a series of review articles on Spanish American letters (published in book form in 1889 as *Cartas americanas* [*American Letters*]), wrote a long and positive review of *Azul*, a collection of poetry and short stories that had come out that year in Valparaiso, Chile. Both the book and the review (written in the form of two letters to Darío) have earned a spot in literary history as landmarks in the development of modernismo, yet neither until now has been read as the foundational moment of a larger shift in cultural authority across the Atlantic. *Azul* and the review it generated represent the first clear instance of modernista position taking, that is, of advancement and gain in symbolic capital, in what was to become an acrid struggle that would be resolved with the imposition of Spanish American modernismo in Spain and the transformation of its literary field, what Bourdieu defines as a "literary revolution" (*Rules* 253).

Two elements stand out in Valera's *Cartas americanas*. The first is the remarkable extent to which the Spanish writer was familiar with Spanish American literary and cultural production. The second is Valera's position as granter of consecration.[1] The two, interconnected, are a necessary point of departure for understanding Valera's texts and their unwitting role in the modernista reversal of colonial dynamics, as we will see in this chapter.

Darío, Valera, and the Old Spanish Tree of Knowledge

Condescending as he is in his positive review of *Azul*, Valera shows a clear, if uneasy, understanding of what Darío's modernismo was and meant. Although the name "modernismo" was not yet consolidated in 1888 and was certainly not yet on the horizon of most Spaniards, what Valera identifies as the main elements of *Azul* are indeed central elements of the movement.[2] The first thing Valera notes is Darío's unabashed cosmopolitanism:

> Si el libro, impreso en Valparaíso en este año de 1888, no estuviese en muy buen castellano, lo mismo pudiera ser de un autor francés, que de un italiano, que de un turco o de un griego. El libro está impregnado de espíritu cosmopolita. Hasta el nombre y apellido del autor, verdaderos o contrahechos y fingidos, hacen que el cosmopolitismo resalte más. Rubén es judaico, y persa es Darío; de suerte que, por los nombres, no parece sino que usted quiere ser o es de todos los países, castas y tribus. (*Obras* 3:290)
>
> [If this book, published in Valparaiso this year of 1888, were not written in very good Castilian, it might as well be by a French, Italian, Turkish, or Greek author. The book is impregnated by a cosmopolitan spirit. Even the name and surname of the author, real or fake and made up, make its cosmopolitanism stand out even more. Rubén is Jewish and Darío is Persian so that, judging by the names, it seems that you want to be, or are, from all countries, castes, and tribes.]

Valera identifies a cosmopolitan spirit in Darío's collection, yet he does so with ambiguous feelings, as he claims that he wants authors to have a "national character" (291). This signature and fascinating trait of Valera's reviews is especially at work in this one: to undermine, or in other instances demote, every opinion he presents as if fearing the implications of what he is saying.

This is a crucial aspect of Valera's writing that must be explored if we are to understand the complexity of Valera's reception of Spanish American texts, as well as the general interaction between Spanish intellectuals and their Spanish American counterparts.[3] Valera was quite aware of his own critical operations and the possible contradictions of his texts, the work of the "critical little devil" he acknowledged in another of his review letters, this one from April 1888, a few months before the first to Darío:

> El diablillo crítico que me atormenta, y por el que estoy no sé si obseso o poseído, no consiente que diga yo, cuando escribo, aquello que quiero decir, sino aquello que él quiere que yo diga; y lo más que logro a veces, y esto es peor, es decir lo que él quiere y lo que yo quiero; de donde resulta, en algo como diálogo, más que discurso, una verdadera sarta o ristra de *antinomias*, según las llaman ahora. (*Obras* 3:238)

> [The critical little devil that torments me and by whom I am either obsessed or possessed, does not allow me to say, when I write, what I want to say, but what he wants me to say; and the most I manage sometimes, and this is the worst part, is to say what he wants and what I want; as a result, mine is a dialogue rather than a lecture, a veritable stream or string of *antinomies*, as they call them now.]

What I find remarkable about the "diablillo crítico" is not only Valera's level of awareness, but also his decision to leave those "antinomias" unresolved. Thus, after showing amazement at the poet's radical cosmopolitanism, he finds the need to reduce it to something much smaller, more concrete, and easier to handle—he criticizes Darío's alleged "galicismo mental" (mental gallicism), the notorious phrase to which the richness of Valera's long text—full of critical insight, anxiety, and contradictions—has been regrettably reduced by literary history (291, 298). Yet the Spanish critic, despite himself, cannot deny his own perceptiveness:

> Y usted no imita a ninguno: ni es usted romántico, ni naturalista, ni *neurótico*, ni decadente, ni simbólico, ni parnasiano. Usted lo ha revuelto todo, lo ha puesto a cocer en el alambique de su cerebro y ha sacado de ello una rara quintaesencia. Resulta de aquí un autor nicaragüense, que jamás salió de Nicaragua sino para ir a Chile, y que es autor tan a la moda de París y con tanto *chic* y distinción, que se adelanta a la moda y pudiera modificarla e imponerla. (291)

> [And you do not imitate anybody: you are neither romantic nor naturalist, neither *neurotic* nor decadent, neither symbolist nor Parnassian. You have turned everything upside down, you have cooked it all in the alembic of your brain and you have extracted a rare quintessence from it. As a result, we have a Nicaraguan author who never left Nicaragua except to go to Chile, and who is such an author *à la mode de Paris* and with such *chic* and distinction that he is ahead of fashion and could indeed modify it and set a new trend.]

Back and forth Valera goes; he wants to turn Darío into just another imitator of French literature but finds himself unable to do so. For him, the American poet is not an imitator, nor can he be compared or circumscribed to any French school, however much they may have contributed to his creation. On the contrary, Darío is not a follower but a leader, an innovator, a trendsetter "ahead of fashion." Ultimately Valera concedes that Darío is just himself and that he has created something new and original: "Usted es usted; con gran fondo de originalidad, y de originalidad muy extraña" (*Obras* 3:290). [You are you, with a great core of originality, a very strange originality.] These words would find an interesting echo in Darío's preface to his next poetry collection, *Prosas profanas* (1896): "Mi literatura es *mía* en mí" (168). [My literature is mine in me.]

Although the Spaniard never actually spells out that Darío is a "modern" writer, modernity is what he sees all over *Azul*. That Valera was a traditionalist and a Catholic did not blind him to the connection between Darío's new way of writing and the philosophical issues of the times: "Con ser su libro de usted de pasatiempo, y sin propósito de enseñar nada, en él se ven patentes las tendencias y los pensamientos del autor sobre las cuestiones más trascendentales. Y justo es que confesemos que los dichos pensamientos no son ni muy edificantes ni muy consoladores" (*Obras* 3:292). [Even though your book is a mere pastime with no pedagogical intention, one can clearly see in it the thoughts and inclinations of the author regarding the most transcendental questions. And it is fair to say that those thoughts are neither very edifying nor very consoling.] In fact, most of the first part of the review is dedicated to describing the experience of modernity that he reads in Darío's text. It is a succinct but insightful description of the effect that science, philosophy, technology, and secularism have had on "modern life." For Valera, under their influence, modern life is characterized by at least two fundamental traits, the disappearance of God and the search for new beliefs and mythologies, and this is exactly what he finds embodied in *Azul*: "Estos dos rasgos van impresos en su librito de usted. El pesimismo, como remate de toda descripción de lo que conocemos, y la ponderosa y lozana producción de seres fantásticos, evocados o sacados de las tinieblas de lo incognoscible, donde vagan las ruinas de las destrozadas creencias y supersticiones vetustas" (293). [These two features are stamped upon your little book: pessimism as the culmination of every description of what we know, and the ponderous and vigorous production of fantastic beings, evoked or taken from the mist of the unknown, where the ruins of destroyed old beliefs and superstitions lay.] In typical contradictory fashion again, the Spanish critic considers the "little book" a mere pastime, then claims that it deals with the most transcendental issues of modernity.

Finally, not only does Valera recognize Darío's cosmopolitanism and modernity, but also he has to admit—and this is the hardest pill to swallow and the apparent source of his ambivalence and anxiety—that neither has anything to do with Spain's current literary production: "Yo no creo que se ha dado jamás caso parecido con ningún español peninsular. Todos tenemos un fondo de españolismo que nadie nos arranca ni a veinticinco tirones." [I do not believe that there has ever been a similar case with a Spaniard from Spain. We all have a core of Spanishness that no one strips us of no matter how hard they try.] Furthermore, Valera, who confesses himself unable and unwilling to think beyond nation, concedes that Darío is bound to become not just a great Nicaraguan writer, but a "glory" of Spanish American letters: "En mi sentir, hay en usted una poderosa individualidad de escritor, ya bien marcada, y que, si Dios da a usted la salud que yo le deseo y larga vida, ha de desenvolverse y señalarse más con el tiempo en obras que sean gloria de las letras hispanoamericanas." [In my opinion, there is a powerful individuality in you as a writer, already well defined, which, if God grants you the long and healthy life that I wish for you, will in time stand out more and evolve into works that will be the glory of Spanish American letters.] Valera painfully admits two important facts. First, that Darío's stature extends beyond his native Nicaragua to the continent and, second, that the continent is no longer politically dependent on Spain, and thus he cannot "demand" anything: "N[o] puedo exigir de usted que sea literariamente español, pues ya no lo es políticamente" (291). [I cannot demand that you be Spanish literarily since you are not so politically.]

Following Valera's own logic (political dependence *would* allow him to demand literary dependence), it is impossible not to connect his explicit desire to see more Spanish influence in Darío's text with a lingering nostalgia for empire. This nostalgia, of course, permeates the entire collection *Cartas americanas* (and the later *Nuevas cartas americanas* [New American Letters] of 1890) and is made explicit at various points by Valera, who has no qualms in openly lamenting the dissolution of the Spanish empire. It could be argued that this longing is also the *razón de ser* of the *Cartas* themselves, an attempt at maintaining cultural authority over the ex-colonies. Indeed, in his dedication of *Cartas* to Spanish prime minister Antonio Cánovas del Castillo, Valera starts with a defense of the Spanish empire, which he follows with a summary of the tumultuous political histories of Spanish America and Spain in the nineteenth century. With political stability now in sight, Valera thinks, cultural understanding must ensue. He can conceive of this cultural unity, however, only under the leadership of Spain: "Porque las literaturas de Méjico, Colombia, Chile, Perú y demás repúblicas, si bien se conciben separadas, *no cobran unidad superior y no son literatura general hispanoamericana* sino en virtud de un lazo para cuya formación es menester contar con la metrópoli" (*Obras* 3:213; my emphasis). [Because, while they can be thought of in separate terms, the literatures of Mexico, Colombia, Peru, and the rest of the republics *do not have a higher unity nor are they Spanish American literature* except by virtue of a tie whose existence necessarily depends on the metropolis.] The insistence of Valera on the role of Spain as leader of and mediator between the republics reveals his underlying anxiety not only over the end of empire but also, and perhaps more importantly, over being irrelevant. What here is merely implicit Valera would fully disclose in the prologue to his next collection, *Nuevas cartas americanas*, dedicated to Antonio Flores, president of Ecuador, where he openly admits that culture is never only about culture, but about politics as well: "Aunque mi propósito al escribir [las cartas] es puramente literario, todavía, sin proponérmelo yo, lo literario trasciende en estos asuntos a la más alta esfera política." [Although my intention in writing (the letters) is purely literary, still, without my attempting it, in these matters literature reaches the highest political spheres.] When he adds a few lines later that everything written in Spanish is "literatura española" [Spanish literature], there is no need for further explanation of his political implications (*Obras* 3:313). It is indeed this cultural/political need for Spain to matter, for Spain to be that which gives meaning to Spanish America, that seems to motivate Valera's anxiety, and it is this vision of a central and dominant Spain that he cannot find anywhere in *Azul*, whose author he foresees, nonetheless, destined to become a glory of "Spanish American letters" and therefore distinct and independent of "Spanish literature."[4]

This precariously balanced set of contradictions breaks down in the Spaniard's closing remarks. He ends the second and last letter on *Azul* with what is almost a plea to the cosmopolitan, modern, Spanish American poet to consider Spain worthy of attention:

> Con el *galicismo mental* de usted no he sido sólo indulgente, sino que hasta le he aplaudido por lo perfecto. Con todo, yo aplaudiría muchísimo más, si con esa ilustración francesa que en usted hay, se combinase la inglesa, la alemana, la italiana, y ¿por qué no la española también? Al cabo, el árbol de nuestra ciencia no ha envejecido tanto que aún no pueda prestar jugo, ni sus ramas son tan cortas ni están tan secas que no puedan retoñar como mugrones del otro lado del Atlántico. (*Obras* 3:298)

> [With your mental Gallicism, not only have I been indulgent, but also I have applauded it for its perfection. Still, I would applaud you even more if, together with that French enlightenment that exists in you, you mixed some from England, Germany, Italy, and, why not? from Spain as well. Ultimately, our tree of knowledge

has not grown so old that it cannot still give juice; its branches are not so short nor so dry that they cannot have offshoots on the other side of the Atlantic.]

Valera began his review by explaining how, "a pesar de la amable dedicatoria" (289) [despite the lovely dedication], he looked at Darío's book "con indiferencia" [with indifference] upon receiving it: "Yo sospeché que era usted un Víctor Huguito, y estuve más de una semana sin leer el libro de usted" (290). [I thought you another little Victor Hugo and spent over a week without reading your book.] However, this image of the old consecrated master receiving a book from an unknown young "imitator" from the ex-colonies gives way by the end of the review to a complete reversal of positions. Valera tries to bribe Darío with more applause (i.e., consecration) so that the latter pays attention to Spain, a barely veiled appeal that cancels the authority of that applause. If Spanish literature is absent, so is the context in which Valera's magisterial position makes sense. The absence of Spanish authority from Darío's collection means the absence of Valera's own; the "death" of Spain is his own symbolic death. The image of Spanish culture as a dying tree that (and here Valera can hardly hide what is the expression of a wish) might still be able to reach across the Atlantic only confirms the crumbling of its/his authority, now in the hands of Darío.

Underlying Valera's text and his disdainful comment regarding Darío's apparent "mental Gallicism," there is a desperate need to preserve the relationship between America and Europe in imperial terms, even as his own review confirms the irreversible end of that relationship. What he first described as cosmopolitan, fully original, and indeed influential, Valera tries to rewrite as a mere shift of European influences. Afraid of the implications of his first impulse, the Spanish critic would rather Darío be bedazzled by France than accept Darío's cultural independence. Yet Valera here is confronted with a problem that goes to the core of the complexities of transnational power and cultural fields in the nineteenth century, as discussed in the previous chapter. For the Spanish novelist seems to be in a catch-22 situation: to dismiss the possibility of Europe losing its cultural supremacy to an American poet who does not follow trends but creates them, Valera must admit that Europe's cultural capital resides in France and that Spanish literature is peripheral to French, an admission that Valera and many other Spanish intellectuals were not ready to make. According to Valera, Darío's cosmopolitan modernity, which is ahead of fashion and could set a new trend, has already outstripped French trends, so that conceivably French writers might eventually follow his lead. Where does that leave Spanish literature? Valera's imperial nostalgia does not allow him to entertain that question openly. For him, in the end, if not Spain, then Germany, England, Italy, or anything European will do. The alternative might be too fearful to utter, while any cultural dependence on Europe might preserve the fiction of empire, converting Spain's potential irrelevance into a contest between European powers and thus leveling the playing field and diluting any recognition of French symbolic power. The implications of what Rubén Darío achieved in *Azul* are indeed groundbreaking for postcolonial literature in the 1880s, and Valera grapples with them as he writes the review. When culture and politics are as inseparable as Valera himself acknowledged, what would happen if Darío, "glory of Spanish American letters" (291), did ultimately impose his own trend? The question lingers, never openly asked or answered, as Valera leaves us with the image of the old Spanish tree, dying and drying up, as it tries to reach across the Atlantic.

The Increasing Presence of Spanish American Literature in Spain

Valera's ambiguities and double rhetoric did not go unnoticed. Mexican Manuel Gutiérrez Nájera, a central figure of the movement and founder of Mexico's *Revista Azul*, one of the most important modernista journals, celebrated Valera's role in introducing foreign literature to Spain, but when it came to Spanish American literature, Nájera considered Valera's *Cartas* thoughtless and condescending. In his essay significantly entitled "El cruzamiento en literatura" (Miscegenation in Literature), Nájera shows his misgivings about Valera's critical work:

> [Valera] ha sido muy útil a la poesía española . . . como *agente de colonización* . . . o si se quiere, como introductor de embajadores. Ora introduce a Valmiki, ora a Goethe; hoy a Shakespeare, mañana a Lessing, y así van sabiendo los poetas de la península que no sólo hay moros y cristianos, flores y espinas, en la literatura. . . . La influencia de [Menéndez Pelayo y Valera] ha sido provechosa, tal como lo sería para los españoles el estudio de la exuberante, libre, espléndida y desordenada poesía sud-americana. Este no lo emprenden: las *Cartas americanas* de Valera, y, más que éstas, los prólogos puestos por Menéndez Pelayo a Anthologias [*sic*] americanas, prueban el altísimo desdén con que nos miran y la impremeditación con que nos juzgan. (291–92; my emphasis; ellipses in first sentence in original)

> [(Valera) has been very useful to Spanish poetry . . . as *an agent of colonization* . . . or, if you'd rather, as an introducer of ambassadors. Now he introduces Valmiki, now Goethe; today Shakespeare, tomorrow Lessing; and thus poets in Spain are slowly finding out that there are more than just Moors and Christians, flowers and thorns, in literature. . . . The influence of [Menéndez Pelayo and Valera] has been beneficial, just as it would be for the Spaniards to study the exuberant, free, splendid, and disorderly Spanish American poetry. This they do not do: Valera's *American Letters* and, even more, Menéndez Pelayo's prologues to his American

anthologies, are proof of the disdainful heights from which they look down on us and the thoughtlessness with which they judge us.]

The reference to colonization is hardly innocent, pointing out as it does Spain's own subaltern relationship to Northern European literatures. It is in Valera's role as "colonizing agent" of Spanish letters that Nájera exhorts him (and, indeed, all Spanish writers) to *also* read and study Spanish American literature, chastising Valera's *Cartas* for the disdain with which they treat their peers across the Atlantic. By placing Spanish American letters on the same level as other European literatures yet above Spain's, Nájera turns the colonial tables on Valera and his remarks about Rubén Darío. Not only does Nájera ignore Valera's Spanish tree but actually encourages the Spaniard to become a "colonizing agent" for Spanish American literature, a task that would require him to accept Spain's colonial cultural position with respect to Spanish America.[5]

Ironically, perhaps, Valera's *Cartas* contributed to that reversal of cultural influence. By the time Darío arrived in Spain in 1892, he already had a considerable amount of cultural capital, due in part to Valera's review. Darío had chosen to include the review in the second edition of *Azul*, published in Guatemala in 1890, thus neutralizing its criticism and capitalizing on its endorsement. He soon made contact in Spain with both prominent established writers (including Valera himself) and younger ones, such as Salvador Rueda. The review of *Azul* marks, then, a turning point in the reception of Spanish American modernista writings in Spain. Certainly some Spanish writers (most notably Salvador Rueda) had already been following the work of their peers across the Atlantic, but Valera's positive review, coming as it did from a highly consecrated writer with a strong and secure position in the field, had a significant impact on the battle over the legitimation in Spain not only of Darío and modernismo, but of Spanish American literature at large.

Juan Valera's reviews came out at a time when the publication of Spanish American works in Spanish periodicals was on the rise as the celebrations of the fourth centennial of Columbus's first voyage approached. In the years following Valera's *Cartas*, not just Rubén Darío but also many other Spanish American authors (from Mercedes Cabello de Carbonera and Clorinda Matto de Turner to Gutiérrez Nájera, Díaz Mirón, Gómez Carrillo, Jaimes Freyre, and Lugones) were increasingly read in Spain. As Almudena Mejías Alonso and Alicia Arias Coello note, in the same periodicals that were publishing the latest from England, France, and Germany, "no es sorprendente encontrar huellas de escritores uruguayos, paraguayos, chilenos, ecuatorianos, y otros, que el tiempo, y otras circunstancias, ha hecho que hoy resulten desconocidos para nosotros pero que en su día aparecieron al lado de otros escritores reconocidos en la literatura mundial como es el caso de Rubén Darío" (246) [it is not surprising to find traces of Uruguayan, Paraguayan,

Chilean, Ecuadorian, and other Spanish American writers who time and other circumstances have obscured, but who, back in their day, appeared on the page next to other world-renowned writers such as Rubén Darío].

The presence of Spanish American cultural production in the Peninsula was creating growing tension and uneasiness in the Spanish cultural field. Such tension is also the best indicator of the upheaval caused by newcomers in the field, since, as Bourdieu reminds us: "To produce effects is already to exist in a field, even if these effects are mere reactions of resistance or exclusion. It follows that the dominants have trouble defending themselves against the threat contained in any redefinition of the right of entry, explicit or implicit, *since they are granting existence, by fighting against them, to those they want to exclude*" (*Rules* 236; my emphasis). As we shall see, the more the dominant Spanish writers fought against the new Spanish American modernistas, the stronger the position of modernismo became.

The Modernista Upheaval in Spain: Clarín and the American Epidemic

Max Henríquez Ureña's appreciation that "las *Cartas Americanas* (1889) de Valera provocaron en muchos incredulidad y asombro" (*Breve* 38) [Valera's *American Letters* (1889) produced in many incredulity and shock] is accurate, but it falls short of representing the violence generated in Spain by Spanish American letters and even by what many perceived as Valera's role in "introducing" them into the field, his role, to use Nájera's metaphor, as a "colonizing agent." Many of Valera's Spanish peers could not read his reviews of Spanish American books without thinking that he was being sarcastic or simply excessively nice. Prominent Spanish novelist and cultural critic Leopoldo Alas (whose pen name was Clarín) could not imagine *any* relationship between America and Spain, cultural or otherwise, if it meant having to "reconocer derechos de nación más favorecida a las bobadas que se le ocurran a cualquier sinsonte bajo el sol de los trópicos" (qtd. in Carbonell 164) [recognize the rights of a most-favored nation to any nonsense that may occur to any mockingbird under the tropical sun]. Clarín goes as far as to equate Valera with Columbus, who, he says, might have decided *not* to "discover" the Americas had he seen the poetry they would produce:

> Pero si [Colón], persona formal, hubiera sabido que lo que iba a doblarse y centuplicarse era la poesía becqueriana, campoamorina, etc.... en todas las pampas y en todos los Andes ... ¡rediós! se hubiera dicho Colón, ahí queda eso; yo no descubro nada. Por eso le digo a don Juan [Valera], es claro que con el mayor respeto, que hace mal en dar alas a esos cóndores de por allí, porque esas vulgaridades altisonantes que a ellos se les ocurren teníamos ya nosotros quien nos las dijera, sin

> necesidad de que nadie se molestara en ir a descubrirles a ellos, lo cual siempre es ocasión de sustos y disgustos. (Carbonell 164–65; second ellipses in original)
>
> [But if (Columbus), a formal person, had known that what would double and even multiply . . . in all the Pampas and all the Andes was poetry in imitation of Becquer, Campoamor, etc., "By Jove!" he would have said, "That's it. I'm not discovering anything." This is why I tell Mr. Juan Valera, with the utmost respect of course, that he is wrong in encouraging the flight of those condors from over there, because we already had people here who could tell us those high-flown commonplaces that they come up with without anyone bothering to go over there and discover them, which is always an occasion for fright and sorrow.]

Valera's ambiguities and imperial contradictions pale in comparison to the verbal violence of Clarín and the anxieties his words embody. In his critique of Valera for "discovering" and "encouraging" Spanish American writers, Clarín's text is also a testament to the complexities, tensions, and inconsistencies generated by Spanish American writers in the discourse of their peninsular colleagues. Whatever Valera's shortcomings, he had made a point in several of his *Cartas* to show the variety and importance of the Spanish American cultural tradition, even once stating that "desde antes de la independencia compite con la metrópoli en fecundidad mental" (*Obras* 3:213) [since before independence, it has competed with the metropolis in mental fecundity]. Clarín, on the other hand, reduces all of America to a natural space allegedly untouched by "civilization," metonymically contained in the Pampas and the Andes. Spanish Americans are dehumanized, described as condors and mockingbirds (*sinsontes*) inhabiting an otherwise empty landscape, able only to imitate the song of others. Yet in complaining about their mimicking back to Spain its own "high-flown commonplaces," Alas betrays an awareness of Spain's own literary irrelevance, and it is this concern that Valera reveals as he explains the animosity his *Cartas* elicited: "Y ¿cómo, a no ser un santo, sin chispa de emulación, no se ha de afligir un poco el poeta de por aquí, a quien tal vez nadie hace caso, y a quien *Clarín* no calificaría de céntimo de poeta, de que yo importe tanto género similar ultramarino, que llegue a secuestrar la escasa atención y aprecio que pudieran concederle?" (389) [And how, unless he is a saint without a spark of emulation, can a poet from here, to whom maybe no one pays attention and whom *Clarín* would not even consider one hundredth of a poet, not be a little upset that I am importing so many similar goods from overseas that could take whatever little attention and estimation he may receive away from him?] Employing an economic metaphor, Valera exposes the competitive nature of the literary field, a market where writers vie for symbolic capital and prestige.[6]

As modernismo imposed its new aesthetic in the following decade, this capital and prestige moved westward toward Spanish America, so that by 1898 Spain had lost not only its political and economic dominance over its last colonies, but also its cultural authority over the entire continent. Furthermore, as younger Spanish writers began to follow the modernista path, Spain's cultural production could be construed as "mimicking" that of the American "mockingbirds." Clarín would be perennially on guard trying to prevent this from happening.

Valera's writings, then, in addition to their central role as mediator between the national and international literary fields, bear witness to the tensions and the virulence of the climate in Spain at the time modernismo arrived. They repeatedly show that literary discussions were embedded in a complicated dynamic and that many Spanish writers were unable or unwilling to consider that Spain might no longer be the cultural center of the Hispanic Atlantic: "Es harto difícil mi empresa de agradar, interesar y persuadir con las *Cartas americanas*. ¿Cómo va a creer quien apenas cree que hay algo bueno en Madrid o Barcelona, que lo hay en Valparaíso, en Bogotá o en Montevideo?" (389) [My task to please, interest, and persuade with my *American Letters* is quite difficult. How is anyone who hardly thinks there is anything good in Madrid or Barcelona going to believe that there are good things in Valparaiso, Bogota, or Montevideo?] Especially, we might add, when some of his colleagues, like Clarín, refused to recognize the existence of urban centers in Spanish America, reducing it to an uninhabited landscape.

Those who, like Clarín, still thought Madrid had any claim to relevance would not have been happy to read Rubén Darío's crónicas on Spain (written for *La nación* of Buenos Aires in 1900 and published in book form as *España contemporánea* in 1902).[7] Here Darío painted a devastating picture of what he saw as Spain's social, economic, and cultural stagnation, as he criticized a general ignorance of the part of the Spanish of anything beyond Spain's borders, and in particular, of Latin American reality. The effect of his crónicas on Spanish readers must have been powerful. For Darío, Madrid's deserted cultural landscape stood in sharp contrast to the cosmopolitanism and open cultural preeminence of Buenos Aires, the "flor colosal de una raza que ha de cimentar la común cultura americana" (*España* 173) [the colossal flower of a race that will build the foundations of a common American culture]. Against Clarín's insecure, backward-looking, and sarcastic tone, Darío presents a triumphalist, future-focused, and secure faith in a "cultura americana," with Buenos Aires, not Madrid, at its epicenter, where Spain is not even relevant. By 1900, and despite many a Spanish critic's shortsightedness at the time, modernismo had consolidated its new position in the Spanish field.

The Removal of Castilian Linguistic Authority

Capitalizing on this state of affairs and under the triad of cosmopolitanism, Latin Americanism, and modernity, modernismo was attaining increasing symbolic capital among an entire generation of young Spanish writers and intellectuals, and was establishing its leadership over the Spanish field. In 1892, Salvador Rueda, an Andalusian poet who initially had enjoyed the sympathetic support of Clarín, proudly published his collection *En tropel* (*Pell-Mell*), with an introductory poem by Darío entitled "Pórtico." In his prologue, Rueda praised the revolutionary stature of Rubén Darío's poetry and celebrated his visit to Spain: "Como sabe el público español, se halla entre nosotros . . . el poeta que ha hecho la revolución en la poesía, el divino visionario, maestro en la rima, músico triunfal del idioma, enamorado de las abstracciones y de los símbolos, y quintaesenciado artista" (qtd. in Ibarra 526). [As the Spanish public knows, the poet who has revolutionized poetry is among us, the divine visionary, the master of rhyme, the triumphant musician of the language, the lover of abstractions and symbols, and quintessential artist.] Later included in Darío's masterpiece collection *Prosas profanas* (Profane Prose), "Pórtico" stands as another important instance of modernista position taking or advancement in the field. At this point, only four years after Valera's reviews, Darío's poems already commanded distinction and prestige among the younger generation of Spanish poets, who, like Rueda and many others after him, found in Spanish American modernismo a much needed literary renewal that the older generation, which held power in the field, strongly resisted.

Clarín, who had been supportive of Rueda and only a year earlier had written a prologue for the poet's *Cantos de la vendimia* (1891), did not hesitate to withdraw his support after the publication of *En tropel*, turning his critical virulence against both the Andalusian poet and the "corrupting" influence exerted by Rubén Darío and his "portico" (Ibarra 525–26). It is for this influence that Clarín would never forgive Darío, fighting him with all his might and with the worst of his insults. For the Spanish critic, modernismo was like a contagious disease. In an article written for Madrid's *El Globo* in December 1893 and reprinted in Buenos Aires's *La Prensa* a month later, Clarín decries again the "corrupting" influence in Spain not only of Darío but also of his fellow Spanish American modernistas: "Me veo en la dolorosa necesidad de deplorar que el simpático y entusiasta poeta Salvador Rueda ande en tan malas compañías, como lo son, sin duda, ciertos escritores americanos, que, a vueltas de cien imitaciones de modas francesas, no son más que los antiguos *sinsontes* disfrazados de *neomísticos* o *simbolistas ipsistas* o el diablo y su madre" (qtd. in Ibarra 531). [I find myself in painful need of deploring that the nice and enthusiastic poet Salvador Rueda keeps such bad company as undoubtedly is that of certain American writers, who, after a hundred imitations of French trends, are none other than the old *mockingbirds* disguised as *neo-mystics* or *self-absorbed symbolists* or who the hell knows what.] For Clarín, Salvador Rueda must run away "de estos señores, en cuanto literatos, *como de la peste*. No les proteja, ni se deje amparar por ellos" (531; my emphasis) [from these gentlemen (as writers, that is) as from the plague. Do not protect them, nor let them protect you]. Forged in a rhetoric of sickness and contamination, Clarín's text is a monument to the anxiety that many consecrated Spanish writers felt over the advent of Spanish American modernismo and its impact on newer generations.[8] As he had with Rueda, in 1897 Clarín tried to dissuade the future Nobel laureate Jacinto Benavente from following modernista language and aesthetics, to which Benavente responded with a passionate defense of Rubén Darío and his mastery of Spanish: "Rubén Darío domina el idioma castellano y al dislocarlo en rimas ricas y ritmos nuevos, no es el desdibujo de la ignorancia, sino el trazo seguro que produce el efecto buscado" (qtd. in Ibarra 535). [Rubén Darío has full command of the Castilian language and when he displaces it into rich rhymes and new rhythms, it is not the blur of ignorance, but the secure stroke that produces the desired effect.]

Although perhaps the most notorious critic, Clarín was not alone in his animosity. In 1896, critic Antonio de Valbuena, author of the column "Ripios Ultramarinos" (Cacophonies from Overseas), said Valera was senile for praising Spanish American writers; another critic, Peris, said that such praise could be explained only as an issue of political diplomacy rather than as one of literary taste (Carbonell 162), yet another symptom of how political the whole debate was. As late as 1907, Julio Cejador y Frauca, a well-known philologist and author of a major history of the Spanish language and literature, launched attacks on modernismo using the same rhetoric of disease Clarín had favored, speaking of "la gangrena del lenguaje empleado por los autores americanos" (qtd. in Fogelquist 60) [the gangrene of the language employed by the American writers]. By then, however, modernismo was well established in the Peninsula and the Bolivian poet Jaimes Freyre could retort:

> Y no proteste el señor Cejador—hay evoluciones literarias que han viajado ya de esta América a su España, y hay quienes en este castellano de América han escrito libros intensos, espirituales, en verbo moderno, flexible, sutil, con lucideces emocionales desconocidas, cosmopolita, rico. . . . la lengua en que escriben Darío, nueva y cristalina; Lugones, inagotablemente rica en expresiones e imágenes, o Díaz Rodríguez, o J. Enrique Rodó, Groussac, preciso y sabio, si no es castellano, no ha de envidiar nada al que sirve al señor Cejador para denostarlo sin . . . conocerlo. (qtd. in Fogelquist 84)
>
> [Mr. Cejador should not protest: there are literary developments that have already traveled from this America to his Spain, as there are those who, in this Castilian from America, have written intense, spiritual books in a modern language that is flexible, subtle, cosmopolitan, and rich, with heretofore unknown emotional lucidity. . . . the language of Rubén Darío, new and crystalline; of Lugones, unendingly rich in idioms and images; or of Díaz Rodríguez, or of J. Enrique Rodó, or of Groussac, precise and wise; if not Castilian, then, this language does not envy at all the Castilian that Mr. Cejador employs to insult it . . . without knowing it.]

Disease, corruption, a plague—for Spanish critics, Spanish American modernismo and the way it was transforming and opening literary language in Spanish were a threat to the perceived purity of "Castilian" and to the linguistic, literary, and cultural authority of the nation. The issue at stake was not so much that Spanish American writers were changing what many in Spain called "la lengua castiza" (purebred language), as this had been happening to some extent at the very least since independence (we can think of the debate between Bello and Sarmiento over the Spanish language); the real issue was that now Spanish American writers had actually come to the Peninsula (both textually and physically), imposed themselves, and Americanized, as it were, the Spanish language *and* Spanish literature.

The more Spanish critics tried to disguise their rejection of Spanish American modernismo as a critique of its alleged infatuation with all things French, the more they revealed their fear of the implications of its Americanism for both Spanish literature and the language itself. In one of his collaborations in the prominent *Revista Ilustrada de Nueva York* published in October 1891, Valera wrestled with this issue, admitting that although "harto sutil entendimiento se necesita, a mi ver, para explicar en qué consista y estribe el *americanismo*" [in my opinion, one needs a very subtle understanding in order to explain what Americanism may be about], nonetheless, "indudablemente lo hay" (424) [it undoubtedly exists]. Like many before and after him, Valera could understand America only from a European framework: "Así como hay cierta solidaridad europea, la cual se sobrepone a las divergencias, rivalidades y odios, [de modo que] prevalece en Europa el fundadísimo orgullo de una civilización superior . . . yo sospecho que este mismo orgullo transplantado al Nuevo Mundo es lo que constituye el americanismo" (424). [Just as there is a certain European solidarity which takes precedence over disagreements, rivalries and hatred, (so that) the well-grounded pride in a superior civilization prevails across Europe, . . . I suspect that this same pride transplanted to the New World is what Americanism is about.][9] Significantly, Valera ends the discussion admitting, however grudgingly, that "América podrá decir a Europa: 'El porvenir es mío'" (424) [America may be able to say to Europe: "The future is mine"], but only as long as it recognizes its European "mother." When "the future" arrived in the form of a novel by Reyles, Valera was not pleased to see that the Spanish American "motherland," again, was nowhere in the picture.

From Motherland to Childishland: The Debate over the Modernista Novel

In Montevideo in 1896, Carlos Reyles published *Primitivo* (Primitive), the first in a series of novels he called *Academias* (Sketches). Although not comparable to *Prosas profanas* or *Azul* in literary significance, *Primitivo* and its successor in the series, *El extraño* (The Stranger; 1897), sparked a significant debate that, as far as debates go, was like nothing *Azul* had ever caused. It involved the most prominent Spanish novelists of the time, with the exception of Benito Pérez Galdós. No small issue in the debate was the prologue, "Al lector" (To the Reader), that Reyles wrote for *Primitivo* and revised for *El extraño*. The polemic was about Reyles's new concept of the modern novel, which he named in his prologue "la novela del porvenir" [the novel of the future].

Directly linked to the experience of modernity, according to Reyles, this new novel was being written in America, and there was nothing remotely like it in Spain, whose novelistic production was both local and superficial: "demasiado epidérmicas para sorprender los ESTADOS DEL ALMA, de la nerviosa generación actual y satisfacer su curiosidad del MISTERIO de la vida" ("Al lector" 9) [too superficial to surprise the STATES OF THE SOUL of the nervous present generation and satisfy their curiosity about the MYSTERY of life]. In other words, Reyles's prologue is as much about the modernista novel itself as about reaffirming a shift in cultural authority from Spain to the American continent. Moreover, Reyles was explicitly aware of what he was doing and anticipated—and in so doing perhaps created—attacks from those who "ofendan e irriten las ideas que las *Academias* puedan sugerir" [may be offended and irritated by the ideas that my *Sketches* may suggest], foreseeing "insultos y zarpadas" (10) [insults and attacks]. In fact, the last image of his prologue is that of a bleeding warrior in the military avant-garde, "que marcha a la conquista del mundo con un corazón en una mano y una espada en la otra" (10) [marching to the conquest of the world with a heart in one hand and a sword in the other]. In Reyles's text there is a powerful reversal of the imperial image that had been haunting Spanish reception of Spanish American literature. His warrior duplicates the iconic figure of the Spanish conquistador, Bible and sword in hand, ready to conquer America. This time around, the world is being conquered eastward, and Spain is the first land discovered and taken over. Religion in the form of the Bible gives way to modernity as experienced by the "modern heart," and sword/pen in hand, the conquistador is now an American. The American claim that "the future is mine" came back to Valera with a vengeance.

Virtually unknown compared to his reviews of *Azul*, Valera's reviews of the *Academias* and the succession of reviews and opinions Reyles's texts generated are far more significant and far-reaching than literary history has acknowledged.[10] The reception of Reyles's novel is a landmark in the history of transatlantic literary relations, as well as in the development of the novel in Spain, much as *Azul* was for the direction of Spanish poetry.[11] In fact, the Reyles and Valera exchange echoes in many ways that of Darío and Valera eight years earlier. Yet, while Darío's poetry came to the Spaniard as a surprise, enough had changed by 1896 for Valera to know that *Azul* had been but the tip of an iceberg approaching the Spanish shores.

Furthermore, Valera never claimed to be a consecrated poet, but he certainly was a consecrated novelist, and this time around it was the novel that was at stake and his own work that was being blatantly dismissed.

Interestingly enough, the Spanish critic chose to begin his review of Reyles's *Primitivo* with a review of Darío's *Los raros* (The Strange), a collection of literary portraits of writers whom Darío considered his peers (not one of whom was Spanish), published that same year in Buenos Aires. Reminding his readers of his own praise of *Azul* because of its "novedad extraña" (482) [strange novelty], this time Valera rejects that same novelty on the grounds that it threatens to destroy Darío: "Si *raro* es el que tiene una *pose* o varias, el que para llamar la atención, seguir la moda o dar la moda, inventa rarezas y extravagancias, yo no celebro a ningún raro. . . . Esto es lo que yo critico y esto es lo que me infunde el recelo de que pueda extraviarse Rubén Darío" (*Obras* 3:482). [If *strange* is someone who has a pose or several, someone who invents strange and extravagant things in order to call attention, follow a trend, or set a trend, I do not celebrate anyone strange. . . . This is what I criticize and this is what fills me with the suspicion that Rubén Darío may go astray.] If Valera chose to bring *Los raros* to the discussion table on *Primitivo*, it must be because he saw a common aesthetic project in them. Reyles, from Montevideo, was making explicit a lack of intellectual curiosity, restlessness, and change in Spain. He was asserting Spanish America's necessary role in the future of Spanish literature. Thus, Darío was not an exception, Valera might have realized, but a leader of the "sangrienta falange" [bloody phalanx] ready to conquer the world. Both Darío and Reyles were confirming that the old Spanish tree that Valera hoped could still reach across the Atlantic had not survived the winds of change.

Change and progress were, in fact, the main issues debated. Valera insisted that change was not, and should not be, a value in literature. He believed in the universality and atemporality of literature and its duty to please and lift readers, instead of what he thought Reyles was proposing, that is, "aterrar y compungir a los lectores como con una pesadilla tenaz y espantosa" (*Obras* 3:524) [to terrorize and sadden readers like a persistent and horrible nightmare]. Indeed, Reyles's concept of the modern novel is, for Valera, an "herejía literaria casi monstruosa" (Obras 2:935) [almost monstrous literary heresy].[12] After his two novels had appeared and been criticized on these grounds by Valera and others, Reyles published an essay in Madrid's *El liberal* entitled "La novela del porvenir" (1897) where, after expanding on his concept and reaffirming his opinions about the state of Spanish narrative, he concludes: "¡[Esta] generación no comprenderá al señor Valera, si le habla de deleitar, de dejar glorificada a la Providencia! . . . ¡El entretenimiento, la moral del libro, los personajes admirables! . . . ¡Qué pueril nos parece todo eso! ¡Qué pueril y ajeno al sentimiento profundo y doloroso de la vida que pone la pluma en la mano del poeta!" (187; ellipses in original) [(This) generation will not understand

Mr. Valera if he talks to them about delighting, about glorifying Providence! . . . Entertainment, the moral of a book, admirable characters! . . . How childish all of this seems to us! How childish and alien to the profound and painful feeling of life that brings the pen to the hand of the poet.] If Valera's authority, and that of Spanish intellectuals with him, had been compromised since Darío's *Azul* in 1888, Reyles's remarks confirm that their authority no longer existed. Furthermore, the notion of the "madre patria" and the paternalistic attitude that many Spaniards had shown toward Spanish Americans are here contested by Reyles, for whom the ideas of Valera's generation are childish ("pueril"). That is, Reyles reverses the maternal image, turning Spain into a child that needs to be guided. The same trope can be found in other modernista texts such as Rodó's 1911 "La España niña" (Baby Girl Spain), in which, adopting a paternal attitude, he explains that he has high hopes for Spain's future. E. S. Morby was absolutely right when he characterized the entire polemic as "a battle between ancient and modern" (119), but it was far more than that. Like every battle fought by modernismo in Spain, this was a battle between Americans and Spaniards for cultural authority, with far-reaching implications for larger postcolonial dynamics.

Throughout the debate, the imperial/colonial issue so prominent in the *Azul* discussion never disappeared. Valera began his last essay on this matter, "Del progreso en el arte de la palabra" (On Progress in the Art of the Word; 1897), with what seems to be a digression on the Cuban war and the dangers the Cuban people were putting themselves in by seeking to sever their ties with Spain (*Obras* 2:936–73). Yet given that it was written by someone who claimed that literary discussions inevitably ended up being about politics, this can hardly be read critically as a digression; it suggests how directly linked were the colonial context, the issue of independence, and the modernista enterprise in the imaginary of many Spanish intellectuals. Eduardo Gómez de Baquero, an up-and-coming critic of the same generation as Reyles and Darío and a regular reviewer of Spanish American books, was not surprisingly the one critic who most agreed with Reyles. Like Emilia Pardo Bazán, he disagreed with Valera's disdain for "trendy fashion" and change, but unlike the Galician writer and her fellow naturalists, he probed the surface of the topic and exposed the issues underlying Valera's discontent: Gómez de Baquero is the only one to acknowledge and discuss the intellectual landscape of Spain itself. Thus, regarding the title of Valera's review—"*El extraño*, última moda de París" (*The Stranger*, the Latest Fashion from Paris)—Gómez de Baquero explains that Reyles should have replied that "el Sr. Valera rendía, a su vez, culto a la última moda de Madrid. Moda de hace algunos años, pues las nuestras duran mucho, sin duda porque como es escaso el movimiento intelectual, las ideas . . . tardan bastante en vulgarizarse, y [no se necesita] variarlas con tanta frecuencia como los de otros países donde se lee y se discute mucho" (136) [Mr. Valera submitted, in turn, to the latest fashion from Madrid; a fashion from a few years ago since ours last a long time, no doubt because since intellectual movement is scarce, ideas . . . take quite some time to spread, and . . . do not need to be varied as frequently as those in other countries where people read and discuss much].

Furthermore, Gómez de Baquero is the only participant in the debate to bring up the colonial issue directly and put in on the table, making explicit what had until then remained only implicit in the Spanish camp:

> Mucho mejor sería para nosotros, y acaso para los americanos de nuestra raza, que España siguiese siendo la metrópoli intelectual de sus antiguas provincias del Nuevo Mundo. No lo es, y ante el hecho sirve de poco la dialéctica. Estas primacías intelectuales no se ganan por títulos históricos, ni por los meros vínculos de consanguineidad y de raza. Requieren una superioridad de cultura que no poseemos con relación a otros pueblos de Europa, y no podemos censurar en justicia a los hispanoamericanos porque busquen inspiración en esos pueblos. Nosotros la buscamos también, y debemos buscarla, puesto que no sería racional que nos privásemos de participar de los beneficios de la ajena cultura por espíritu de casta o por exagerado amor a tradiciones muertas. (137)

> [It would be much better for us, and perhaps for the Americans of our race, that Spain keep being the intellectual metropolis of its old provinces in the New World. It is not, and no dialectics can change that fact. Intellectual preeminence is not gained by historical titles, nor by the mere links created by blood and race. It requires a superiority of culture that we do not possess in relation to other people of Europe, and we cannot censure the Spanish Americans, in all fairness, because they look for inspiration among those people. We do too, as we should, since it would be irrational to deprive ourselves of the benefits of other cultures because of a spirit of caste or an exaggerated love for dead traditions.]

Acknowledging Valera's imperial nostalgia and its echoes in Clarín, Pardo Bazán, and others, Gómez de Baquero exposes the rhetoric of the "madre patria" and Spain's claim to cultural leadership as an empty gesture, based on dreams of the past rather than on achievements of the present.[13] Nonetheless, even Gómez de Baquero cannot think outside his own eurocentrism and postcolonial anxiety. He resists accepting modernismo as "strangely original," to use Valera's old phrase, and able to impose trends. Instead, while willing to give up any claim to cultural preeminence (thus sanctioning the death of Valera's "Spanish tree"), Gómez de Baquero repeats Valera's initial operation of transferring the dependency relation to other European powers. However, for Gómez de Baquero, Spanish literature is also dependent on other European literatures. In this sense, there is a notable difference between this younger critic and the established popes of Spanish letters, which did not go unnoticed by Spanish American modernistas. Regarding another review by Baquero in which he praised Rubén Darío's poetry, Amado Nervo happily said: "No nos tienen acostumbrados a este lenguaje los críticos españoles, que viven aún bajo la influencia de la técnica meticulosa y un poco lamida de Núñez de Arce o de la técnica erizada de prosaísmos de Campoamor—dos grandes poetas por otra parte" (qtd. in Fogelquist 86). [We are not used to this kind of language in the Spanish critics, who still live under the influence of the meticulous and a bit affected technique of Núñez de Arce or of Campoamor's technique, so full of prosaic thorns—two great poets, on the other hand.]

The younger generation of Spanish writers and critics was indeed embracing the modernista renovation, but as in the case of Gómez de Baquero, they did so by maintaining an uneasy relationship with the idea that the renovation was coming from America. The heavily politicized language of literary debates, the constant encoding of these discussions in colonial and imperial language, and an underlying anxiety regarding an open acknowledgment of Spain's debts to Spanish American letters would characterize Spanish discourse for years to come. For Spanish critics and writers, it was much easier to follow Valera's first approach and, in the end, narrate the Spanish American transformation of Spanish letters as a pan-Hispanic opening to other "European" literatures. (As we see later in this chapter, that is the view that would survive in scholarly approaches to Spanish literature of the period.) For Spanish American writers, however, it could not be any clearer that it was the transatlantic impulse and presence of Spanish American modernismo that shook Spanish culture from its slumber. Even while disputing Darío's leadership in the context of the American continent, José Enrique Rodó had no doubt regarding the role of the Nicaraguan poet and his fellow Spanish Americans in waking up, healing, and transforming Spain.

Modernismo and the American Mentoring of Spanish Youth

Rubén Darío as Prospero

When Rodó wrote his essay about Darío in 1899, as the latter was sailing again toward Spain, the Uruguayan critic ended his text with the certainty that modernismo, in which Rodó included himself, was a "sign of renewal." Rodó leaves readers with the powerful image of Darío arriving in Spain, where he is to become a figure not unlike Rodó's own Próspero in *Ariel* (1900), a teacher of a new generation of Spaniards in need of a new leader:

> El poeta viaja ahora, rumbo a España. Encontrará un gran silencio y un dolorido estupor, no interrumpidos ni aún por la nota de una elegía, ni aún por el rumor

> de las hojas sobre el surco, en la soledad donde aquella madre de vencidos caballeros sobrelleva, menos como la Hécube de Eurípides que como la Dolorosa del Ticiano, la austera sombra de su dolor inmerecido. Llegue allí el poeta llevando buenos anuncios para el florecer del espíritu en el habla común, que es el arca santa de la raza; *destáquese en la sombra la vencedora figura del Arquero*; hable a la juventud, a aquella juventud incierta y aterida, cuya primavera no da flores tras el invierno de los maestros que se van, y enciéndala en nuevos amores y nuevos entusiasmos. Acaso, en el seno de esa juventud que duerme, su llamado pueda ser el signo de una renovación; acaso pueda ser saludada, en el reino de aquella agostada poesía, su presencia, como la de los príncipes que, en el cuento oriental, traen de remotos países la fuente que da oro, el pájaro que habla y el árbol que canta. (*Obras completas* 79–80)
>
> [The poet is now traveling to Spain. He will find a great silence and a painful stupor, uninterrupted by even the note of an elegy or even the rustling of the leaves on the furrow, in the solitude where that mother of vanquished knights bears the austere shadow of her undeserved grief, less like Euripides' Hecuba than like Titian's *Mater Dolorosa*. Let the poet arrive there bearing good news for the blossoming of the spirit in our common speech, which is the Holy Ark of the race; *let the victorious figure of the Archer stand out from the shadows*; let him speak to the youth, that uncertain and chilled youth whose spring produces no flowers after the winter of the old masters who now leave; and let him ignite it with new loves and new enthusiasms. Perhaps his call may be the sign of a renewal in the bosom of that sleepy youth; perhaps his presence may be hailed in that kingdom of withered poetry, like that of the prince who, in the oriental tale, brings the fountain of gold, the talking bird, and the singing tree from remote lands.]

Carefully ventriloquizing Darío's voice, Rodó presents an image of the poet loaded with modernista symbolism from *Prosas profanas*, the poetry collection Rodó was reviewing in his essay. From Darío's poem "Año Nuevo" (New Year), Rodó cites the verse about the divine Archer, Sagittarius the Centaur, associated not only with wisdom and human progress, renovation, and new years as in the poem, but also with Chiron, the great healer and teacher of Greek mythology and the protagonist of Darío's "Coloquio de los Centauros" (Colloquium of the Centaurs). Darío is depicted, then, as the foreign master, healer, and new leader of Spain. Traveling to the east, like Saint Sylvester in Darío's "Año Nuevo," the poet becomes a new pope, builder of a new Vatican, and founder of a new creed.[14] A savior, Darío is also a sort of Christ figure who will bring light where there are only shadows, warmth to a numb and barren generation, love and enthusiasm to awaken Spanish youth from their slumber. Alluding at the end to what is perhaps one of the most emblematic modernista poems, Darío's "Sonatina," Rodó turns Darío into its Prince Charming, who rescues the poem's princess from death. Like the princess's clavichord in the poem, Spain's own lyre is mute. In Rodó's vision Darío stands out, above all, as a new voice in a space where there is only silence and emptiness. All allusions to Spain are connected to silence and paralysis, while Darío is the carrier of a new common language, "the Holy Ark of the race," a new Ark of the Covenant, a new gospel for the next generation of writers. Like the "Holy Spirit" over the apostles and Mary, Darío is descending upon the silent youth of Spain and granting them the biblical gift of tongues. Intertwining Greek and Christian mythologies, Rodó creates a Darío that is both Chiron and Christ, but depicts a Spain that is not Hecuba but Mary, and, like her, an empty vessel to be filled by God.[15] In a magnificent parallel of the Christian conundrum, Rodó's text crafts a Darío who is both son and father of Spain, savior and creator.

Whatever issues Rodó might have had with Darío regarding the direction of the movement in America, it is perfectly clear that, when it came to the transatlantic thrust of modernismo and its place in Europe, Rodó closed ranks with Darío and understood the extraordinary significance of the revolution that modernismo was carrying out in the ex-metropolis. Indeed, from the literary battlefield of the Peninsula, Salvador Rueda saw in Rodó's essay on Rubén Darío the expression of a common cause and yet another manifestation of the modernista renewal of literary expression. For Rueda, the essay was like nothing a Spanish critic could produce, and he confessed in a letter to Rodó that it had made him bitterly sad to realize that "en España no tenemos críticos con esa altura de miras, dotado de esa elegancia suprema y, sobre todo, de esa amplitud de criterio de Ud.: su cerebro me parece un bosque en el cual pueden entrar todos los vientos, todas las corrientes, todos los perfumes, todos los pájaros, por vario y distinto que sea su plumaje" (qtd. in Ibarra 536) [in Spain we have no critics with such high-mindedness and vision, gifted with such supreme elegance and, above all, with such a capacity for understanding as yours: your brain seems to me like a forest in which all winds may enter, all currents, all perfumes, all birds, no matter how varied and different their plumage]. Striking in Rueda's letter, moreover, is the way he incorporates and perpetuates the aesthetics and worldview of both Darío and Rodó. The language, metaphors, and cosmopolitan openness are all modernista. In this way, Rueda detaches himself from the Spanish critics in a position-taking move, openly lamenting the state of the Spanish literary field and looking to America for inspiration.

Rubén Darío as the Embodiment of America

Compared to Rueda, literary history has taken a less open approach to Rodó's essay about Rubén Darío. Instead of a critical mind open to all winds, literary history has favored the construction of a more limited vision of Rodó as the Americanist critic of modernismo's cosmopolitanism. Isolating and stressing Rodó's claim that

Darío was not *the* poet of America, literary history has created a largely fictional view of Rodó's Americanism and Darío's cosmopolitan modernismo as contradictory forces. Yet Rodó had written one of the most brilliant articulations of the cosmopolitan spirit of modernismo in his defense of Reyles's novels three years before his essay on Darío, and he would do the same in his most famous book, *Ariel*, the following year. Americanism, on the other hand, the conviction that they were creating a pan-Spanish American literature, had been a central part of modernismo from its very beginnings, from Martí to Darío himself. There was tension, to be sure, but it was not between Americanism and cosmopolitan modernismo, but rather between Rodó and Darío as two agents of modernismo. In Rodó's essay, the American origin of modernismo is never a matter of debate, nor does Rodó claim to oppose modernismo. Rodó was challenging Darío for leadership *within* the movement: this rivalry was an internal struggle for symbolic capital in a movement that had already attained a strong position in the literary field in both Spanish America *and* Spain. Darío was rapidly gaining international recognition and, as I have shown, Rodó's admiration for him and his acute sense of how important Darío's role in Spain was cannot be questioned. Rodó's critique, then, may have been motivated less by any real dislike of Darío's work than by Rodó's self-interest in advancing his own position in the shifting literary field. By challenging Darío, Rodó hoped to grant himself a position of authority within modernismo.

Struggles in the literary field are directly connected to what Bourdieu calls habitus, the set of dispositions of any given agent according to class, education, origin, and so on. With this in mind, I suggest that the issue of origin and ethnicity might have been a factor in Rodó's challenge to Darío's leadership. Rodó, a white Creole intellectual from the River Plate, a region that prided itself on its Europeanness and cosmopolitanism, might have had some misgivings in granting full authority as leader of such a radically cosmopolitan yet clearly American movement to a mestizo-mulatto from Nicaragua. To some extent at least, the issue at stake for Rodó might have been *who* could define and best represent the otherwise unquestioned "Americanness" of modernismo. Following this line of thought, Rodó's *Ariel* (1900) should be considered another act of position taking, as Rodó used to his own advantage the Ariel-Caliban metaphor employed by Darío in *Los raros* (1896) and in the chronicle "El triunfo de Calibán" (Caliban's Triumph; 1898) and turned the Shakesperean opposition into an entire book about the future of Latin America.

In any event, even if Rodó was not, most established and up-and-coming intellectuals in Spain were very aware of Darío's ethnicity. Valera wrote Ménendez Pelayo that Darío had "bastante del indio sin buscarlo, sin afectarlo" (qtd. in Fogelquist 69) [much of the Indian character in him, without seeking it, without feigning it]. Notorious is Unamuno's remark that "a Darío se le ven las plumas del indio debajo del sombrero" (qtd. in Fogelquist 69) [Darío's Indian feathers can be seen under his hat], and in a less sarcastic if certainly not less racist tone, "Rubén Darío es algo digno de estudio; es el indio con vislumbres de la más alta civilización, de algo resplendente y magnífico, que al querer expresar lo inexplicable balbucea" (69) [Rubén Dario is something worthy of study; he is the Indian with inklings of the highest civilization, of something resplendent and magnificent, who, in trying to express the inexplicable, babbles].[16] Novelist Pío Baroja said that "Darío es escritor de mucha pluma. Se nota que es indio" (qtd. in Iwasaki) [Darío is a writer with a prolific feather (pen). You can tell he is an Indian], while Juan Ramón Jiménez, upon meeting him, described him as "oscuro, muy indio y mogol de facciones" (qtd. in Fogelquist 70) [dark, with very Indian and Mongol features], and added "me pareció más pequeño, más insignificante" [he looked to me smaller, more insignificant].[17] It seems that the Nicaraguan poet and his racial heritage were perceived as the very embodiment (in its most literal sense) of America in the eyes of the Spaniards. The extent to which Darío's body was an unsettling signifier in Spain, whatever the generation of writers, cannot be overemphasized. After all, it was this "Indian" who had arrived in Spain in 1892, four centuries after Columbus sailed in the opposite direction, looking down on Spanish culture and its "backwardness," whom Rodó had depicted as a messiah for the youth of Spain, and who himself would claim to have revolutionized Spanish literature.

The Spanish Literary Field Transformed

As Bourdieu explains, once a new set of producers imposes itself, the entire field changes: "The whole space of positions and the space of corresponding possibilities, hence the whole problematic, find themselves transformed because of it: with its accession to existence, that is, to difference, the universe of possible options finds itself modified, with formerly dominant productions, for example, being downgraded to the status of an outmoded or classical product" (*Rules* 234). That was certainly the situation in Spain, where options were progressively transformed by Spanish American modernistas and new writers began to emerge, while once-dominant writers, those who most violently fought against the "tropical mockingbirds," lost their position and capital in the field or transformed themselves to retain relevance, that is, to stay in the game. Such was the case, for instance, of Pardo Bazán, who, despite her strong commitment to naturalism, would move away from it and closer to modernismo in her later novels (Whitaker). New Spanish writers took advantage of the innovations brought about by Spanish American modernismo to accumulate symbolic capital, writers who came to prominence in the first decade of the twentieth century, from Juan Ramón Jiménez, Antonio Machado, and Ramón del Valle-Inclán to Miguel de Unamuno, Azorín, and Jacinto Benavente.

For more than a decade, most up-and-coming writers in the Peninsula had been devouring every Spanish American modernista writing they could get their hands on. According to Juan Ramón Jiménez, his friend and fellow writer Francisco Villaespesa, who corresponded with Spanish American authors, owned a significant collection of Spanish American works. In the 1890s the two young poets enthusiastically read modernista texts from all over the continent: poetry and fiction by Guillermo Valencia from Colombia, Ricardo Jaimes Freyre from Bolivia, Manuel Díaz Rodríguez from Venezuela, Amado Nervo from Mexico, and Leopoldo Lugones from Argentina (Henríquez Ureña, *Breve* 508). Villaespesa would later acknowledge: "Es indudable que los poetas americanos no solo son conocidos y admirados en España, sino que de cierto modo influyeron en el actual renacimiento de nuestras letras" (qtd. in Fogelquist 87). [There is no doubt that the American poets are not only known and admired in Spain, but that in a certain way they influenced the present renaissance in our letters.] Jiménez himself began his writing career with more or less fortunate imitations of Colombian modernista José Asunción Silva (García Morales).

The importance of Spanish American modernista poetry in Spain has been widely acknowledged, but the impact of modernismo was revolutionary, altering the totality of the Spanish field. In theater, playwrights as different as Benavente, who was awarded the Nobel Prize in 1922, and Valle-Inclán, by far Spain's most important playwright of the period, were among the first to embrace modernismo. As for Spanish narrative production, upon his return from Mexico, Valle-Inclán, who would later say that Mexico made him a writer (Reyes 70), published the collection of short stories *Femeninas* (Feminine) in 1894, the first example of modernista prose written by a Spaniard. In 1895, as he wrote *En torno al casticismo* (On Cultural Purity) and in the midst of the debates on modernismo and its renovation of Spanish, Unamuno expressed, in terms close to those of the debates, the need to renew the language: "El viejo castellano . . . necesita, para europeizarse a la moderna, más ligereza y más precisión a la vez, algo de desarticulación, puesto que hoy tiende a la anquilosis" (qtd. in Henríquez Ureña, *Breve* 523). [In order to Europeanize and modernize it, old Castilian needs to be at once lighter and more precise; it needs some disarticulation, because of its present tendency to anchylosis.] Like Valera's tree, Spanish literary language seemed to be in need of new life, and he had little doubt about where that new life was coming from: "Nuestra lengua nos dice allende el gran mar cosas que aquí no dijo nunca" (qtd. in Henríquez Ureña, *Breve* 99). [Our language tells us things from across the great sea that it never told us here.] Despite his declared distaste for the term *modernismo*, Unamuno wrote many positive reviews of Spanish American modernista books, including Manuel Díaz Rodríguez's novels *Ídolos rotos* (Broken Idols, 1901) and *Sangre patricia* (Patrician Blood, 1902), both of which he praised together with Díaz Rodríguez's earlier *Cuentos de color* (Colored Stories, 1899).

The relationship between Spanish and Spanish American writers had grown exponentially by 1902, when Unamuno published *Amor y pedagogía* (Love and Pedagogy); Azorín, *La voluntad* (The Will); Baroja, *Camino de perfección* (The Way to Perfection); and Valle Inclán, *Sonata de otoño* (Autumn Sonata)—by then the point of reference for the new generations of Spanish novelists was no longer realism but modernismo.[18] In 1902, Valle-Inclán published an article on modernismo, as did Baroja (who was notoriously anti-American) in 1903, defending the term in ways close to those used by Darío and other Spanish American modernistas. In 1906, Amado Nervo testified to the veritable revolution taking place in Spanish letters under the influence of Spanish American modernismo:

> Pasa España, en el momento presente, por un periodo de transición, en el cual se diseña con claridad la influencia de literaturas menos inmovilizadas que la literatura ibérica. Esta influencia acabará por cambiar totalmente el arte español, infundiéndole nueva vida y vigor nuevo. No se quejen de ellos los críticos peninsulares, pues asisten acaso a la evolución que ha de devolver a su literatura la universalidad que ha perdido. Y ciertamente van de América las brisas que orean sus huertos. (qtd. in Fogelquist 85–86)
>
> [At present, Spain is undergoing a period of transition, in which the influence of other literatures less stagnant than Iberian literature is clearly visible. This influence will end up changing Spanish art completely, infusing it with new life and vigor. Critics from the Peninsula ought not to complain, since they are witnessing a development that will give back their literature the universality that it has lost. And certainly, the breeze that is airing out their garden comes from America.][19]

Time and again, Spanish American writers referenced the Americanist impulse behind this renovation, which even those Spanish critics who embraced the new aesthetic had a hard time recognizing. Yet, as is the case with literary change, fighting Americanism only acknowledged its existence in the field.

Focused exclusively on the notion of national literature, Bourdieu never considers the role played by foreign literatures, that is, outside agents. His model of the literary field assumes that each national cultural field functions in a sort of vacuum or bubble, unaffected by external agents, rules, and symbolic capital. But much like economic capital, symbolic capital is not constrained by national boundaries. In fact, this transnational dimension of the circulation of symbolic goods is essential to understanding the workings of cultural fields and the nature of the struggles in those fields, even when one is interested in analyzing only a single national context. This is all too clear when studying the debates surrounding the advent of Spanish American modernismo in Spain. From Valera's complaints on what he considered mere "trendiness" to Gómez de Baquero's criticism of Spanish isolation and provincialism, the issue of "copying" foreign literary models is central to the struggles within the Spanish literary field at the turn of the century. Bourdieu failed to notice that since literature was inseparable from nationhood in the nineteenth century, the implications of transnational cross-pollinations were, as Valera himself noted, inevitably political as well. Issues of national prestige and distinction are also fundamental to the way transnational influences work and are valued. This is crucial to understanding modernismo's reception in Spain not only at the time, but also since.

In the Spanish literary establishment, it was difficult enough to accept that Spain could no longer claim the status of intellectual metropolis; French literary influence was a hard pill for some to swallow, but the dominance of Spanish America, Spain's colony not long ago, was for most simply unacceptable. This point can hardly be overemphasized. In *La imitación colectiva*, Jesús Torrecilla has shown that nineteenth-century Spanish cultural production was profoundly mediated by the place of France and French culture in the Spanish imaginary. As Torrecilla argues, Spanish literary discourse was marked by the tension between attraction and rejection of a modernity that many identified with France, which was at least a European nation. The arrival of Spanish American modernistas under the banner of modernity and on a mission to transform Spanish language and literature was inconceivable.

Cultural power might have shifted within Europe, but it was always European. There was no historical precedent for an ex-colonial subject to assert cultural authority over the former metropolis and claim to modernize it. To acknowledge that influence openly amounted to granting Spanish America cultural authority and prestige, and Spanish writers and intellectuals (with notable exceptions, no doubt) were not ready to admit the end of the colonial dream. Moreover, in the context of nineteenth-century racial discourses, the racist attitude shown by many Spanish writers toward the Spanish Americans can be explained not only in terms of imperial nostalgia, but also, and concomitantly, in relation to Spain's own subaltern place in the new Euro-American racial divide. For many Spaniards, then, to admit a position ancillary to Spanish American literature and language, when literature and language were considered the ultimate expression of the character and value of a people, meant admitting a position at the margin of the margins.

Modernismo: A Literary Revolution in the Transatlantic Literary Field

The presence of Spanish American modernismo was making Spain's peripheral position clear, but, as with all drastic literary changes, factors external to the literary field gave the final impulse to the consecration of modernismo in Spain and to the reconfiguration of the Spanish national imaginary that the movement had prompted. Embedded in the field of power as the literary field is, according to Bourdieu, changes in the field need external sanction: "In effect, even if they are largely independent *in their principle* (meaning in the causes and reasons determining them), the clashes which unfold inside the literary (etc.) field always depend, *in their outcome*, happy or unhappy, on the correspondence they have with external clashes (those which unfold at the core of the field of power or the social field as a whole)" (*Rules* 252). In the transatlantic Hispanic literary field, that is, in both the Spanish American *and* the Spanish literary fields, modernismo brought about what Bourdieu calls a successful revolution, which for its success required the help of events external to the field: "A successful revolution in literature . . . is the product of the meeting between two processes, relatively independent, which occur in the field and outside it. The new heretical entrants . . . can usually only succeed in imposing recognition of their products by virtue of external changes." Two of these changes stand out for Bourdieu as the most decisive. The first is "the appearance of new categories of consumers" (253). In the case of the modernistas, as we have seen, this occurred through the slow process of "familiarization" begun in the early 1880s—creating and capitalizing on a new audience for their literary products, first in Spanish America and soon afterward in Spain. In competition with other literary practices, both local and foreign, modernismo combined elements (e.g., modernity, cosmopolitanism, and Americanism) that appealed to a considerable sector of the growing reading public, which was largely associated with the expanding urban centers. At the same time, the modernistas familiarized that public with new literary aesthetic practices that readers, in their turn, would eventually demand.

The second important external factor in Bourdieu's model is "political ruptures, which change the power relations at the heart of the field" (*Rules* 253). A well-known political rupture was indeed a central factor in the rise of modernismo to dominance: the War of 1898. The political rupture caused by the war, its wide-ranging transnational implications for both North and South, was the most important external force that consolidated the modernista literary revolution in the transatlantic Hispanic field. In the case of Spain, the war of 1898 made patently evident the end of Spanish hegemony. From Darío to Reyles, from Gutiérrez Nájera to Díaz Rodríguez, the Spanish American critique of Spain's stagnation and provincialism, of its material "backwardness," and of the emptiness of its imperial dreams, found undeniable evidence in what soon was called in Spain "the disaster." The Spanish defeat made clear the need for change and ultimately sanctioned a newer generation of writers and intellectuals who pointed to the inadequacy of old models, a generation born under the influence of modernismo. Despite the misgivings of some about their American peers, young Spanish writers turned the advances made by modernismo into their own. In Spanish America, the Cuban War and the confirmation of U.S. imperialism consolidated the consecration of the modernista generation and their Spanish Americanist impulse; in Spain, the war had a similar effect. There, it helped debunk established writers like Valera, Pardo Bazán, and Clarín, whose projects were deemed inadequate for the new state of affairs by a group of writers who immediately capitalized on the effects of the war and the so-called "problema de España" (problem of Spain). They would become known as the "Generation of 1898."

In sum, the Spanish military and political defeat in Cuba, Puerto Rico, and the Philippines served only to confirm and validate the literary and cultural defeat that had already taken place in Spain under the influence of modernismo. Modernismo gave Spanish writers an entirely new aesthetic and ideological framework from which to write and rethink the meaning of Hispanicness, Spain, and their place in a changing political and cultural global order. Modernismo meant for Spanish American writers their final consecration in the transatlantic literary field and the distinction of being the first movement to reverse directionality and alter European literary developments. Thus, modernismo produced an unprecedented transformation in the cultural field of the nation that not long before had been Spanish America's imperial metropolitan center, helping prompt a profound national crisis in Spain, a period of national self-reflection. This relocation of authority across the Atlantic has haunted Spain ever since.[20]

Toward the Erasure of Spanish America

Of Imperial Ghosts and European Membership

That the war of 1898 was a traumatic experience that contributed to a crisis in the Spanish national imaginary is a well-known fact of Spanish cultural history, although only recently have literary and cultural studies begun to explore the full scope of its implications and the place of the Spanish American ex-colonies in that crisis. Even so, the active role of Spanish American letters, and of modernismo in particular, have remained rather unexplored. Notable in their approach to the question of Spanish nationalism and the role of Spanish America in Spain's post-imperial imaginary at the turn of the century are Robin Fiddian's "Under Spanish Eyes: Late Nineteenth-Century Postcolonial Views of Spanish American Literature" (2002), Ángel Loureiro's "Spanish Nationalism and the Ghost of Empire" (2003), and Joseba Gabilondo's "Historical Memory, Neoliberal Spain, and the Latin American Postcolonial Ghost" (2003). Although quite different in scope, the three essays offer insightful readings of the way Spanish intellectual discourse of the nineteenth and early twentieth centuries was haunted by empire and of the role the Spanish American ex-colonies had in the construction of Spanish identity. There is, however, an important absence in these studies: Spanish Americans themselves. Fiddian, Loureiro, and Gabilondo analyze the Spanish imperial ghost and the place of Spanish America in the Spanish imaginary as if these had resulted from a self-generated process of identity construction.[21] That is, these critics examine Spanish America exclusively as a Spanish construct, never contemplating the existence of a real Spanish American agency that may have prompted, influenced, or otherwise mediated Spanish national imaginaries.[22] As I have pointed out, however, this agency is central to the process. Spanish intellectuals were not creating an image of Spanish America in a vacuum, but confronting the real presence of Spanish American writers and intellectuals in Spain who were changing the way Spanish literature ought to be written and forcing Spaniards to face the present. To ignore this fundamental element and pay attention only to the imperial discourse of Spanish intellectuals, as if they were writing on a blank slate rather than anxiously responding to a powerful Spanish American discourse, runs the risk of unwittingly reproducing the imperial move under critique.

A similar risk lies behind the also recent critical approaches that have aimed to relocate Peninsular modernismo in the context of Anglo European modernism. As valuable and necessary as this critical stance undoubtedly is to correct the ethnocentric impulse behind Anglo European modernism (a result itself of nineteenth-century racial discourses), this relocation has been carried out, unfortunately, by largely ignoring the transatlantic dimension of modernismo and its origin in Spanish America. Thus, unwittingly or not, critics are removing Spanish modernismo from its context of production and further erasing the magnitude of the Spanish American enterprise, as well as the uniqueness of the Hispanic "postcolonial condition." Take, for instance, Germán Gullón's early exasperated comments on this issue: "¿Hasta cuando durará el ostracismo de la literatura española del conjunto de las europeas? ¿En qué momento pediremos que nos incluyan con plenos derechos en las nóminas de Occidente? J. R. Jimenez y T. S. Eliot . . . deben ir emparejados al igual que Virginia Woolf . . . y Miguel de Unamuno, sin que frunzan ceños ni se experimenten disparidades" (16). [How long will the ostracism of Spanish literature from the set of European literatures last? At what point will we demand to be included with full rights in the catalogues of the West? J. R. Jiménez and T. S. Eliot must go together and so must Virginia Woolf and Miguel de Unamuno, without any frowning or disagreement.] It is undeniably true that the concept of modernism has been theorized by exclusion. Yet there is something troublesome in pleading for inclusion in "Europe's" select club, especially in doing so by turning the peninsular back on Spanish America's modernismo.[23] This approach, nonetheless, is rapidly gaining ground in peninsular studies. It is difficult not to see the political, economic, and cultural context of contemporary Spain mediating the scholarly writing of modernismo. As Spain has become a full member of the European Union and its "modernity" finally secured and recognized, its literary and cultural production has also undergone a revision: the old privileging of the so-called Generation of '98 (strongly associated with the Franco regime) has given way to an understanding of the period according to prevalent definitions of "European" modernism. In other words, the modernism of Peninsular modernismo is presented as further evidence (and reassurance) of Spain's "Europeanness."

In contrast (and the irony of the situation cannot be missed), many Spanish Americanists have found themselves grappling with the issue of modernism, doubting its existence in Spanish America (or delaying its appearance to the narrative "boom" of the 1960s), and looking at their peninsular colleagues with a certain envy: "In contrast to critics working in the field of modern Peninsular fiction, *we are patently at a disadvantage*. In Spain, the notion of a Generation of 1898 has been, despite some opposition, progressively incorporated into a wider concept of modernismo, and this in turn has begun to be presented as a variant of Anglo American Modernism" (Shaw 395; my emphasis). As a result, Spanish American criticism has gone through much juggling of terminologies, chronologies, and texts and often a good deal of self-deprecation in order to "fit" into a concept that originated in Spanish America in the first place.[24]

Spanish Denial and the Invention of a Debate

Much of this criticism has been mediated by the contested existence of the so-called Spanish Generation of 1898 in Spain. Indeed, the almost century-old debate on the validity of the term "Generation of '98" and its opposition to modernismo can be seen as a foundational critical instance whose pervasive influence can still be traced in recent critical trends, even among those clearly trying to break away from it and its regrettable effects on Spanish literary criticism. For, despite the apparent antagonism between the two main critical stances on the debate, both are haunted by the same imperial ghost that prevents them from thinking of Spain as anything other than the center of the Hispanic Atlantic.

One approach opposed the Generation of '98 to modernismo, very loosely based on Azorín's coinage of the term "Generation of '98" in 1912 and represented by Pedro Salinas, Guillermo Díaz Plaja, Pedro Laín Entralgo, and many others since. Although it kept the association between modernismo and Spanish America almost intact, it did so by trivializing it, reducing modernismo to a mere formalist game in contrast to the alleged seriousness and profoundness of the Generation of '98.[25] The official take on the period for most of the twentieth century, this categorization would pay good service, willingly or unwillingly, to Francoist ideology and unfortunately has marked until now our understanding of most turn-of-the-century literary production.

The other approach, the so-called epochal view, was best developed and argued by Ricardo Gullón and traced in Spain to Juan Ramón Jiménez and Federico de Onís, who claimed that modernismo was the pan-Hispanic expression of a universal crisis. This approach exposed the provincial shortcomings of the Generation of '98 fallacy (to use John Butt's words) or invention (to use Gullón's). Nonetheless, it did so only by erasing the central role of Spanish American writers and by presenting modernismo as a *simultaneous* pan-Hispanic opening to "European" currents. Moreover, according to Jiménez and Ricardo Gullón, this general moment of literary and intellectual renovation was the result only of the alleged original impulse of nineteenth-century Spanish poets Gustavo Adolfo Bécquer and (to a lesser extent) Rosalía de Castro (R. Gullón, *Direcciones* 32). In this way, Jiménez and Gullón ultimately traced the pan-Hispanic epochal view back to Spain, locating there the "true" origin of modernismo and further erasing Spanish America's centrality and authority. Almost a century after Valera, Gullón affirmed: "Hasta el modernismo casi sólo podía hablarse de literatura española, ya fuese escrita dentro o fuera de la Península; a partir de él, la realidad es otra: surge la literatura hispánica, con divergencias saludables, pero con integración genuina. . . . Y lo esencial es, a mi juicio, la simultaneidad con que el impulso renovador aparece en Andalucía como en Chile, en Cuba como en Colombia" (34–35). [Before modernismo, one could only speak of Spanish literature, be it written within or outside the Peninsula; from modernism on, reality is different: Hispanic literature is born, with salutary differences but with genuine integration. . . . And the essential thing is, in my view, the simultaneity with which the renovating impulse appears in Andalusia as in Chile, in Cuba as in Colombia.] The epochal view thus did an excellent job revealing the "invención del '98," but only by inventing its own self-satisfying version of a Becquerian pan-Hispanic modernismo.[26]

The source of these critical operations can be found in the complex development of modernismo in the Peninsula. Spanish American writers had radically transformed the Spanish field and made possible the rise of a new generation of producers who followed their aesthetic and philosophical lead. Nonetheless, the politics and ideologies of the postcolonial context were such that most of those producers would eventually refuse to acknowledge the influence of their transatlantic peers after modernismo was established in the Spanish field and the previous generation demoted. For many Spanish writers and intellectuals, denial seemed a better option.[27] Rather than accept the loss of literary authority, they chose either to ignore it or, in some notable cases, to launch an attack on the very Spanish American writers who made the existence of their work possible.[28]

"Sangre de Hispania fecunda": The Inverted Conquest and the Silence of Spain

The very idea that the epochal view was formulated by Jiménez and Onís is a sign of Spanish bias. Long before them, Spanish American writers had used the term "modernismo" to refer to a general or universal shift in the relationship between art and modernity. Among these, Venezuelan novelist Manuel Díaz Rodríguez wrote one of the most interesting theorizations of modernismo to date in his 1908 book *Camino de perfección*. In this text, Díaz Rodríguez exposed the growing amnesia of some Spanish writers as they tried to erase their debt to Spanish America's transforming presence in Spain and the Spanish literary field: "Bueno es decirlo porque muchos afectan desconocerlo, cómo se dio el caso de una especie de inversa conquista en que las nuevas carabelas, partiendo de las antiguas colonias, aproaron las costas de España. De los libros recién llegados por entonces de América, la crítica militante peninsular decía que estaban, aunque asaz bien pergeñados, enfermos de la manía modernista" (61). [It is important to say it because many pretend not to know it: that a kind of inverted conquest took place in which the new caravels, departing from the old colonies, set course for the coast of Spain. Militant critics from the Peninsula used to say that the books then recently arrived from America were, although quite well drafted, sick with modernist mania.] Recalling the language of disease and contamination that had permeated the critical discourse of Clarín's generation on Spanish American letters and confronting Spanish "amnesia" and imperial denial, Díaz Rodríguez turns the colonial metaphor on its head and conjures the powerful image of the inverted conquest. This idea of modernismo as a conquest in reverse evoked all the earlier remarks of his fellow Spanish American modernistas, from Darío, Reyles, and Rodó to Gutiérrez Nájera, Jaimes Freyre, and Nervo, concretizing them along with the imperial nostalgia of many Spanish intellectuals into one lasting and powerful metaphor. It is also an image that foregrounds the unprecedented shift in directionality that Spanish American modernismo meant and that many of Díaz Rodríguez's Spanish peers feared.[29] Cultural change was now traveling east and conquering Europe.

The Spanish denial of influence that Díaz Rodríguez pointed out in 1908 was so strong that even basic chronologies sometimes were distorted to make Spanish American writers the ones following the Spanish lead. Díaz Rodríguez himself had already had to deal with such critical juggling when he was accused of copying Valle-Inclán:

> Hubo un gacetillero zascandil que dijera cómo yo era un simple imitador de Valle-Inclán. . . . De haber un imitador, no podía serlo quien fue primero en escribir y publicar, por lo que la pretendida acusación al cambiarse por pasiva, equivalía a una confesión involuntaria de una influencia que no se ha confesado nunca. Es el caso de repetir que, si la hubo, semejante influencia no aparejaba inferioridad a quien la sufría. Y fuera absurdo usar de ese término ante la originalidad y el estilo incomparable del maestro de las *Sonatas*. (qtd. in Henríquez Ureña, *Breve* 509)

> [There was a mean penny-a-liner who said that I was a mere imitator of Valle-Inclán. . . . Were there an imitator, it could not be the person who wrote and pub-

lished first, so that the intended accusation turned around was equivalent to an involuntary confession of an influence that has never been confessed. But I insist that, if there was any influence, it did not mean inferiority for the recipient. It would be absurd anyway to use that word in the face of the originality and incomparable style of the master of the *Sonatas*.]

Forced to defend himself, Díaz Rodríguez managed to leave open the possibility of his unacknowledged influence over the Spanish novelist *and* to assert Valle-Inclán's genius, all the while making clear that influence and originality are not incompatible. Moreover, Díaz Rodríguez exposed the anxiety behind the accusations by pointing out "a never confessed influence."

Díaz Rodríguez would be accused of plagiarism again, this time by Spanish critic Joaquín López Barbadillo regarding his *Camino de perfección* (The Way of Perfection). In 1917, the year of Rodó's death and one year after Darío's, López Barbadillo apparently criticized the author of *Ariel* for praising Díaz Rodríguez's *Camino*. These remarks coincided with a diatribe by novelist Pío Baroja against Spanish American letters and Spanish Americans themselves in words that made those by Clarín about Darío seem almost friendly:

> Sucede, que, a veces, en un pueblo nuevo se reune toda la torpeza provinciana, con la estupidez mundial, la sequedad y la incomprensión del terruño con los detritos de la moda y de las majaderías de las cinco partes del mundo. Entonces brota un tipo petulante, huero, sin una virtud, sin una condición fuerte. Este es el tipo americano. América es por excelencia el continente estúpido. El americano no ha pasado de ser un mono que imita. . . . La misma falta de simpatía que siento por los hispanoamericanos experimento por sus obras literarias. Todo lo que he leído de los americanos, a pesar de las adulaciones interesadas de Unamuno, lo he encontrado mísero y sin consistencia. . . . ¡Qué oleada de vulgaridad, de snobismo, de chabacanería nos ha venido de América! (qtd. in Alazraki 756)

> [It happens that sometimes in new nations all the provincial turpitude merges with worldly stupidity, the land's own dryness and lack of understanding with the detritus of fashion and nonsense from all five parts of the world. It is then that a type is born: petulant, empty, without any virtue, without a strong character. This is the American type. America is the stupid continent par excellence. The American has not gone beyond being an imitating monkey. . . . The same lack of sympathy that I feel for the Spanish Americans, I feel for their literary works. Everything I have read by Americans, despite Unamuno's calculated flattery, I have found miserable and without consistency. . . . What a wave of commonplaces, of snobbism, of vulgarity has come to us from America!]

Regarding Díaz Rodríguez's *Camino de perfección* and its rewriting and defense of Hispanic history and modernity, Baroja had complained that the Venezuelan novelist had no right to defend Spain.[30] Used to it by now, Díaz Rodríguez saw through these maneuvers and insisted, this time far more forcefully, on exposing their fallacy and the pettiness of their imperial denial. In an open letter to Baroja and López Barbadillo, the Venezuelan novelist denounced the Spanish refusal to publicly accept and honor the role of Spanish American letters in transforming those of Spain. For him, Baroja's attitude was but a symptom of his small-mindedness and of Spain's provincialism, backwardness, and xenophobia: "Así, [los hispanoamericanos] hemos ido a todas partes, viajado por muchos países, aprendido otras lenguas, probado y saboreado extrañas culturas, todo para que a la vista de un Baroja, nuestra sana y generosa inquietud se resuelva en mueca de simios" (*Camino* 152). [Thus, we Spanish Americans have gone everywhere, traveled in many countries, learned other languages, tried and tasted strange cultures, all so that, in Baroja's view, our healthy and generous restlessness comes down to a simian gesture.]

Little seemed to have changed in the ideological reaction of many Spanish writers to their Spanish American counterparts. The "mockingbirds" of Clarín were now Barojas's "imitating monkeys," metaphors aimed at defining Spanish Americans as imitators, as culturally dependent. Díaz Rodríguez exposes the tactic behind the peninsular writers' attacks by calling attention to their contradictions and turning Baroja's pejorative comments against Spain. He uncovers the maneuver behind this strategically evasive amnesia and insistently reinstates the reversal of influence that had taken place:

> No ha sido exclusivamente, sin embargo, simiesca vanidad nuestra actitud, porque ya dio su fruto en sazón para la misma España. Suelen hablar hoy a menudo, los escritores peninsulares, de su generación literaria del 98, sin recordar como debieran que ese renacimiento o florecer español despertó bajo la viva corriente—llámesela modernismo o como quiera llamársela—renovadora de la prosa y el verso castellano, que partió de nuestra América a fijarse y quedar desde entonces representada ante España en la hora y el nombre de Rubén Darío. (*Camino* 152)
>
> [However, our attitude has not been exclusively simian vanity since it has already borne ripe fruits in Spain itself. Writers from the Peninsula today talk frequently of their literary generation of '98, not remembering as they should that that Spanish renaissance or blossoming awoke under the lively current—call it modernismo or however you may want to call it—that renewed both Castilian prose and verse, and that left our America to root and remain since then represented in Spain in the times and name of Rubén Darío.]

For Díaz Rodríguez there is no doubt about the effort Baroja and his peers were making to erase any trace of Spanish American influence or authority. Díaz Rodríguez highlights the derivative nature of Spanish literature, calling attention once again to the politics of naming and the equivalence of modernismo and the "Generation of '98." A successful and influential novelist, Díaz Rodríguez reminds Baroja, a novelist himself, that modernismo's profound renovation was not limited to poetry but extended to Spanish narrative as well, a renovation that, rather than a passing fancy, came from Spanish America to stay ("fijarse y quedar") in Spain. In short, it was permanent and ultimately undeniable. Much as Rodó had done in the concluding paragraph of his essay on Rubén Darío, Díaz Rodríguez turns Darío into a Christlike figure and depicts the poet leading a generational group of apostles and the entire American continent. Like Christ, Darío is represented sharing his bread/body and bringing salvation to Spain:

> Y es muy posible que aun después de haber provocado al frente de su generación, y con América, el más preclaro encendimiento de las letras en España, hoy, como hace el padre Cejador, le negase la generalidad, o se afectase ignorar su nombre y su obra, de no haber el poeta vivido luengas temporadas en Madrid, y partido, con periodistas y escritores madrileños, el pan y la sal, un pan y una sal que fueron seguramente argentinos o nicaragüenses, iberoamericanos en suma. (153)

> [And it is quite possible that even after Rubén Dario, leading his generation and with America, produced the most brilliant enlightenment of letters in Spain, today the majority might deny him, like Father Cejador does, or pretend not to know his name and his work, had the poet not lived in Madrid for long periods and had he not shared bread and salt with journalists and writers from that city, a bread and salt that surely came from Argentina or Nicaragua, Iberian America in any case.]

The religious metaphor of Darío breaking bread with his Spanish peers is loaded with meaning. Díaz Rodríguez references the colonial discourse of salvation, but, reversing the imperial gesture that had been present in Spanish critics like Clarín, salvation now comes from America. The reference to bread and salt, associated in the biblical tradition with hospitality, speaks to the lack of welcome in Spain, its xenophobia: ignoring or pretending not to have known Darío, Spaniards are new versions of both Peter and Judas, negating and betraying him and the renovative impact of modernismo.

For all his focus on Darío here, however, we should not think that Díaz Rodríguez limits the scope of modernismo to the Nicaraguan poet. Darío may embody its greatness, but Díaz Rodríguez is careful to affirm that an entire generation and a whole continent were with him. Darío was not alone, nor was modernismo a one-man phenomenon. Working through metonymy, the Spanish denial of Darío-Christ is the refusal to recognize Spain's debt to all Spanish American writers: "Apenas dos o tres voces vergonzantes y tímidas nombraron en España a Rodó antes de su muerte. Y hoy mismo viven en Madrid hispanoamericanos eminentes que en España se ignoran" (*Camino* 153). [Barely two or three timid and embarrassed voices named Rodó in Spain before his death. Even today, there are eminent Spanish Americans living in Madrid that are ignored in Spain.] Furthermore, Díaz Rodríguez emphasizes that the dependency of Spain on Spanish America is not only cultural but also economic and material: here, bread and salt are at once Spanish American symbolic and material goods that Spain depended on and consumed.[31] Díaz Rodríguez, as other Spanish American modernistas had done before him, turns the Spanish colonial discourse on its head by transforming the "motherland" into a dependent, if not a child, that needs to be nourished both intellectually and physically. In sum, Díaz Rodríguez's text places Spain in a colonial position with respect to a metropolitan Spanish America.

Indeed, aware of the anxieties of Spanish intellectuals regarding Spain's new place in the transnational field of power, that is, its loss of political and cultural importance, as well as their fears about becoming culturally, economically, and materially peripheral to what not long ago were Spain's own colonies, Díaz Rodríguez does not allow Baroja the possibility of thinking Spain only marginal to the most powerful countries of Europe:

> Atisba [Baroja] la verdad, cuando por el hecho de hallarse España, según él dice, fuera de la corriente, considera provincianos a los españoles, para caer inmediatamente en error cuando imagina que solo son tales con relación a alemanes, ingleses y franceses. De ser provincianos, para no abandonar el símil del novelista, lo son igualmente respecto a otros pueblos de América y Europa. Y como entre estos hay algunos de origen español que no la padecen, me alegro de no ver en la cerrazón como la llama Baroja, o estrechez de vista, ningún irreducible defecto de raza. (*Camino* 149)
>
> [(Baroja) glimpses the truth when he considers that Spaniards are provincial because, as he says, Spain is out of the loop, only to immediately make the mistake of imagining that they are so only in relation to the German, the English, and the French. If they are provincial—using the simile established by the novelist himself—they are equally so in relation to other people in America and Europe. And since among these others there are some of Spanish origin, I am happy to see that that close-mindedness, as Baroja calls it, that narrow field of vision, is not an irreducible defect of the Spanish race.]

By bringing up prevalent racial discourses, Díaz Rodríguez is performing a double move. On the one hand, he is questioning the validity of those discourses by canceling the then-prevalent association between "backwardness" and the Hispanic people. On the other hand, and just as important, he is reversing the locus of enunciation of "Hispanicness" by affirming the centrality of Spanish American nations over the Peninsula. He places those same Spanish American nations (as well as other European nations) on the same level as Germany, England, and France.

Following the tradition of Darío's journalistic writings collected in *España contemporánea*, Díaz Rodríguez is merciless with Baroja and the state of affairs in Spain:

> Tratase más bien de una simple ausencia casi absoluta de instrucción popular, de suerte que, aparte la limitación propia del medio picaresco donde ha vivido, en la cortedad irremediable de vista con que el señor Baroja no alcanza a ver más allá de los Pirineos, y que es la misma estrechez de visión de la aldea, del cacicazgo, de la patriecita, columbramos el reflejo natural de la misma estrechez de visión de un pueblo que marcha a tanteos y tropezones por entre la densa y verdadera cerrazón de tinieblas de la más honda incultura. (*Camino* 149)
>
> [It has to do with a simple and almost absolute absence of public instruction, so that in the irremediable shortness of vision that prevents Mr. Baroja from seeing beyond the Pyrenees, that same narrowness of vision of the village, of the *cacicazgo*, of one's little homeland, we can make out, aside from those limitations typical of the picaresque environment in which he has lived, the natural reflection of the same narrowness of vision of a people that fumbles around and stumbles about in the dense and true close-minded darkness of the most profound lack of any education.]

From an environment like this, nothing worthy may emerge, according to Díaz Rodríguez. Citing Joaquín Costa's despair about the Spanish lack of education and Pardo Bazán's complaint about the lack of readers in Spain—"Pregúntese a nuestros editores, libreros, autores: dirán que su salvación está en el mercado de América" (150) [Ask our editors, booksellers, and authors: they will tell you that their salvation lies in the American market]—Díaz Rodríguez goes a step further: "Sin variar ni alterar la esencia, cambiemos la palabra [Mercado] y escribamos cultura" (150). [Without varying or altering its essence, let's change the word "culture" for "market."] Díaz Rodríguez, then, proceeds to demolish Spain's intellectual landscape in literature, science, and the arts—just when the members of the Generation of '98 are at the height of their literary production. For him, in Spain there is only "un poco de literatura selecta sumergida en un mucho de gallofa y literatura pésima y barata" (150) [a bit of good literature submerged in a pool of garbage and cheap and terrible literature].

Given what he sees as the situation in the Peninsula, finally the Venezuelan novelist virtually expels Spain from the Hispanic community until it is ready to catch up with the rest. While it does so, he exhorts the Spaniards to improve Spain, to work for Spain and thus for all of the Hispanic community: "Pretendo solo que, entre tanto no se enteren de nuestra geografía, ni sepan de nuestra historia y hasta afecten ignorarnos, trabajen por España y para España, que así trabajarán al fin y al cabo para todos, buena y lealmente" (155). [My only intention is that, while they have no idea about our geography, know nothing about our history, and even pretend to ignore us, they work for the benefit of Spain, since that way they will, after all, be working well and faithfully for us all.]

For Díaz Rodríguez, not all is lost in the Peninsula, however; he appeals to another Spain buried "en medio de la estrechez de visión, de la mentalidad limitada y de la rudeza de las maneras, propias de la general incultura" (*Camino* 156) [in the midst of this narrowness of vision, limited intelligence, and rudeness of manners typical of the general lack of education]. Recalling Darío's famous poem "Salutación del optimista," Díaz Rodríguez focuses on that other, submerged Spain, concluding his essay by reclaiming Spain despite itself and appealing to a transatlantic cultural space:

> Así como Felipe IV, Carlos II y Fernando VII no fueron toda España, tampoco son toda España los López, Baroja y compañía: son estos a lo sumo el espumarajo, la pavesa, el detritus, el alga inánime y errátil, cuanto necesaria y fatalmente flota en aquel ancho mar que, con sus corales y perlas del fondo, con sus archipiélagos y continentes de la superficie, con sus tempestades y calmas, con sus maravillas e impurezas, condensara un gran poeta de América en este numeroso y henchido verso triunfal: "Ínclitas razas ubérrimas, sangre de Hispania fecunda." Y no debemos renegar de tan ilustre sangre, por más que todos los Barojas insistan en que reneguemos de ella. (157)
>
> [Just as Spain cannot be reduced to Phillip IV, Charles II, and Ferdinand VII, it cannot all be reduced to Lopez, Baroja, and company: they are, at most, the foam, the dying spark, the detritus, the inanimate and erratic algae that necessarily but fatally floats in that wide sea that, with its corals and pearls in its depths, with its archipelagos and continents on the surface, with its tempests and calmness, with its wonders and impurities, was condensed by a great American poet in one crowded and swollen triumphant verse: "Distinguished, fructiferous races, blood of prolific Hispania." And we should not reject such illustrious blood, however much Baroja and his cronies insist that we reject it.]

Ruthless in his critique of Baroja "and company" as the scum of the sea, Díaz Rodríguez constructs a poetic and hopeful image of the Hispanic Atlantic. Building an image of Spain from the standpoint of Spanish America, he performs the recurring modernista move of colonial reversal by recreating Spain as saved by its ex-colonies, an image, as I show in the next chapter, suitable for their own interests in the battle against Anglo Saxon supremacist racial discourse and U.S. imperialism.

Rescuing Spain from itself, as it were, and confirming the location of Hispanic cultural authority in America, Díaz Rodríguez ends his open letter by confirming the persistence of the "great silence" that Rodó, almost two decades earlier, noted in Spain as Darío sailed across the Atlantic in 1899:

> Y a las diatribas que de España nos vengan, así ellas nos vinieren de un escritor altísimo, y no alcanzo a ver muchos en medio de tanto prosista anémico y tanto poeta mediano, podremos contestar victoriosamente como esta vez con un verso de Rubén o una frase de Rodó. ¿Quién puede hoy en España reemplazar a Rubén, el gran poeta? ¿Quién puede en España reemplazar cumplidamente a Rodó, el gran ensayista? Si la muerte de esos dos hispanoamericanos ilustres ha sumido en profundo silencio a la América, ese hondo silencio es también silencio de España. (*Camino* 157)
>
> [And to the diatribes coming from Spain, even if they come from an excellent writer (and I do not manage to see many among so many anemic prose writers and so many mediocre poets), we will answer victoriously, this time with a verse by Rubén or a sentence by Rodó. Who can replace Rubén, the great poet, today in Spain? Who in Spain can fully replace Rodó, the great essayist? If the death of these two illustrious Spanish Americans has immersed America in a profound silence, that deep silence is also the silence of Spain.]

In this profusion of "silencios," Díaz Rodríguez's voice is the only heard. In the absence of Darío, the great American poet, and Rodó, the great American essayist, Díaz Rodríguez seems to assume the place of the great American novelist. If Spanish American poetry and essay are respectfully silent, so should they be in the ex-metropolis, because as Rodó had before him, Díaz Rodríguez suggests that Spain does not have its own voice. The voice of America now speaks for Spain. The Hispanic Atlantic speaks from America, and Spain must respectfully recognize both its debt to that voice as well as its subaltern cultural position. In this way, Díaz Rodríguez's essay could be understood as a unique postcolonial gesture as it makes the pan-Hispanic discourse America's own and, in so doing, reveals the ex-metropolis as silent and empty, a mere vessel that is now filled with meaning from across the Atlantic, much as Rodó had envisioned in 1899. If Spain had written America four hundred years earlier, it was now the Americans who were writing, as we shall see next, Spain, Hispanicness, and the modern Atlantic.

CHAPTER 4

Rewriting Modernity, Authoring Spain

> We must take absolutely seriously the fact that the racial theories of the nineteenth and twentieth centuries define communities of language, descent and tradition which do not, as a general rule, coincide with historical states, even though they always obliquely refer to one or more of these. This means that the dimension of universality of theoretical racism . . . plays an essential role here: it permits a "specific universalization" and therefore an idealization of nationalism.
>
> —Etienne Balibar, "Racism and Nationalism"

> The power to narrate, or to block other narratives from forming and emerging, is very important to culture and imperialism, and constitutes one of the main connections between them.
>
> —Edward Said, *Culture and Imperialism*

By 1900, Spanish American modernismo had attained consecration in the transatlantic literary field and was reaching the height of its prestige. Indeed, not long before, Spanish American writers had sought legitimation and recognition from the Spanish establishment, leading Amado Nervo to complain that no American poet could be considered such until a Spanish writer said so. By the end of the century, however, the tables had turned. Many young Spanish writers looked up to their Spanish American peers, seeking their approval and respect in what amounted to an unprecedented reversal of authority in the Hispanic literary field. While in 1888 it had been Rubén Darío who sent his book for Valera's seal of approval, in 1900 it was young Spanish poet (and future Nobel laureate) Juan Ramón Jiménez who addressed Darío as "Maestro" and begged him for a prologue (Darío, *Epistolario* 132). That same year, the young and still unknown Jiménez was one of many young writers who looked across the Atlantic to José Enrique Rodó, not just with admiration, but in search of recognition:

> Una misteriosa actividad nos cojía a algunos jóvenes españoles cuando hacia 1900 se nombraba en nuestras reuniones de Madrid a Rodó. *Ariel*, en su único ejemplar conocido por nosotros, andaba de mano en mano sorprendiéndonos. ¡Qué ilusión entonces para mi deseo poseer aquellos tres libritos delgados azules, pulcros, de letra nítida roja y negra: *Ariel, Rubén Darío, El que vendrá*! Después, en 1902, tuve ya una carta inestimable de Rodó por mis pobres *Rimas* enfermas. Luego, para mí solo, sus libros aquellos anhelados. (Rodó, *Obras completas* 1408)
>
> [A mysterious activity seized some of us young Spaniards when, around 1900, the name of Rodó was uttered at our meetings in Madrid. *Ariel*, in what was the only copy known to us, would circulate from hand to hand, surprising us. How I desired to own those three small books, thin, blue, delicate, in neat black and red font: *Ariel, Rubén Darío, El que vendrá* (That Who Will Come)! Later, in 1902, I finally received an invaluable letter from Rodó about my poor, sickly *Rhymes*. And then, all to myself, those books of his I so craved.]

Indeed, in 1902, Jiménez sent Rodó his *Rimas* and a letter addressing the Uruguayan intellectual as "Dear Master" (1408).[1] *Ariel*, the programmatic text of Latin Americanism that Rodó had addressed to "the youth of America" warning them against the threat of a growing "nordomanía" [North mania], was likewise eagerly read by the youth of Spain, who also considered Rodó their maestro, their Prospero.

In 1892, only a decade earlier, Juan Valera had not quite known what to do with the term "americanismo," as we have seen. Thinking of Europe, he managed to gain a sense of common history and a common purpose. He went as far as to imagine, only to later dispel the thought, that the future could actually be American. Between September 1891 and March 1892, Valera, who had served as Spanish ambassador to the United States between 1884 and 1886, wrote a series of crónicas under the title *Cartas de España* for the prestigious *Revista Ilustrada de Nueva York* (*New York Illustrated Magazine*). This magazine, which soon became one of the most emblematic of modernismo even if it was not a modernista project per se, was founded on precisely the "americanismo" that had puzzled the Spanish critic.[2] *La Revista* had been conceived as a "publicación de ancha base, de gran espíritu, genuinamente americana, que los sirva a todos por igual en su despertar enérgico a la vida colectiva" (qtd. in Chamberlin 4) [a genuinely American publication with a wide base and a great spirit that serves everyone equally in their energetic awakening to a collective life]. Indeed, both the appellation "nuestra América" [our America] that José Martí made famous in its pages, as well as "nuestra raza" [our race], were common terms used to refer to the community of readers of *La Revista*.

When the magazine came out in the mid-1880s, it promised to reveal to its readers "el secreto de esta maravilla de nación" [the secret of this wonder of a nation], referring to the United States. But by 1891, the attitude of the magazine had drastically changed, and that secret seemed less wonderful than anticipated. That year, the magazine published Martí's "Nuestra América" in the January issue, and in December, just before introducing a new section of crónicas by Spanish novelist Pardo Bazán, the editors stated:

> LA REVISTA espera ver colmado uno de sus deseos más ardientes, cual es el de hacer de sus páginas poderoso torna voz para los más escogidos miembros de la gran familia hispano-americana que, por desdicha, no ha ocupado hasta hoy este palenque sino para traducir y exagerar dolorosas disidencias cuya imprudente prolongación y criminal envenenamiento comprometerían a la larga superiores intereses comunes a toda la raza. En presencia de la anglosajona, que por su superioridad industrial indiscutible nos menosprecia, y por cálculo nos espía en cada una de nuestras caídas, españoles de América y de España deben aparecer unidos, siquiera sea en el terreno literario, mantener sus tradiciones, perseguir sus propios ideales, y afirmar en este nuevo mundo revelado a la civilización cristiana, la parte de influencia que de derecho le corresponde por semejantes títulos. (qtd. in Chamberlin 8)
>
> [LA REVISTA hopes to see one of its most burning desires satisfied: to turn its pages into a powerful sounding board for the most select members of the great Spanish American family, who, unfortunately, have occupied this tribune only to translate and exaggerate painful disagreements; prolonging this criminal poisoning is imprudent and would, in the long run, compromise higher interests common to our race. In the presence of the Anglo-Saxon race, who scorn us because of their indisputable industrial superiority and with calculation spy on us each time we fall, the Spanish people of America and Spain must appear united even if only in the literary terrain, keep their traditions, follow their own ideals, and affirm in this New World revealed to Christian civilization, the share of influence to which they are rightfully entitled.]

The great Spanish American family whom the magazine addressed was under threat. The editorial echoes the words of Martí nearly a year earlier: unity against fragmentation, common cause against an enemy lurking outside—Martí's "tiger outside" and "the disdain of the formidable neighbor" (*Selected* 294, 295)—and the importance of ideas in the battle for America. This Spanish American family, however, had a new member: Spain. Rather than the "madre patria" (that androgynous parent so dear to Spanish discourse of the time), Spain seemed like a sibling in this large family defined by race. This act of bringing Spain into the American family was remarkable. Many Spanish intellectuals (as well as those in Spanish America attached to the conservative tradition) insisted on the need for Spanish America to reunite culturally with the "motherland," to come home, like the prodigal son. At the turn of the century, however, many Spanish American writers who refused to come home performed the opposite move: they turned Spain into a part—a province, as it were—of America.

The phrase "españoles de América" (Spaniards from America), in common use at the time, altered in meaning depending on how it was used and who used it. For many Spanish intellectuals the term was loaded with imperial overtones, as we have seen. It was as cultural as it was territorial; it was the reminder and remainder of empire. For turn-of-the-century Spanish Americans, however, it was an act of appropriation of "Hispanicness" for themselves, and it was loaded with racial overtones. In the editorial, the term "Spanish," rather than attempting to erase "American" (as Valera or Clarín might have done), was Americanized in an effort, if not to erase, to combat or contain the "Anglo-Saxon" advance. Bhabha's concept of mimicry does not apply here; the analogy is more that of a baton in a relay race taken from, rather than given by, a spent runner who is no longer an active part of the race but who remains part of the team. It is paternalism in reverse, telling the ex-imperial power that it is, to play on Bhabha's words, "almost the same but not quite" (Bhabha 90). In the process, of course, the meaning of "Hispanicness" itself was also changed. It is within this context, only a few years after this 1891 editorial, that Juan Ramón Jiménez and the Spanish youth were enthralled with Rodó's Americanism and Manuel Díaz Rodríguez found himself in the position of telling some of his Spanish peers what "Hispanicness" was all about.

The ultimate goal was the survival of the race in America, which the editors had earlier called "la tierra del porvenir" (qtd. in Chamberlin 7) [the land of the future]. The future was at stake, and for the editors the future was in America; it was for America, not for Spain, that the Spaniards must also work. The entire Hispanic race was under surveillance and in danger, and the lurking enemy was not just the United States but the Anglo-Saxon race. Here, the Anglo-Saxon race stands in metonymic relation to the United States; the source of that metonymy lies in Europe, for Anglo-Saxonness traces the United States back to England, much as the construction of the South as "Spanish America" is based on a metonymic operation. In both instances, European heritage is the source of (racial) authority, while America is the battleground.

In *Culture and Imperialism*, Edward Said states that "the power to narrate, or to block other narratives from forming and emerging, is very important to culture and imperialism, and constitutes one of the main connections between them" (xiii). In this chapter, I explore the construction of imperial and anti-imperial cultural narratives in the Americas at the turn of the century, when the concept of race became a central element in the discursive battles over the meaning of modernity in the nineteenth century. In modernismo studies, the recurrence of the "Latin race" as a topic and the increasing presence of a pan-Hispanic discourse have been largely considered of anecdotal importance at best (and, at worst, as another symptom of the Spanish American intellectual-colonized mind). I will first discuss how important the belief in the superiority of the Anglo Saxon race was to the imaginary of the United States, to its self-fashioning as both empire and embodiment of modernity, and to the discursive and political violence exerted over the rest of the continent to its south. I will show how Spanish American modernistas built a counter narrative to Anglo Saxon discourse that theorized a different understanding of modernity, using the Spanish Renaissance to connect the Americas to southern European cultural tradition. Finally, I will discuss how as modernism gained symbolic capital and attained a dominant position in the transatlantic field, and as the United States attained a dominant imperial position in the international field of power after the war of 1898, the focus on a specifically Hispanic modern tradition became stronger within modernista discursive production. Within this frame, I argue, Spain was then imagined from across the Atlantic as the birthplace of a modern project that, now spent in the Peninsula, continued its path in Spanish America.

The Racial Construction of the (Anglo) American Empire

The imaginary of empire, so present in the relationship between Spain and Spanish America, was not exclusive to the South Atlantic. In England, a somewhat similar operation took place, which speaks, on the one hand, to the anxieties and scars left in Europe by the successive acts of independence and nation building in the Americas and, on the other hand, to the way transatlantic relationships were increasingly encoded in and understood through racial claims. Much as postindependence U.S. culture thought of itself as fundamentally British, the British imaginary viewed the United States in many ways as an extension of England and "Englishness." Charles Dilke, a British radical liberal, spoke of "England round the world" when traveling through the United States, Canada, and English-speaking colonies elsewhere in 1866–1867, and John Robert Seeley in *The Expansion of England* (1883) "developed Dilke's ideas by giving them a history, rewriting the history of England so that its colonial activities became central to its history, rather than a peripheral add-on as had hitherto been the case" (Young 36, 37). Britain was to embark on a process of rethinking its national identity in which new notions of empire were to play a central role: "Imperialism emerged in the 1880s and 1890s for the first time as a positive term in British culture by being linked to the idea of an imperial federation of people of British descent now living in settler colonies: it involved constituting a new British national identity that would encompass all people of Anglo-Saxon descent scattered all over the world" (35).

Despite obvious differences between the Spanish empire, which was all but gone, and the British, which was in expansion, empire was at the core of the articulation of the relationship of both nations toward the American republics. As in Spain, in Britain, "this concept of a greater empire was haunted profoundly by the experience of American independence in 1776" (Young 35). Although still expanding its imperial ambitions, Britain was not free from imperial nostalgia toward the United States: "It was envisaged that the United States might in some way re-enter the fold, thus healing what Seeley characterized as the tragic 'schism in Greater Britain.' "[3] Cecil Rhodes, a British colonialist who made his fortune in South Africa, created the now prestigious Rhodes scholarships to be granted to members of the elite in the United States in the hope that by going "to study at Oxford they would recognize the profound ties that bound them to the larger framework of Anglo-Saxon civilization" (38).[4] In studying the place of the United States in the British imagination, Armstrong, Fagge, and Lockley have recently argued that not only before but also after independence, Britons saw America as an extension of British society, in which different factors could bring about certain differences, which "meant that Britons back home could gauge the effect of each of these changes on an essentially 'British' society" (2). As the nineteenth century progressed, the category of race gained even greater prominence and provided the ideological framework for the reformulation of transatlantic bonds between what British colonial secretary Joseph Chamberlain had called the "two great branches of the Anglo-Saxon race" (qtd. in Joll 97), that is, Britain and the United States.

Cecil Rhodes lamented the departure of the United States from a British empire that in his megalomaniacal fantasy should rule the world, but his fears that the British ex-colony might forget its Anglo-Saxon roots were unfounded. From such philosophers as John Fiske and such social scientists as John William Burgess, to such senators as Carl Schurz and such religious leaders as Josiah Strong, not only were Anglo Americans not forgetting their racial heritage, but also they were claiming that their race was flourishing in the United States.[5] Josiah Strong is a paradigmatic and significant example, since the success of his book *Our Country* (1885) and his personal campaign so attracted the attention of the public that some of his contemporaries considered his book as influential as *Uncle Tom's Cabin* (Muller 487). General secretary of the Evangelical Alliance for the United States for twelve years, Strong had noteworthy political ties, for he became a close friend of Theodore Roosevelt, the assistant secretary of the U.S. Navy during the Spanish-American War and future president of the United States (see Muller, Berge).

Strong could have been responding in these words from *Our Country* to Rhodes's worries about the United States:

> It may be easily shown, and is of no small significance, that the two great ideas of which the Anglo-Saxon is the exponent are having a fuller development in the

> United States than in Great Britain. . . . Furthermore, it is significant that the marked characteristics of this race are being here emphasized most. Among the most striking features of the Anglo-Saxon is his moneymaking power—a power of increasing importance in the widening commerce of the world's future. We have seen, in a preceding chapter, that, although England is by far the richest nation of Europe, we have already outstripped her in the race after wealth, and we have only begun the development of our vast resources. (221)

For Strong, although both nations were unrivaled, the United States was the land of the Anglo-Saxon future, where the race was developing strongest and most powerfully. The ultimate proof of U.S. superiority was, according to Strong, in moneymaking and commerce. In his argument we find three elements common to U.S. imperialist rhetoric since: liberty, commerce, and progress, usually conceived of as inseparable. In the nineteenth century, these three elements were tied to the power of the Anglo-Saxon people. In this way, Anglo-Saxonism, modernity, and imperial expansion became heavily intertwined, as can be seen in Strong's text:

> There are no more new worlds. The unoccupied arable lands of the earth are limited, and will soon be taken. . . . Then will the world enter upon a new stage of its history—the final competition of races, for which the Anglo-Saxon is being schooled. Long before the thousand millions are here, the mighty centrifugal tendency, inherent in this stock and strengthened in the United States, will assert it. Then this race of unequaled energy, with all the majesty of numbers and the might of wealth behind it—the representative, let us hope, of the largest liberty, the purest Christianity, the highest civilization—having developed peculiarly aggressive traits calculated to impress its institutions upon mankind, will spread itself over the earth. If I read not amiss, this powerful race will move down upon Mexico, down upon Central and South America, out upon the islands of the sea, over upon Africa and beyond. And can any one doubt that the result of this competition of races will be the "survival of the fittest"? (222–23)

Strong's Darwinian vision of the competition of the races and the final victory of the Anglo-Saxon, particularly "aggressive" and already being "schooled" for the contest, is symptomatic of the centrality of race in U.S. imperial discourse. His vision of a future in which the Anglo-Saxon race will conquer the world seamlessly combines science and religion, Darwin and the Bible, so that the survival of the fittest is encoded in biblical terms and recalls God's mandate to humankind: "Be fruitful and multiply, and replenish the earth and subdue it" (Gen. 1:28). Christianity was indeed central to Strong's views (he was a missionary, after all), and not every variety but only Protestantism. In fact, in Strong's text, anti-Catholicism is almost as strong as his racism. Thus, not surprisingly, the conquest was to begin southward, where he saw racial inferiority compounded with Catholic ideology. Indeed, as 1898 approached, Strong was to be one of the most outspoken advocates of the war against Spain for, according to Berge, "Strong stated that many undesirable characteristics of the 'so-called Latin races . . . are due to . . . religious training' " (ellipses in original). For Strong, there might not be more new worlds, but the existing world was going to be, like the title of his book, entirely *Our World*.

Racial discourse and the belief in the superiority of the Anglo-Saxon race permeated nineteenth-century public life and politics in the United States, affecting both sides of the ideological spectrum, used equally well by those who, unlike Strong, opposed imperial expansion.[6] That was the case of journalist and U.S. senator Carl Schurz, who in the Senate debate about the annexation of the Dominican Republic in 1871 asked: "Is the incorporation of that part of the globe and the people inhabiting it quite compatible with the integrity, safety, perpetuity, and progressive development of our institutions which we value so highly?" (*Speeches, Correspondence* 78). His answer was of course a negative one, formulated on racist grounds similar to those that sustained the kind of projects that Strong, on the imperialist side of the spectrum, epitomized:

> You cannot exterminate them all. . . . You must admit them as states, not only to govern themselves, but to take part in the government of the common concerns of the Republic. Have you thought of it, what this means? . . . Fancy ten or twelve tropical States added to the southern States we already possess; fancy the Senators and Representatives of ten or twelve millions of tropical people, people of the Latin race mixed with Indian and African blood; people who . . . have neither language nor traditions nor habits nor political institutions nor morals in common with us; fancy them sitting in the halls of Congress, throwing the weight of their intelligence, their morality, their political notions and habits, their prejudices and passions, into the scale of the destinies of this Republic; and, what is more, fancy the Government of this Republic making itself responsible for order and security and republican institutions in such States, inhabited by such people; fancy this, and then tell me, does not your imagination recoil from the picture? (Schurz, *Speeches, Correspondence* 93, 98–99)[7]

Although seemingly not an option, that the mere thought of extermination could come up is striking. Regardless of the speaker or writer's position on the issue of empire, Anglo-Saxon supremacy remained a central point, and the discursive violence aimed at Spanish America in these discussions cannot be overstated.

Time and again, Spanish Americans were written out of the modern, written out of the future. The power and pervasiveness of the Anglo American narrative of modernity resulted in the continual exclusion of Spanish Americans from that narrative, an exclusion perceived as embodied in the very name of the continent.

When recounting her travels through the United States in the 1860s, Argentine writer and intellectual Eduarda Mansilla noted that

> la raza que se da á sí misma el nombre de Americana, . . . no consiente en que los Latinos, que hemos formado también nuestro mundo, en este hemisferio, nos llamemos sino Hispano americanos. . . . Intolerantes y orgullosos, como severos puritanos, los hijos de la Unión no creen sino en sí mismos, y ni siquiera dan fe, ni hacen justicia, al progreso real de nuestras Repúblicas. Nosotros les llamamos, con cierta candidez, *hermanos del Norte;* y ellos, hasta ignoran nuestra existencia política y social. (qtd. in Urraca)[8]
>
> [the race that calls itself "American" . . . does not allow that we, the Latin people, who have built our world also in this hemisphere, call ourselves but Hispanic American. . . . Intolerant and proud, like severe puritans, the children of the Union believe in no one but themselves and do not acknowledge, or do justice to, the real progress of our Republics. We call them with naïveté *brothers and sisters of the North* while they ignore our political and social existence.]

There is no acknowledgment in the North that "America" names an entire hemisphere; instead the name is stripped from its southern half, whose political and social life, whose "progreso real," seemed to be erased together with its name.[9] As early as the 1860s, Mansilla witnessed with a certain amount of outrage how name, race, and modernity were written in the United States as the same thing, the positive of the Spanish American negative. In the 1880s, as Martí was writing crónicas from the United States and Josiah Strong pontificating on the superiority of the Anglo-Saxon race and its divine call to dominate the world, the identification between Anglo America and "modernity" seemed to be complete.[10] The U.S. imperial project was well under way, as the editors of *La Revista Ilustrada de Nueva York* warned its readers.

Returning to the editorial with which I opened this chapter, we can now better understand its context. The editors were indeed performing a metonymical operation by calling the United States "la raza anglosajona," but they were doing it in reverse, as it were, calling the trope what it was, a hegemonic rhetorical device. In other words, the *Revista Ilustrada* was exposing the identification between America, Anglo-Saxonness, and modern progress ("superioridad industrial") as a rhetorical device of empire. It was against this force, both discursive and physical, that the editors addressed the "gran familia Hispano-Americana."

In this rhetorical battle, the confrontation between the two Americas can also be read as the confrontation between two modernities. In the second part of this chapter, I will argue that modernismo's critical stance against the United States is not a confrontation with "modernity," as is often assumed, but with the Anglo

American definition of modernity, which modernistas saw as lacking balance: it was excessively materialistic and more concerned with possession and consumption than with knowledge, justice, and progress. Ultimately, for them, Anglo American modernity was more destructive than constructive and a rhetorical trap of imperialism. In opposition, modernistas reclaimed a more inclusive concept of the modern, an idea of progress as a continuation of a process begun in the Renaissance with its ties to classical Latin and Greek cultures and the discovery of America. This idea of modernity did not exclude material and technological elements, but it was not exhausted by them. Such a move by the modernistas is directly related to the wider debate over the Latin and Anglo-Teutonic races taking place in the West at the time, yet it does not coincide exactly with the terms of that debate nor is it restricted by them. On the one hand, Spanish American intellectuals saw themselves as part of a larger geocultural discontent with Anglo American modernity and its increasing influence worldwide. On the other, Spanish American modernista expression and formulation of modernity was anchored in an increasingly specific Hispanic tradition, and strongly mediated by a sense of urgency vis-à-vis the cultural and political influence of the United States and its imperial ambitions in the region.

As Said argued, narrative has a central place in the relationship between culture and imperialism, both as a reproducer of imperial thought and as an act of resistance. In "Nuestra América," José Martí spoke with urgency about a developing war of ideas, a war more powerful than the conventional type. While Martí warned against growing U.S. imperialism, he was also pointing at the relationship between culture and power, a relationship at the core of Pierre Bourdieu's theory. For Bourdieu, the field of power is composed of both economic and cultural capital, the two principles of hierarchy, for "the principle mode of domination has shifted from overt coercion and the threat of physical violence to forms of symbolic manipulation" (Swartz 82). Bourdieu calls it "symbolic violence" when "every power who manages to impose meanings and to impose them as legitimate by concealing the power relations which are the basis of its force, adds its own specific symbolic force to those power relations" (Bourdieu and Passeron 4). According to his model, all symbolic capital carries social distinction and is power driven.

The struggle for symbolic capital in the Americas was also a power struggle. For the United States, it was the justification for its growing imperial ambitions. For Spanish America, it was a defense against those ambitions, against economic and political aggression, and against the possibility of erasure. It was a struggle over the future of America and over America as the future. Europe, although mostly associated with the past, was an essential component of this struggle over symbolic capital, in which the future was legitimated by the past in the form of racial/cultural heritages that were flourishing in the Americas. As we have seen, that was the case in the constructions of the United States as the place where the Anglo-Saxon race was achieving its greatest potential. In Spanish America, it was the cultural tradition of the Latin race, and specifically the Spanish race, which, if in decline in Spain itself, was succeeding in America. Thus, Spain became the source of a different genealogy of the modern that, rather than veering northwest as Hegel had suggested, continued southwest to Latin America. To the extent that northern narratives of empire were perceived as built on fear of hybridity and from a drive toward homogenization, Spanish American narratives of resistance were based, to a considerable extent, on what Said identified in another context as "breaking down the barriers between cultures" (Said 216).

Of Modern Demons and Monsters: Ariel and Caliban

Conceiving Alternative Histories

When José Martí told the history of humankind to the young readers of *La Edad de Oro* (The Golden Age), the children's magazine he published in 1889, he took an unusual approach, explicable perhaps by the youth of his intended audience. He narrated world history as the history of houses: "Ahora la gente vive en casas grandes, con puertas y ventanas, y patios enlosados, y portales de columnas: pero hace muchos miles de años los hombres no vivían así, ni había países de sesenta millones de habitantes, como hay hoy" (86). [Now people live in big houses, with doors and windows and tiled courtyards and columned portals; but thousands of years ago men did not live like this, nor were there countries with sixty million people like today.][11] The contrast between "now" and "thousands of years ago" leads Martí to embark on an explanation of how we came to live in these houses. He writes, in doing so, his own narrative of the birth of modernity, which he locates in the Renaissance.

In this history lesson through houses, Martí describes the variety of human dwellings from Japan to Mexico, from Germany to South Africa, providing an account of history that progresses not east to northwest, but multidirectionally. In Martí's text, Africa and Asia are as central to the story as are Europe and the Americas: "Estudiando se aprende eso: que el hombre es el mismo en todas partes, y aparece y crece de la misma manera, y hace y piensa las mismas cosas" (*Edad* 89). [Studying, one learns these things: that man is the same everywhere, and looks and grows up in the same way, and does and thinks the same things.] That is, we are all equal, we just build different types of houses.

Martí speaks of the three "ages" of mankind (Stone, Bronze, and Iron), yet he makes sure to clarify that they are not always and necessarily consecutive but can coexist: "En España, hay familias que viven en agujeros abiertos en la tierra del monte: en Dakota, en los Estados Unidos, los que van a abrir el país viven en covachas, con techos de ramas, como en la edad neolítica: en las orillas del Orinoco, en la América del Sur, los indios viven en ciudades lacustres, lo mismo que las que había hace cientos de siglos en los lagos de Suiza" (*Edad* 90). [In Spain, there are families who live in holes opened in the mountain side; in Dakota, in the United States, those who are expanding the country live in huts with roofs made of branches, as in the Neolithic Age; on the banks of the Orinoco River, in South America, the Indians live in cities built over the water, like those in the lakes of Switzerland hundreds of years ago.] Martí writes against both the Hegelian fantasy of a history that moves northward and whose spirit is embodied in a particular people, and Darwinian interpretations of history as the survival of a fitter North. In his text, time is fluid, as are the connections between time and space. According to his story, some peoples followed a sequence, while others skipped an entire age. Thus, against a Eurocentric conception of history, in Martí's text Americans were in the Iron Age by the time the Europeans arrived:

> Hay pueblos que han llegado a la edad de hierro sin pasar por la de bronce, porque el hierro es el metal de su tierra, y con él empezaron a trabajar, sin saber que en el mundo había cobre ni estaño. Cuando los hombres de Europa vivían en la edad de bronce, ya hicieron casas mejores, aunque no tan labradas y perfectas como las de los peruanos y mexicanos de América, en quienes estuvieron siempre juntas las dos edades. (91)
>
> [There are people who have arrived at the Iron Age without going through the Bronze Age because iron is the native metal and they started working with it without knowing of the existence of copper and tin in the world. When European men lived in the Bronze Age, they managed to build better houses, although not as well-worked and perfect as those built by Peruvians and Mexicans in America, who went through the two ages at the same time.]

Indeed, linearity appears in Martí's history as a phenomenon specific to Europe, rather than a universal timeline; more noticeable in northern than southern Europe, linearity is a result of cultural isolation and lack of intercultural exchange: "En los pueblos de Europa es donde se ven más claras las tres edades, y mejor mientras más al Norte, porque allí los hombres vivieron solos, cada uno en su pueblo, por siglos de siglos" (93). [In the peoples of Europe is where the three ages can be seen more clearly, the more to the North, the clearer, because there men lived alone, each in their own village, for centuries and centuries.]

In Martí's lesson, there is a persistent distinction between North and South. All humans may be equal, but climate is not, "porque el hombre que nace en tierra de árboles y de flores piensa más en la hermosura y el adorno, y tiene más cosas que decir, que el que nace en una tierra fría, donde ve el cielo oscuro y su cueva en la roca" (*Edad* 89) [because the man born in a land of trees and flowers thinks more about beauty and adornment, and has more things to say than the man born in a cold land, where all he sees is a dark sky and his cave in a rock]. Thus, using environmental explanations, Martí writes against the grain of the biologic thought that so informed texts from Montesquieu to Senator Schurz and portrays the southern climate, rather than the northern, as conducive to art and thought. In a hardly innocent pattern in Martí's peculiar telling of universal history, the North is consistently associated with isolation, backwardness, and lack of ideas: "Cuando los romanos tenían palacios de mármol con estatuas de oro, y usaban trajes de lana muy fina, la gente de Bretaña vivía en cuevas, y se vestía con las pieles salvajes, y peleaba con mazas hechas de los troncos duros" (93). [When the Romans had marbled palaces with golden statues and dressed in very fine wool, the people of Britain lived in caves and dressed in skins of wild animals and fought with maces made of tree trunks.] By contrast, from Mesoamerica to Egypt and from India to Spain, it is both in the South and through cultural miscegenation that human houses have become better and more beautiful.

Martí's history lesson ends in the Renaissance, when

> los cristianos empezaron a no creer en el cielo tanto como antes. Hablaban mucho de lo grande que fue Roma: celebraban el arte griego por sencillo: decían que ya eran muchas las iglesias: buscaban modos nuevos de hacer los palacios: y de todo eso vino una manera de fabricar parecida a la griega, que es lo que llaman arquitectura del "Renacimiento." . . . Eran tiempos de arte y riqueza, y de grandes conquistas, así que había muchos señores y comerciantes con palacio. Nunca habían vivido los hombres, ni han vuelto a vivir, en casas tan hermosas. (*Edad* 103)

> [Christians began to believe in Heaven less than before. They spoke a lot about how great Rome was; they celebrated Greek art because of its simplicity; they said that there were too many churches and looked for new ways to build palaces. Out of all this, a new way of building similar to that of Greece came about, which is what they call the Renaissance in architecture. . . . Those were times of art and wealth and of great conquests so that there were many lords and merchants living in palaces. Never had men lived before, nor have they lived again, in such beautiful houses.]

In his text, the Renaissance marks the beginning of modern secularism and a return to Greek and Roman ideas and aesthetics. It was a time of flourishing art, thought, and commerce. In this history of humankind through houses, Renaissance houses have never been surpassed. The name of the children's magazine itself, *La Edad de Oro*, evokes simultaneously the Golden Age of Greek Arcadia and the

Spanish Golden Age. For Martí, it was a time of openness and cultural mixture, of Roman, Greek, Moorish, and Gothic houses all at once (103). It was a time of heroes, but also of conquest, and as Martí reaches the end of what has so far been a mostly happy story, he chooses to show what we could call with Walter Mignolo the "darker side of the Renaissance":

> En nuestra América las casas tienen algo de romano y de moro, porque moro y romano era el pueblo español que mandó en América, y echó abajo las casas de los indios. Las echó abajo de raíz: echó abajo sus templos, sus observatorios, sus torres de señales, sus casas de vivir, todo lo indio lo quemaron los conquistadores españoles y lo echaron abajo, menos las calzadas, porque no sabían llevar las piedras que supieron traer los indios, y los acueductos, porque les traían el agua de beber. (103–4)

> [In our America, the houses have something of Roman and Moorish houses because Moors and Romans were the Spanish people who came to govern in America and destroyed the houses of the Indians. They razed them to the ground, they destroyed their temples, their observatories, their towers, their houses, everything Indian was burned down and destroyed by the Spanish conquerors, except the roads, because they did not know how to carry the stones that the Indians had brought, and the aqueducts, because they brought them drinking water.]

What is remarkable about Martí's rewriting of history is that 1492 ends world history, which stops at this time of stark contrast, of the most beautiful houses ever made in Europe, and of Europe's violence against and destruction of the houses and cities of others, the Indians. Instead of an account of the subsequent four hundred years, readers face a blank space on the page (almost as if being asked to reflect on what they have just read), followed by a brief conclusion that brings us back to the "Ahora" with which the text began:

> Ahora todos los pueblos del mundo se conocen mejor y se visitan: y en cada pueblo hay su modo de fabricar, según haya frío o calor, o sean de una raza o de otra; pero lo que parece nuevo en las ciudades no es su manera de hacer casas, sino que en cada ciudad hay casas moras, y griegas, y góticas, y bizantinas, y japonesas, como si empezara el tiempo feliz en que los hombres se tratan como amigos, y se van juntando. (*Edad* 104)

> [Nowadays all the peoples in the world know each other better and they visit each other; and each people has their way of building, depending on whether it is cold or hot, or on their race. Yet what seems new in the cities is not how houses are

> built, but that in each city there are Moorish, and Greek, and Gothic, and Byzantine, and Japanese houses, as if the happy times when all men come together and treat each other like friends were beginning.]

This blank space, the narrative end, and the lack of change in the way houses are built draw a direct line to the "nowadays," marking the Renaissance as the arrival at the present of modernity. They are part of the same moment; the conquest leads us seamlessly and without delay or deviation to today. In Martí's history of the world, modernity is, like 1492 when it began, both light and dark: born out of the double impulse of the creation and destruction of beauty, modernity is racially and culturally mixed and also a time when the very concept of one world is possible. This idea of one world also allows Martí to articulate a final utopian fantasy of globalization devoid of violence, of multicultural cities and cross-cultural friendships. Or perhaps this global happiness is a mirage, make-believe, as the ominous "como si" (as if) might signal, as the chronicle he wrote on Coney Island upon his arrival in the United States some years earlier seems to indicate.

Consuming Modernity: Coney Island or "The Belly of the Monster"

In 1881, Martí visited Coney Island, the recently developed recreational area and beach south of Brooklyn in New York City, and wrote a piece about it for Bogotá's newspaper *La Pluma*.[12] Within and beyond U.S. borders, Coney Island's growing reputation as a marvel had whetted his interest. Julio Ramos's classic reading of Martí's chronicle understands it as a text about the modern city and modernity at large, but "Coney Island" is not about New York, or about any modern city—Coney Island, after all, is composed of "cuatro pueblecitos" (103) ["four little towns" (*Selected* 90)].[13] It is, rather, a text about the United States. As Óscar Montero insightfully says: "Is the United States the greatest nation in the world or the greatest show on earth? This is the question Martí put before his readers after his visit to Coney Island, not long after his arrival in New York City" (21). From its first lines, the chronicle establishes a metonymic relationship to the country: Coney Island *is* the United States. Of course, all Martí's *Escenas norteamericanas* (North American Scenes) are ultimately about the United States, and that is precisely my point: Martí is not observing "modernity" at large, which also assumes that Martí is positioned outside the modern; rather, he is reflecting on U.S. modernity. If in *La Edad de Oro* Martí writes about the past and how we arrived at the present, in "Coney Island" Martí wonders about the future. What he faces and fears is not modernity but its Anglo American manifestation; he fears that Anglo American modernity may become the future of *all* modernities. Martí's chronicle is about the possibility that the light and dark that moved modernity for centuries might be resolved in favor of the latter (for, as we shall see, Coney Island is a dark place despite its many lights, a mirage of happiness). His chronicle is about the possibility that the modern world might become one large Coney Island.

Martí describes the scene in Coney Island with a sense of surprise, almost of awe. The source of this feeling is not so much admiration—although there is a certain amount of that in his text—as incomprehension. If there is one theme that stands out in his description of the people in the park, it is consumption, or rather, contentment through consumption. Stands, a circus, dining areas, sensual pleasure, bodily pleasures—the entire Coney Island becomes for Martí a feast for the senses, to be sure, but an excessive feast: "Aquella gente come cantidad, nosotros, clase" (107). ["Those people eat quantity, we, class" (93).] There is a certain obsession with food and eating in his description of Coney Island, where the image of the large dining rooms returns in the text time and again. Excess in consumption, excess in happiness, excess in satisfaction. Coney Island seems to be the U.S. version of Arcadia, a distorted version of the Golden Age that named his children's magazine: "¡Qué correr del dinero! ¡qué facilidades para todo goce! ¡qué absoluta ausencia de toda tristeza o pobreza visibles!" (106). ["What spending of money! What opportunities for every pleasure! What absolute absence of any visible sadness or poverty!" (92)] Sadness and poverty exist, to be sure, and Martí takes care to make visible to the reader what seems invisible to the happy crowd: the poor and their children "como devorados, como chupados, como roídos" (105) ["gnawed, devoured, consumed" (91)]), by cholera, the black minstrels and the "desventurado hombre de color que, a cambio de un jornal miserable, se está día y noche con la cabeza asomada por un agujero hecho en un lienzo esquivando con movimientos ridículos y extravagantes muecas los golpes de los tiradores" (107) ["unfortunate man of color, who, in exchange for a paltry day's wage, stands day and night with his head poking out through a piece of cloth, dodging the pitches with ridiculous movements and extravagant grimaces" (93)]. In "Coney Island," Martí recalls the ghosts of the Anglo American narrative of modernity, those absent from the glee of consumption but on whose labor and suffering it is founded.[14] They are what haunts Coney Island, and Martí gives them presence. Their estrangement from the excess of consumption also creates an implicit connection between them and those from the outside who, like Martí himself, also feel disaffected by the spectacle of Coney Island, that is, from the United States and Anglo-Saxon modernity.

Drawing a distinction between a "we" and a "they," Martí writes a "we" that includes Latin America but is not limited to it. As Montero notes, Martí refers to "people everywhere whose history and whose values give them pause before the easy glee and uneven prosperity of the United States" (33). This "we," then, seems to imply a globalizing gesture by which Martí separates Anglo American modernity from the rest of the world.

> Otros pueblos-y nosotros entre ellos-vivimos devorados por un sublime demonio interior, que nos empuja a la persecución infatigable de un ideal de amor o gloria; y cuando asimos, con el placer con que se ase un águila, el grado del ideal que perseguíamos, nuevo afán nos inquieta, nueva ambición nos espolea, nueva aspiración nos lanza a nuevo vehemente anhelo, y sale del águila presa una rebelde mariposa libre, como desafiándonos a seguirla y encadenándonos a su revuelto vuelo. No así aquellos espíritus tranquilos, turbados sólo por el ansia de la posesión de una fortuna. (106)
>
> [Other peoples—ourselves among them—live in prey to a sublime inner demon that drives us to relentless pursuit of an ideal of love or glory. And when, with the joy of grasping an eagle, we seize the degree of ideal we are pursuing, a new zeal inflames us, a new ambition spurs us on, a new aspiration catapults us into a new and vehement longing, and from the captured eagle goes a free, rebellious butterfly, as if defying us to follow it and chaining us to its restless flight. Not so these tranquil spirits, disturbed only by their eagerness to possess wealth. (92)]

Who is this "sublime demon" that devours everyone except the complacent crowd of Coney Island? From the text itself, it is obvious that this is not a demon of the Christian tradition; this is no devil. To understand Martí's demon we need to go back farther, to the Greek tradition so often mentioned in his texts, the tradition of the *Edad de Oro* (itself a Greek myth). This demon comes from Socrates, who notoriously claimed to have been gifted by Apollo with a secret inner voice or inner demon that prevented him from doing wrong. I believe Martí's text establishes an intertextuality with one of Plato's most famous dialogues, the *Cratylus*, in which Socrates explains to Hermogenes who the demons are:

> *Soc.* Do you not remember that [Hesiod] speaks of a golden race? . . . He says this about it: Since this race has been eclipsed by fate/they are called sacred daimons; / They live on earth and are good, / Warding off evil and guarding mortal men. . . . I don't think he's saying that the golden race is by nature made of gold, but that it is good and fine. I consider it a proof of this that he calls us a race of iron. . . . So don't you think that if someone who presently exists were good, Hesiod would say that he too belonged to the golden race? . . . Are good people any different from wise ones? . . . It is principally because daimons are wise and knowing (daêmones), I think, that Hesiod says they are named 'daimons' ('daimones'). In our older Attic dialect, we actually find the word 'daêmones.' So, Hesiod and many other poets speak well when they say that when a good man dies, he has a great destiny and a great honor and becomes a 'daimon,' which is a name given to him because it accords with wisdom. And I myself assert, indeed, that every good man, whether alive or dead, is daimonic, and is correctly called a 'daimon.'

Her. . . . But what about the name 'hero'? ('hêrôs')? What is it?

Soc. . . . It expresses the fact that heroes were born out of love (erôs). (26–27)[15]

Martí's sublime demon is, then, a combination of wisdom, goodness, and heroism and thus connected to knowledge, ethics, and love, three elements that are an integral part of Martí's imaginary (and of his own messianic self-fashioning). Martí's description of the demon subsumes all those qualities in the act of desiring, a desire that is never satiated, particularly one that does not respond to capitalist logic. In this way, the sublime demon becomes the very act of desiring and of searching itself, an act of production of knowledge, justice, and love. Martí's demon could be read in a sense akin to a Deleuzian desiring machine, that is, always in the process of production and of change, not defined by lack, and constantly shifting its aim to new goals ("when . . . we seize the degree of ideal we are pursuing, a new zeal inflames us, a new ambition spurs us on").[16]

This concept of desire is directly related to Martí's prologue to the "Poema del Niágara" written a year later, in which he describes modern ideas "like coral and like starlight and like waves of the sea" (*Selected* 44–45), moving in multiple directions and always in motion. Indeed, there is a notion of progress in Martí's metaphor of the demon that is not understood as consumption or satisfaction, but as a quest, an incessant desire, like the movement of waves. Martí finds none of these things in Coney Island. The global "we" is possessed by a sublime demon; the crowd is "disturbed only by their eagerness to possess wealth" (92). There is contentment, satiation, and possession, but no ambition to reach "an ideal of love or glory," no restlessness. In Martí's text, Coney Island is "awesome" precisely because of its absence of knowledge, of justice, of love. There is only one exception: the children playing by the seaside, who "esperan en la margen a que la ola mugiente se los moje, y escapan cuando llega, disimulando con carcajadas su terror, y vuelven en bandadas, como para desafiar mejor al enemigo, a un juego de que los inocentes, postrados una hora antes por el recio calor, no se fatigan jamás" (105) ["wait along the shore for the roaring wave to drench them, and flee as it reaches them, hiding their terror behind gales of laughter, then return in bands—the better to defy the enemy—to this game of which these innocents, prostrate an hour earlier from the terrible heat, never tire" (91)].[17] This is the only instance in the text where anyone has a sense of community and purpose, of heroism, facing their fears and returning to wrestle with the never-ending waves. The word "innocents" is not so itself: it implies an ethical stance. The "we," like the children, are possessed by the demons, by the spirit of golden men, the spirit of the "Golden Age." In Coney Island, on the contrary, the "they" are moved by gold itself. For Martí, "aquella gran tierra está vacía de espíritu" (106) ["this great land is devoid of spirit" (92)]. "They" are not possessed by a demon, but instead seek to possess.

Against the image of the sublime demons and the innocent children, the chronicle closes with the image of the monster. When the night comes and it is time to return to the city, "como monstruo que vaciase toda su entraña en las fauces hambrientas de otro monstruo, aquella muchedumbre colosal, estrujada y compacta se agolpa a las entradas de los trenes que repletos de ella, gimen, como cansados de su peso, en su carrera por la soledad que van salvando" (108) ["like a monster emptying out its entrails into the ravenous jaws of another monster, this immense crush of humanity squeezes onto trains that seem to groan under its weight in their packed trajectory across the barren stretches" (94)]. In this powerful image, Martí insists one last time on consumption and excess in a conception of modernity that has lost all drive for knowledge, justice, and love, and has become a monstrous system that consumes its people only to vomit them up again in an endless cycle of consumption and disgorgement.[18]

It is not surprising that Martí alludes to Plato's *Cratylus* in "Coney Island." It is a dialogue about language, about origins and change in language, about the connection between words and things, to paraphrase Foucault. As Cathy Jrade and others have shown, for Martí, as for modernismo, language is central. Language is a way of communicating and of knowing, a way of searching for lost connections.[19] In Martí's vision of Coney Island, however, there is no communication; there is only noise—"las orquestas, los bailes, el vocerío, el ruido de olas, el ruido de hombres, el coro de risas" (108) ["orchestras, dances, chatter, surf sounds, human sounds, choruses of laughter" (94)]. It is not language that spills from the mouths of the monsters but human vomit and the groans of the trains, which, rather than vehicles of communication, are surrounded by solitude.[20]

There is always a distance in Martí's observation of Coney Island, as if to avoid being sucked into the spectacle, being consumed by the monster. Martí's act of writing his chronicle, his emphasis on language, his creation of a global "we," his identification with the innocent children and their sense of community are all ways of resisting the monster. But his ultimate fear is that "their" modernity may prevail over "ours": "Si son más duraderos en los pueblos los lazos que ata el sacrificio y el dolor común que los que ata el común interés; si esa nación colosal, lleva o no en sus entrañas elementos feroces y tremendos; . . . eso lo dirán los tiempos" (103). ["Are ties of sacrifice and shared suffering more lasting within countries than those of common interest? Does this colossal nation contain ferocious and terrible elements? . . . Only time will tell" (89).] "Coney Island" is in many ways a foundational text of modernismo, a reflection on the shifting definition of modernity, a text about the failings and yet the power of Anglo American modernity.

Martí's chronicle is framed by a reference to the flow of information in a shrinking world. According to Martí, every North American newspaper is full of "descripciones hiperbólicas de las bellezas originales y singulares atractivos" ["hyperbolic descriptions of the original beauties and unique attractions"] of Coney Island and already "los periódicos franceses se hacen eco de esta fama" (103) ["echoes of its fame have reached the French newspapers" (90)]. The emphasis that Martí places on the echoing effect of French newspapers (the sentence stands out as its own paragraph) is not casual and points out both the powerful effect of discourse in shaping realities and the fear of reproduction, the fear that the echoing of discourse may be followed by the echoing of actions: is France, the center of nineteenth-century cultural prestige, becoming an Echo enamored of a Narcissistic United States, absorbed by its own beauty?

Martí's text, written for a Latin American newspaper, participates in spreading the word of "la prosperidad maravillosa de los Estados Unidos del Norte" (103) ["the marvelous prosperity of the United States of the North" (89)], across the globe. However, all is not marvelous in Martí's account, which rather than echo the descriptions of U.S. newspapers provides an uneasy depiction of Coney Island. He stops the flow of information and redirects it. To the "hyperbolic description of the original beauties" of North American newspapers, Martí opposes his own hyperbolic descriptions of a monstrous future. In the struggles for cultural capital within the international field of power, Martí's texts are an example of position taking and, using Said's terms, a counternarrative of resistance that, "far from being merely a reaction to imperialism, is an alternative way of conceiving human history" (216) and, we may add, of imagining the future. Montero has remarked that, "like a first-rate journalist, Martí wanted his readers to make up their own minds; but like a good teacher, he also wanted to nudge them in the right direction" (23); when it came to proposing an alternative conception of human history, Coney Island and the history lesson for the readers of *La Edad de Oro* shared this pedagogical impulse.

Ariel and Caliban, or the Future of the Americas

Also in a pedagogical framework, José Enrique Rodó would attempt his own rewriting of history and modernity and his reflections on the future. *Ariel* (1900), a text that soon became iconic, provided a new framework from which to read Latin American identity; its influence reverberates today.[21] In a pedagogical text explicitly written for Latin American youth, Rodó appropriates and rewrites the three main characters of Shakespeare's *Tempest* (Prospero, Ariel, and Caliban). Prospero's is the main narrative voice, the teacher talking to his students. He begins his lesson by invoking the guiding spirit of Ariel as the symbol of culture, spirituality, and beauty, which Prospero (and the text) associates with the Latin cultural tradition and opposes to the corporal figure of Caliban, embodiment of the materiality and utilitarianism of the North. Thus, Martí's sublime demon and consuming monster are reincarnated in Rodó's Ariel and Caliban.

Like Martí's demon, the spirit of Ariel in Rodó's text is associated with knowledge, ethics, and heroism: "Ariel triunfante, significa idealidad y orden en la vida, noble inspiración en el *pensamiento*, desinterés en *moral*, buen gusto en arte, *heroísmo* en la acción, delicadeza en las costumbres. Él es el héroe epónimo en la epopeya de la especie" (228; my emphasis). [Triumphant Ariel means idealism and order in life, noble inspiration in thought, generosity in morals, good taste in art, heroism in action, kindness in customs. He is the eponymous hero of the epic of the species.] In Rodó's text, Ariel is explicitly the spirit of progress: "El porvenir es en la vida de las sociedades humanas el pensamiento idealizador por excelencia" (226). [The future is the idealizing thought par excellence in the life of human societies.] In contrast, Caliban is the "símbolo de sensualidad y de torpeza" (139) [symbol of sensuality and turpitude]. In line with Martí's demon and monster, Ariel and Caliban represent restlessness versus contentment, desire versus possession and consumption.

In Rodó's essay, Caliban is not associated exclusively with the United States but is a symbol of Anglo-Saxon utilitarianism, of which the United States is, nonetheless, the paradigmatic example: "Si ha podido decirse del utilitarismo que es el verbo del espíritu inglés, los Estados Unidos pueden ser considerados la encarnación del verbo utilitario" (*Ariel* 196). [If it has been possible to say that utilitarianism is the word of the English spirit, the United States can be considered the flesh of the utilitarian word.] The United States "quiere imponérsenos como suma y modelo de civilización" (215) [wants to impose itself on us as sum and model of civilization]. Regardless of Rodó's claim that his book was not about the opposition United States and Latin America, as it was immediately read upon its publication, *Ariel* encourages the reader to see the U.S. model as a calibanesque modernity, not least because, even if not explicitly acknowledged, Rodó's use of these symbols builds on their earlier use by Argentine Paul Groussac and, especially, Rubén Darío.[22] Finally, *Ariel* is a text about the future, and the future is clearly located in the Americas, while Europe remains the locus of the past. As in the case of Martí's Socratic "sublime demon," the spirit of Ariel is traced in Rodó's essay to southern Europe and to Greek thought and culture. The spirit of Caliban, on the contrary, is the "English spirit" of northern Europe, the embodiment of "nordomanía" (North mania). The struggle between both is, ultimately, the struggle between South and North, a battle that is to be decided in the Americas, not as the irreducible other of Europe but as its future. In this light, *Ariel* is a book about European genealogies and American possibilities.

Although the idea of Ariel/Caliban might have come to Rodó from Groussac and Darío, Rodó places it in dialogue with a longer tradition of political readings of Caliban, in particular with those by French writers Ernest Renán and Alfred Fouillée (Brotherston 3–6). Like Fouillée, Rodó situates himself against Renán's aristocratic nostalgia. Moreover, Rodó finds democracy consubstantial with "nuestra América." "La obra de la Revolución . . . en nuestra América se enlaza además con las glorias de su Génesis" (*Ariel* 178). [The work of the Revolution is tied to the glories of the Genesis of our America.] Implicitly taking up the idea of *translatio imperii*, the future is to be decided in America, the land of the Revolution, of democracy, of the future. What kind of democratic society and what kind of future are questions *Ariel* reflects upon. In this battle for the future, however, the past is also at stake: that is, for Rodó, a danger posed by the "triumph" of Caliban in the United States is that it aims both to impose itself onto others and to rewrite the past—"¡Ellos aspirarían a revisar el Génesis para ocupar esa primera página!" (214) [They would aspire to revise Genesis in order to occupy its first page!]—as if responding to Josiah Strong's biblical rewriting of the Anglo-Saxon race as following God's command to take over the earth.

In turn, Rodó performs his own rewriting of history, based neither on science nor on biblical myths, but on a Latin/Hispanic cultural heritage perceived as Latin America's responsibility for the future:

> Tenemos—los americanos latinos—una herencia de raza, una gran tradición étnica que mantener, un vínculo sagrado que nos une a inmortales páginas de la historia, confiando a nuestro honor su continuación en lo futuro. El cosmopolitismo, que hemos de acatar como una irresistible necesidad de nuestra formación, no excluye, ni ese sentimiento de fidelidad a lo pasado, ni la fuerza directriz y plasmante con que debe el genio de la raza imponerse en la refundición de los elementos que constituirán al americano definitivo del futuro. (*Ariel* 220)
>
> [We, the Latin Americans, have a racial heritage, a great ethnic tradition to keep, a sacred bond that links us to immortal pages of history, entrusting its continuation in the future to our honor. Cosmopolitanism, which we must accept as an irresistible necessity of our formation, excludes neither that sentiment of fidelity to the past, nor the directing and materializing force with which the genius of our race must dominate in the recasting of the elements that will constitute the definitive American of the future.]

Rodó was not exceptional in tracing a racial/cultural heritage to Europe, of course; the narrative construction of the United States as empire was largely based, as we have seen, on the premise of the alleged superiority of the Anglo-Saxon race, whose source of authority was ultimately in Europe as well. The future in both North and South was constructed as the necessary consummation of a genealogy that justified it. There is no doubt that Rodó was thinking of race through the categories established in the dominant discourses at the time. However, ethnic difference in his text is not presented as a claim to racial superiority in Darwinian terms as was often the case in Anglo American discourse. There seems to be nothing biologically determined in the category of the Latin race, which is instead construed historically: the Latin race is defined as the result of a cultural tradition, an accumulation of historical achievements. The survival and continuation of that tradition, as well as the memory of its past, is what *Ariel* is foregrounding. The "nordomanía" against which Rodó writes his pedagogical essay, the failed modernity that he sees in Caliban, poses for him the danger of losing both the past and the future of that cultural heritage, as the United States rewrites that past and attempts to "impose itself on us as sum and model of civilization." Moreover, although for Rodó there is no doubt that Latin culture must prevail in the shaping of a Latin American future and must function as its guiding force, his conception of race stands in contrast to northern notions of purity and insists that the cosmopolitan influence is a necessity. Rodó was not necessarily advocating internal miscegenation, to be sure; in his vision of the future, the Latin race remains a hegemonic force. Nonetheless, the "American of the future" is bound in his text to be composed of an amalgam of elements. Rodó's understanding of culture and ethnicity contests both the biologist concept of the "survival of the fittest" put forth by northern discourses and the related idea of "decadence" and "degeneration" prevalent, as Litvak has shown, in much of the contemporary debate about the Latin race taking place in Europe.

Montero has suggested that Martí's appeal to the "we" versus the "they" of the United States in "Coney Island" was an act of "radical democracy" (33). Rodó's text to the American youth in *Ariel* might have been less radically democratic, but it certainly cannot be reduced either to an "aristocratic pastime as the model for a Spanish American cultural identity" (Aching, *Politics* 113), or to an "antipragmático y aristocrático manifiesto de la latinidad, . . . un síntoma del *desencuentro* de estos intelectuales con la modernidad (parafraseando una expresión de Julio Ramos)" (Jáuregui 445) [antipragmatic and aristocratic manifest of *latinidad*, . . . a symptom of these intellectuals' diversion from modernity (to paraphrase Julio Ramos's expression)].[23] Rodó was concerned with the power of the Anglo-Saxon discourse of modernity both outside *and* inside Spanish America. He was concerned with the growing distinction of Anglo American cultural capital and the process of cultural reproduction (Bourdieu and Passeron) taking place in Spanish America under the leadership of intellectuals like Sarmiento, whose admiration for the United States and the Anglo-Saxon race was virtually unconditional, as he showed repeatedly, from his *Viajes* (Travels; 1845–1847) to his *Conflicto y armonía entre las razas* (Conflict and Harmony among the Races; 1883).[24] The internalization and reproduction of Anglo American discourses of superiority helped shape official discourses in Latin America that, as Ramos says, "ante la pregunta—qué somos—respondían 'Seamos Estados Unidos'" (*Desencuentros* 237) ["would respond to the question 'What are we?' with 'Let us be the United States'" (*Divergent* 259)]. As Gordon Brotherston says in his classic introduction to *Ariel*, Rodó feared that the hypnotizing force of the North might turn Spanish America into its calibanesque slave (15).

Nordomanía and the Fear of Cultural Reproduction

The pedagogical mode in which Martí and Rodó chose to rewrite history shows a concern as much with what Martí called the "tigre de afuera" [tiger outside] as with the "tigre de adentro" [tiger inside]; in other words, with those who had internalized and reproduced Anglo-Saxon discourse, thus preventing Spanish Americans from two tasks that Martí and the modernistas considered the cornerstone of the region's survival in the global order: to know themselves and to be known by others (Mejías-López, "Conocer"). Modernista texts like Martí's and Rodó's exist within a complex network of discourses, in which they occupy a shifting and sometimes ambiguous position. They are narratives of resistance inasmuch as they contested the symbolic violence exerted by northern Anglo-Saxon discourses, that is, to the extent that they proposed a different understanding of history and modernity. As such, their pedagogical function implies an intervention in the struggle for symbolic capital within the system of cultural reproduction in which education plays a central role. Martí's and Rodó's attempt to educate the youth is, then, an attempt to challenge the reproductive power of Anglo American discourse in Spanish America and to produce, instead, a different sense of history and identity that they believed to be empowering rather than disenfranchising.

In efforts like this, however, many modernistas often exerted their own symbolic violence and engendered a new system of cultural reproduction. In other words, modernistas aimed to challenge Spanish America's subalternity with regard to external powers but sometimes did so by affirming in different degrees the hegemonic position of the Latin cultural/racial heritage over other subaltern cultural/racial heritages. As Ramos explains in his excellent reading of Martí's "Nuestra América": "La literatura efectivamente armaba una defensa contra el imperialismo, contra la amenaza de 'ellos': la modernidad expansiva de los Estados Unidos y, a la vez, los discursos internamente colonizadores de los 'letrados artificiales.' Pero esa defensa del 'ser,' articulada desde la literatura, implicaba un nuevo recorte—jerarquizador y subordinativo—de la heterogénea experiencia americana" (*Desencuentros* 243). ["Literature effectively harnessed a defense against imperialism, against the threat of 'they,' which signified at once the expansive modernity of the United States and the internal colonizing discourses of the 'artificial letrados.' But this defense of 'being,' articulated from within the emergent sphere of literature, implied a new frame—hierarchical and subordinative—of the heterogeneous American experience" (*Divergent* 264).]

This "defense of 'being,'" however, was not particular to Latin America, but also had been taking place in the cultural, scientific, and political fields of the Anglo-Atlantic, hierarchizing and subordinating the heterogeneous experience, not only of the Americas but also of Europe and indeed of the globe. In "Nuestra América," Martí calls attention to precisely the relationship between the two phenomena: the attitude of what he calls "artificial intellectuals" (like Sarmiento) is presented as part of a ladder of distinction that placed the Anglo-Saxon race at its top, leaving everyone else to emulate it. For many Hispanic Creoles, the self-hatred generated by this symbolic hierarchy of race led to transferring similar thinking "down the ladder" to mestizos, Indians, and blacks; it led to "disowning the Indian mother," as Martí puts it. Martí makes this very clear in his essay and further emphasizes the dangerous interconnectedness of racist discourses, the notion that denying one's Indian mother is part of a continuum that connects this attitude to the genocidal practices in the United States, a country that "ahoga en sangre a sus indios" (*Nuestra* 13) ["drowns its own Indians in blood" (*Selected* 289)]. This also means that, given the occasion, the United States might "poner en ella [nuestra America] la codicia" (22) ["begin to covet her (our America)" (295)], deeming the Latin American nations "perecederas e inferiores" (22) ["perishable and inferior" (296)].[25] Implied is the fear that the bloodbath might not stop in the North but continue south. In other words, the idea that under the principle of "the survival of the fittest" the United States might one day not just take over but exterminate its neighbors to the south was, for many at least, a real possibility and a clear and present danger, exacerbated after 1898.[26]

Whatever their insufficiencies and ideological short circuits, the importance of Martí's and Rodó's texts should not be downplayed, especially in relation to competing internal and external discourses in the cultural/power field. Both Martí and Rodó challenged the homogenizing force of northern discourses, as well as their rejection of any sort of cultural/racial miscegenation or hybridity. As we shall see next, this representational gesture is relevant in relation not only to Anglo American imperialism and the internal "letrados artificiales" à la Sarmiento, but also to old imperial cultural ties with Spain, to the notion of "Hispanicness" and the very authority to speak from and about "Hispanic" cultures.

1898: Ariel and Caliban at War

Brotherston believes that Rodó is closer to Martí than to Darío because he considers that the issue of Latin and Spanish races that he sees as so prevalent in Darío's *Cantos* are secondary to Rodó's general concern for "human emancipation" (15). I suggest, instead, that the Latin and Hispanic cultural heritage are of primary importance as strategies to argue for that very emancipation in *Ariel*. As I have shown, the Latin cultural tradition and its place in the future of America is a central component in the text and its formulation of two modernities. "Hispanicness" is nonetheless the necessary condition, the source, as it were, of the "herencia de raza" (*Ariel* 220) [racial heritage]. For Rodó, Spain and Spanish America are joined by their common inauguration of the modern spirit. Thus, on the occasion of the tercentenary of the death of Cervantes, he explains:

> El descubrimiento, la conquista de América, son la obra magna del Renacimiento español, y el verbo de este Renacimiento es la novela de Cervantes. La ironía de esta maravillosa creación, abatiendo un ideal caduco, afirma y exalta de rechazo un ideal nuevo y potente, que es el que determina el sentido de la vida en aquel triunfal despertar de todas las energía humanas con que se abre en Europa el pórtico de la edad moderna. (*Obras completas* 1211)
>
> [The discovery, the conquest of America, are the great work of the Spanish Renaissance, and the logos of this Renaissance is Cervantes' novel. The irony of this wonderful creation, demolishing an outdated ideal, affirms and exalts a new and powerful ideal, the one that determined the meaning of life in that triumphant awakening of all human energies that opens in Europe the portico of the modern age.]

Although Spanish America and Spain are here unified in the birth of modernity, this great Spain is a thing of the past, like a "casa lejana, de donde viene el blasón esculpido al frente de la mía" (740) [distant house from whence comes the coat of arms sculpted over the front door of mine]. It was precisely this Spain of the past that occupied the central place in the symbolic use of Ariel and Caliban in Groussac's and Darío's texts, upon which Rodó built the essay that would, finally, grant him full consecration in the Hispanic literary field.

Two years before Rodó reappropriated these Shakespearean characters, Rubén Darío had written a text announcing "El triunfo de Calibán" (The Triumph of Caliban) in the aftermath of the U.S. intervention in the Cuban War of Independence, turning it into the "Spanish-American" War. In his text, Caliban takes center stage as the embodiment of Anglo America: "El ideal de esos calibanes está circunscrito a la bolsa y a la fábrica. Comen, comen, calculan, beben whisky y hacen millones. Cantan ¡Home, sweet home! y su hogar es una cuenta corriente, un banjo, un negro y una pipa" ("Triunfo" 454). [The ideal of those calibans is limited to the stock market and the factory. They eat, eat, calculate, drink whisky and make millions. They sing "Home sweet Home!" and their home is a checking account, a banjo, a black man, and a pipe.] Darío's appraisal of U.S. modernity closely resembles Martí's earlier depiction of Coney Island and its focus on consumption and contentment alongside human dispossession.

Yet Darío's text explicitly presents the battle as a confrontation between the Anglo-Saxon and the Hispanic races, so that when he returned to the Ariel-Caliban opposition the following year in his short story "D.Q.," Ariel was transformed into a specifically Hispanic figure—Don Quixote defeated by a Caliban in the form of "un gran diablo rubio, de cabellos lacios, barba de chivo, oficial de los Estados Unidos, seguido de una escolta de cazadores de ojos azules" (144) [a large blond devil, with straight hair and a goatee, a U.S. officer, followed by an escort of blue-eyed hunters]. The Socratic sublime demon, the Shakespearean spirit of Ariel, and the Cervantine Don Quixote are thus variations of the same trope, of a vision of modernity that goes beyond materiality and consumption and is conceived as both an epistemological and ethical quest.[27] As modernismo achieved consecration in the transatlantic literary field, and after the "disaster" of 1898, there was a shift in the main focus of modernista writers from the Latin race to Hispanicness, as Spain, now "conquered," was increasingly construed as a symbol of modernity. A symbol that was now, significantly, crafted in America.

Rewriting Spain: Modernity and the Atlantic

Scholars have treated constructions of Spain and Hispanicness in this period almost exclusively in connection with the so-called Generation of '98 and the rethinking of Spanish identity. Generally disregarding the impact of modernismo and of Spanish American letters in the Peninsula, '98 studies (and those focused more generally on Spain's turn of the century) have remained partially blinded to the broader context of Hispanic textual production. One such context is the proliferation of images of Spain and Hispanicness produced across the North and South Atlantic during the nineteenth century and particularly around the war of 1898.

In her book *Spain's Long Shadow: The Black Legend, Off-Whiteness, and Anglo American Empire*, María DeGuzmán has demonstrated just how central discursive constructions of Spain have been to the ethnic imaginary of the United States and its own imperial self-fashioning:

> The construction of Anglo American identity as "American" has been dependent on figures of Spain. Figures of Spain have been central to the dominant fiction of "American" exceptionalism, revolution, manifest destiny, and birth/rebirth; to Anglo-America's articulation of its empire as antiempire (the "good" empire that is not one); and to its fears of racial contamination and hibridity. Figures of Spain have been indispensable to the constitution, elaboration, and even interrogation of these dominant fictions. I use the term "figure" to mean historical personage as well as image and rhetorical device. (xii)

DeGuzmán's study further shows "that what had always been taken as simply 'American' is as ethnically inflected as the cultural production of what is habitually marked 'ethnic' or 'others' " (xxiv). Her statement points to the naturalization of the metonymy in which the name of the whole (America) stands for the name of the part (Anglo America), the same metonymic operation exposed by the editorial of the *Revista Ilustrada* discussed at the beginning of this chapter. According to DeGuzmán, mediated by the Black Legend, figures of Spain worked in two opposite ways in the Anglo American imaginary: by identification and by rejection. That is, the United States conceived of itself as the successor of the Spanish empire, while defining itself against constructions of Spain. Using psychoanalytic theory, DeGuzmán explains that Spain functioned simultaneously as alter ego/imago and as totem. As a totemic figure, Spain was a parental figure that "inspires a certain degree of awe and also provokes anxiety of influence and mixed responses of memorialization and rebellion, similar to those elicited by England" (xv). As alter ego/imago, figures of Spain have also been constructed as "the image in the mirror experienced as external threat rather than internalized reassurance. . . . Anglo Americans created a fantasy of racial purity through the representation of Spaniards as figures of morally blackened alien whiteness or *off-whiteness* and doomed hibridity" (xviii; xxiv).

DeGuzmán does not explore the possibility and its implications that this second function of the figures of Spain in the Anglo American imaginary did not originate exclusively in relation to the "Hispanicness" of Spain itself, but also to another much closer "Hispanicness," that is, from the "Spanish" American half of the continent, the half which, according to Mansilla, was allowed to be called only "Hispano" America. She hints at this possibility, however, when she states: "After all, Spain was in the Americas, and in North America itself in New Spain/Mexico and the Spanish borderlands. 'Spanish' America was and still is the territorially and demographically larger portion of the Americas" (xv). DeGuzmán is mostly concerned in her study with the United States and its internal ethnic imaginary, particularly in relation to the Latina/Latino community.[28] I believe, however, that the core of her argument should be extended beyond internal affairs, for it can help us understand the centrality that representations of Spain and Hispanicness had in modernista textual production and the place of these representations in their development of a narrative of modernity to counter the Anglo-Saxon model. Similar to what DeGuzmán describes regarding U.S. literary and cultural production, modernismo took up the task of rewriting Spain from across the Atlantic, albeit in the opposite way. Their constructions of Spain would become a symbolic battleground for the discursive struggles over the meaning of modernity in the Americas.[29]

Imagining the Future: The Dystopian Impulse in Martí's *Ominous Friendship*

As we saw in the history lesson of *La Edad de Oro*, for Martí modernity began in the bright and dark of the Golden Age of the Spanish Renaissance and the destruction wrought in the Americas, which created the notion of one world, where isolation was no longer possible. In "Coney Island," Martí pondered the future, the discursive power of Anglo American modernity and its possible echoes, the possibility of the world's becoming one monstrous Coney Island. Yet he left the question about the future unanswered, concluding that "only time will tell" (89). In his only known published novel, *Amistad funesta* (Ominous Friendship; 1885), Martí imagined the answer. He wrote an end to the story in which the "monster," moved by jealousy and greed, killed the "sublime demon." A romance—a *folletín*—*Amistad funesta* is the story of a love triangle in an unspecified Spanish American city. The protagonist, Juan Jerez, has "la luminosa enfermedad de las almas grandes, reducida por los deberes corrientes o las imposiciones del azar a oficios pequeños" (*Lucía* 115) [the luminous illness of great souls reduced to small jobs by everyday duties or accidental impositions].[30] Engaged to his cousin Lucía despite his misgivings about her selfishness and lack of idealism, he also becomes the mentor or protector of Sol, a young woman whose father's and brother's deaths left her family in financial trouble.[31] Growing increasingly jealous of Sol, whom everyone, including Lucía herself, admires, Lucía kills Sol on the final page of the novel. In the heavily metaphoric language of the text, the relationship between Lucía, Juan, and Sol can be read as more than a love story.

Lucía, like Caliban, is defined by her physicality and sensuality, and moved by the need to possess the object of her desire.[32] For her, desire is not a productive force but an obsession: "Lucía, en quien un deseo se clavaba como en los peces se clavan los anzuelos, y de tener que renunciar a algún deseo, quedaba rota y sangrando, como cuando el anzuelo se le retira queda la carne del pez" (120). [Lucia, snagged by a desire like a fish by a hook, would be broken and bleeding if she had to renounce any of her desires, like the flesh of the fish when the hook is removed.] Lucía works against Juan's "sublime demon," so that when Juan tells her that he is like the young man in Longfellow's poem "Excelsior," climbing with a flag always higher and against all odds, Lucía responds: "¡Ah no! pero tú no me aparatarás a mí de ti. Yo te quito la bandera de las manos. Tú te quedas conmigo. ¡Yo soy lo más alto!" (167). [Oh no! but you won't take me away from you. I'll take that flag from your hands. You stay with me. I am the top!] Lucía is, then, like the crowd in Coney Island, "disturbed only by their eagerness to possess" ("Coney" 92). Associated with darkness, poison, vipers, and tigers, Lucía can be read within Martí's imaginary as an embodiment of the complacent monster of his earlier *crónica*, and as both the tiger inside and outside "Nuestra América." By contrast, Sol is described as pure spirituality, "un ser de esferas superiores" (*Lucía* 160) [a higher being], who becomes an inspiring—if chaste—force for Juan. Sol, then, can be read as the embodiment of the "sublime demon." In Martí's novel, however, the demon is of Spanish origin.

Despite the novel's brevity (three chapters and fewer than a hundred pages), Martí devotes the entire second chapter to an apparent digression from the main plot, a fairly detailed description of Sol's family, where we learn that Sol is the daughter of a Spaniard who had to leave Spain because of his liberal ideas (137). A noble and honest republican, don Manuel found refuge in America, where he was able to continue writing "sus azotainas contra la monarquía y vilezas que engendra, y sus himnos, encendidos como cantos de batalla, en loor de la libertad, de que los 'campos nuevos y los altos montes y los anchos ríos de esta linda América, parecen natural sustento'" (139) [his attacks against the monarchy and the vileness it engenders; his hymns, as inflamed as war songs, in praise of a freedom that "seems naturally nourished by the new fields and the tall mountains and the wide rivers of this beautiful America"]. Don Manuel and his only son, Manuelillo (who, notably, dies when he is sent back to Spain to study), are both touched by "ansias de redención and evangélica quijotería" (144) [a yearning for redemption and an evangelical quixotism]. They are Quixotes, like Juan Jerez himself.[33] The novel creates a clear continuity between don Manuel and Juan, who becomes the protector of Sol after her father's death. The idealism of don Manuel and his son likewise moves Juan Jerez, who spends his life helping others and working as a lawyer in defense of indigenous communities.[34]

Sol is represented as the embodiment of the idealistic, liberal, and heroic tradition that Juan finds so inspiring but that Lucía resents and ultimately destroys: seeing Juan walk into a party holding Sol by her arm, Lucía grabs a gun and shoots Sol. In his analysis of the novel as a reflection on literary language and metaphors, Aníbal González has argued that the text relates Lucía to the world of appearances and artificiality, as opposed to the natural light of the sun/Sol. Following this reading, we note that shortly before Lucía kills Sol, the narrator connects artificial light with the United States in the character of Mr. Sherman, who is in charge of bringing "la luz eléctrica" [electric light] to the party.[35] It is under this light that Lucía shoots Sol. Through the fictional world of romance, Martí imagines the final confrontation of two modernities, of North and South, the monster and the sublime demon, Caliban and Ariel. Lucía's final act signals what Darío would call "el triunfo de Calibán" over the "evangélica quijotería" of Ariel.

Given that he fought and died for Cuban independence from Spain, it may seem far-fetched to argue that Spain would have any positive value in Martí's imaginary of modernity. However, this is not the "real" Spain, which has killed Manuelillo and whose environment forced Sol's father to emigrate to America in the first place. Instead, it is a formulation of Spain and Hispanicness anchored in a heroic and idealistic reading of *Don Quixote*. What Martí performs in his text is a symbolic gesture (whose importance cannot be overlooked, as it represents more than a third of the novel and introduces a new subplot): a notion of Hispanicness as a particular incarnation of the modern spirit that, if spent in Spain, lives on in Latin America—albeit under threat—like don Manuel, his daughter Sol, and Juan.

As *Amistad funesta* shows, the modernista construction of Spain and the quixotic spirit of Hispanic modernity is indeed present from the earliest examples of the movement. Cervantes' novel also lies behind the structure of Rubén Darío and Eduardo Poirier's early folletín *Emelina* (1887) and its firefighter hero, as well as behind the heroic dreams of Martí in "Sueño con claustros de mármol" (I Dream of Marble Cloisters) from *Versos sencillos* (Simple Verses; 1891–1894). Similarly, José Fernández, the protagonist of Silva's *De sobremesa* (After Dinner; 1896), is explicitly presented as a Don Quixote in search of his Helena-Dulcinea, and so is Julio, the protagonist and "last representative of a knightly and glorious race" of Máximo Soto-Hall's *El problema* (The Problem; 1899).

The Voice of the Master: *Songs of Life and Hope*

One of the most important elements of the modernista renovation of literary language in Spanish was the refashioning of the late medieval and Golden Age literary tradition of Spain, from the *alejandrino* verse and the *romance* structure, to the poetry of Quevedo and Góngora and the prose of Cervantes and Santa Teresa. But constructions of Golden Age Spain as the embodiment of the modern gained a new impulse and became more openly expressed after the war of 1898 and the definitive consolidation of modernismo across the Hispanic literary field. It was then that modernismo further developed an image of Spain for which Spain itself was ultimately irrelevant. This was apparent as early as Darío's "El triunfo de Calibán" (1898), where Spain is explicitly deployed as a foil, as a tool of Spanish American discourse:

> "Y usted ¿no ha atacado siempre a España?" Jamás. España no es el fanático curial, ni el pedantón, ni el dómine infeliz, desdeñoso de la América que no conoce; la España que yo defiendo se llama Hidalguía, Ideal, Nobleza; se llama Cervantes, Quevedo, Góngora, Gracián, Velázquez; se llama el Cid, Loyola, Isabel; se llama la Hija de Roma, la Hermana de Francia, la Madre de América. (455)

> ["And have you not always attacked Spain?" Never. Spain is not the fanatical priest, nor the great pedant, nor the unhappy teacher, disdainful of an America that he does not know; the Spain that I defend is called Hidalguía, Ideal, Nobility; it is called Cervantes, Quevedo, Góngora, Gracián, Velázquez; it is also called the Cid, Loyola, Isabella; it is called the Daughter of Rome, the Sister of France, the Mother of America.]

Darío's gesture in 1898 is a self-conscious act prompted by a rhetorical question that emphasizes, in its context, the discursive construction of Spain as the symbol of a different kind of modernity. Modernismo had imposed itself in the transatlantic literary field in part by claiming the modernization of Spanish letters and, by extension, of Spain itself, thus functioning as a catalyst for the rethinking of national identity that young Spanish intellectuals were to undertake (see Chapter 3). The war of 1898 was the external event that consolidated the modernista revolution in the Spanish field. By 1898, Darío occupied a place of authority on both sides of the Atlantic, and it is from that place that he writes, furthering that authority in the act of writing. Acknowledging his own criticisms of Spain ("Y usted ¿no ha atacado siempre a España?"), Darío was positioned to define the "true" Spain and what it meant. Spain, thus, becomes a rhetorical device in the discursive war between North and South in which the "real" Spain matters little. In this sense, rather than thinking of Cuba from the standpoint of Spain, as Carlos Jáuregui (447) has suggested, reading this text through the neocolonial lens, I contend that Darío thinks of and reinvents Spain from the standpoint of America.

The most famous expression of what we could call the strategic convergence of Ariel and Don Quixote as embodiments of the modern spirit that opposed Anglo-Saxon modernity is, without a doubt, Darío's *Cantos de vida y esperanza* (1905; published in English as *Songs of Life and Hope* [2004]), in many ways the counterpoint to Darío's other great book on Spain, *España contemporánea* (Contemporary Spain; 1901), the collection of crónicas written for Argentina's *La nación* in which he portrays a devastating picture not of the imagined, but of the "real" Spain.[36] In this way, the Nicaraguan poet authors both the past and the present of Spain. In *Cantos*, Darío first reasserts his authority to speak, as he affirms his leadership of modernismo and the triumph of the movement across the Atlantic—"Tanto aquí como allá el triunfo está logrado" (*Poesías* 625). [Both here and there triumph has been achieved.] His choice of the word "triumph" evokes the title of his earlier chronicle, so that if the United States triumphed over Spain militarily, Spanish America triumphed over Spain culturally. In both instances, Spain itself stands defeated and becomes simply the symbolic battleground of modernity in the Americas.

His authority and that of the movement established, in *Cantos* Darío expands in poetic form what he had created in "El triunfo de Calibán," that is, a vision of Spain that stands in contrast to the values of Anglo American modernity and that reclaims the first modern spirit of the Renaissance and the Spanish Golden Age. From the first self-referential poem, "Galatea Gongorina," to his questioning of the swan in the first poem of the section "Los cisnes" (The Swans), Darío builds a genealogy with Americans as the heirs of the classical and Spanish traditions and builds a bridge between past and present, between Europe and America:

> A vosotros mi lengua no debe ser extraña.
> A Garcilaso visteis, acaso, alguna vez . . .
> Soy un hijo de América, soy un nieto de España . . .
> Quevedo pudo hablaros en verso en Aranjuez. (*Poesías* 648; ellipses in original)

[To you my language should not be foreign,
Perhaps you saw Garcilaso, once . . .
I'm a son of America, I'm a grandson of Spain . . .
Quevedo spoke to you in verse in Aranjuez. (*Songs* 109)]

The innovation of the Spanish past is now part of the Spanish American present. The revolution that Garcilaso de la Vega brought about in Spanish letters in the sixteenth century, when he imported the hendecasyllabic verse and other Italian forms, is explicitly connected to the modernista revolution. Hispanic modernity is no longer the realm of Spain, but of America, and it is there where Hispanicness is redefined and constructed.

After the introspective first poem about his own poetic and personal trajectory, Darío inserts his famous "Salutación del optimista" (The Optimist's Salutation), a poem not about Spain but about its American descendants, who are not one but many "races." Darío invokes a notion of race that is plural and, as I mentioned earlier, characterized by cultural heritage rather than biological determinism. Thus, Darío implicitly contrasts the fear of racial mixing that we saw in Strong and Schurz, "the fear of racial contamination and hibridity" (xii) that DeGuzmán identifies behind Anglo American constructions of the United States as empire, although not directly named in the poem, with the multiplicity of the "inclitas razas ubérrimas" (*Poesías* 631) ["distinguished, fructiferous races" (*Songs* 63)]. This stance is nowhere clearer in *Cantos* than in what is perhaps its most famous composition, "A Roosevelt" (To Roosevelt). In this poem, Darío not only builds an opposition between Spanish America and the United States, but also makes the category of race a central component of that contrast. While Roosevelt and his countrymen are depicted a "soberbio y fuerte ejemplar de tu raza; . . . hombres de ojos azules y alma bárbara" (640–41) ["a strong and splendid specimen of your kind; . . . men of Saxon eyes and barbarous souls" (85, 87)], Spanish America is presented as a crucible of indigenous and Mediterranean cultural traditions now under threat: "Eres los Estados Unidos, / eres el futuro invasor / de la América ingenua que tiene sangre indígena / que aún reza a Jesucristo y aún habla en español" (640). ["You're the United States, / you're the future invader / of the guileless America of indigenous blood / that still prays to Jesus Christ and still speaks in Spanish" (85).] Another composition, "Al Rey Óscar" (To King Óscar), addressed to the Swedish King, creates a similar contrast between the "Sire de ojos azules" ["Blue-eyed Sire"] and a "raza de oro" (633) ["Golden race" (67)] whose history is a conflictive accumulation of the classical, the Christian, the Arabic, and the indigenous. From the Pyrenees to the Andes, the Alhambra, Lepanto, Otumba, Perú, and Flandes, Darío creates in the poem a pluri-cultural geography of the Spanish race.

Spain is, indeed, a central symbol in Darío's *Cantos*. The collection is a masterful exercise in the construction of a powerful image as a weapon in a discursive battle that is omnipresent in the book. Yet *Cantos* is, in many ways, a book about Spain without Spain. That is, the Spain carefully crafted by Darío is an object of the past, an idea rather than a reality, but an idea that is meant to affect the present. Spain in *Cantos* is akin to Martí's "sublime demon" and Rodó's "Ariel"; it is the conceptualization of a different modernity, of a different vision of progress and of the future:

> ¡Mientras el mundo aliente, mientras la esfera gire,
> mientras la onda cordial alimente un ensueño,
> mientras haya una viva pasión, un noble empeño,
> un buscado imposible, una imposible hazaña,
> una América oculta que hallar, vivirá España! (*Poesías* 634)
>
> [As long as the world draws breath, as long as the sphere turns,
> as long as the cordial wave nourishes a daydream,
> as long as there is a lively passion, a noble endeavor,
> a sought-after impossibility, an impossible feat,
> a hidden America to find, Spain will live on! (*Songs* 69)]

These famous verses of "Al rey Óscar" epitomize the conflation of the different *modernista* symbols of modernity (the demon, Ariel, Don Quixote) into one: Spain.

But *Cantos* is a book about Spain without Spain in another, perhaps more significant, way. Many of the poems about Spain are, in a sense, doubly mediated by the foreign gaze: first by Dario's own, and second by that of others, be it Roosevelt, King Óscar, or Cyrano de Bergerac. Spain is the *object* of conversation, but Spain does not have its own voice. On the contrary, Darío is always explaining Spain to its others. Darío's poetic voice is, in fact, one of the most striking elements of this collection. His is the voice of the master; he has the authority to say and not to say, to praise and to condemn. From the beginning to the end of the book, that masterly voice that writes and explains Spain is American. Spain becomes a malleable object in his hands as he orchestrates its construction as a symbol. It is the mestizo Darío and the cosmopolitan Darío, Darío the "meteco," the barbarian, the Darío that in 1888 rejected the old Spanish tree of Valera, who now recreates that very tree and lends his own authoritative voice to the old masters, to Góngora and Velázquez who, in "Trébol" (Clover), are able to speak only through Darío.[37] Darío speaks to Goya, makes Cervantes his own, and prays to the Christ figure of Don Quixote in the "Letanía a Nuestro Señor Don Quijote" (Litany of Our Lord Don Quixote). In *Cantos*, published seventeen years after *Azul*, it is America that replants the Spanish tree and creates Spain, not the reverse.

The Way of Perfection: A Genealogy of Modernity and a Definition of Modernism

Against the "Yanquizarse" of the Globe

"De los pueblos modernos, el pueblo español es aquel en quien se ha encarnizado más la injusticia" (85) [Of all the modern people, the Spanish people is the one who has been attacked more viciously by injustice], says Venezuelan Manuel Díaz Rodríguez in *Camino de perfección* (The Way of Perfection; 1908), alluding simultaneously to Spanish modernity and the way Spain and Spanish history had been written in North Atlantic discourse. This thought can be considered the motivating force of his book. If *Cantos* was a construction of Spain as a symbol of modernity, Díaz Rodríguez's book is a major elaboration of that symbol, a critique of northern depictions of Spain and Hispanicness, and a further rewriting of both. In the introduction, Díaz Rodríguez tells his reader: "Retén, sobre todo, la saludable admonición que, de estas páginas, de cuando en cuando surge[, en] *medio al progresivo y universal yanquizarse de la tierra, cuando los hombres y pueblos han hecho del oro el único fin de la vida*" (7–8; my emphasis). [Keep, above all, the healthy admonition that springs from these pages from time to time[, in] the midst of the progressive and universal Americanization of the earth, when men and people have turned gold into the only goal of life.]

Díaz Rodríguez sees himself working against what seems to be a global process of "yanquizarse" [Americanization] and places his work under the protection of "el verbo de Teresa de Jesús y bajo la santa advocación de Nuestro Señor Don Quijote" (8) [the word of Saint Theresa of Avila and under the saintly advocacy of Our Lord Don Quixote], echoing Darío's "Litany of Our Lord Don Quixote" in *Cantos*. The mystic and the idealistic knight, two central figures of the Spanish Golden Age, here embodying the search for knowledge and the search for justice, also stand in this text as the two engines of a modernity that is the opposite of the possession and consumption that seems to characterize the "yanquizarse de la tierra." Under the verbal guidance of Saint Theresa, from whom the title of the book *Camino de perfección* is taken, Díaz Rodríguez divides his essay into four chapters, each dealing with one main topic: language, science, modernismo, and race. Although apparently separate elements, there is clear cohesion and progression in his text, and they all lead to Spain in the final chapter.

On the Openness of Language

Díaz Rodríguez begins by building an argument on the power of language and against anyone who thinks in terms of rules and norms, who perceives change as "palabrería" [verbiage] and calls "modernista a cuanto no ha comprendido y le parece nuevo" (13) [modernista anything that he does not understand and sees as new].[38] Díaz Rodríguez presents two main contentions about language. The first, evocative of Martí's prologue to the "Poema del Niagra," is that language is a living and transformative thing that must be experienced, not a dead object that can be reduced to a dictionary: "Inútil decirle de las palabras que son como casas, o como seres leves y armoniosos. Jamás ha entrado él en una palabra como en un jardín, ni se ha bañado en una palabra como en una fuente, ni ha subido por una palabra como quien trepa un monte, ni se ha asomado a ninguna palabra a vivir un rato siquiera ante la perspectiva de otro mundo" (15). [A useless task it is to tell him about words that are like houses, or like light and harmonious beings. Never has he stepped into a word like one does into a garden, nor has he swum in a word like one does in a spring, nor has he climbed a word like one scales a mountain, nor has he looked through any word in order to live in another world's perspective for a while.] Language is active communication, hence fundamentally popular and democratic: "Las palabras, en verdad, son la invención y el instrumento necesarios del vulgo" (15). [Words, in truth, are the necessary invention and instrument of the common people.] Words are not just the house of ideas but ideas themselves "que llegaron a concretarse cada cual en su propia arquitectura" (14) [that became concretized each into its own architecture].

Thus, following the romantic tradition, language is the expression of a worldview, and meaning is ever changing, depending on who inhabits the houses of language, which, "además de su arquitectura, que llevan en sus formas y líneas, tienen perfume y color, sonido y alma" (14) [in addition to their architecture, carried in their form and lines, have perfume and color, sound and soul]. Language is subjective, then, and central to thinking and knowing. With the excuse of defending his use of the words *orgullo* (pride) and *vanidad* (vanity) in an earlier book, Díaz Rodríguez embarks on a discussion reminiscent of the baroque on the difference between pride and vanity. Referring to Gracián and especially to Fray Luis de Granada's dictum "soy lo que soy" [I am what I am], Díaz Rodríguez explains that while vanity is related to the concern for appearances, pride is a form of self-knowledge: "El poseído de vanidad no dice como el orgulloso y el humilde: *soy lo que soy*. . . . Porque lo esencial para él es oírse en la lengua de los otros, que su nombre suene, y para ello, cuando nadie lo suena, se pone él mismo a sonarlo, como tambor de titiritero. . . . No así el orgulloso: Quiere ser lo que es, no lo que quieren los otros que sea" (22). [The man possessed by vanity does not say, like the proud and the humble, *I am what I am*. . . . Because the essential thing for him is to listen to himself in the tongue of others, for his name to echo, so that, when no one echoes it, he himself echoes it like a puppeteer's drum. . . . It is not the same for the proud, who wants to be who he is and not whomever others want him to be.] This discussion allows Díaz Rodríguez to connect language to self-knowledge, to finding and exploring self-expression, that is, one's own worldview. In so doing, he also implicitly refutes the idea of modernismo and its linguistic exploration as a copy or echo of European trends and as simply an issue of "style."

It is then not surprising that Díaz Rodríguez's second contention about language has to do with cosmopolitanism. As "Don Perfecto," who thinks of himself as the "guardian" of language, Díaz Rodríguez mocks those who oppose modernismo in the name of the purity of the Castilian language: "Si no ¿Cómo oponerse a los diablos modernistas que están convirtiendo el castellano en pura algarabía y jerigonza? ¿No pretenden haber devuelto al habla, que estaba según ellos en chochez y estagnación, como vieja doncella paralítica, la libertad, el ritmo y la gracia del movimiento? ¿No dicen de sí mismos que trajeron al idioma calor, belleza y música?" (32). [If not, how to oppose those modernista devils who are turning the Castilian language into pure babble and gibberish? Do they not claim that they have returned liberty, rhythm, and freedom of movement to the language, which was, according to them, senile and stagnant like an old paralytic maid? Do they not say that they brought warmth, beauty, and music to the language?] The issue at stake is the use of neologisms and Gallicisms. Díaz Rodríguez contests the conception of language as a closed space and refers back to the Spanish Golden Age in order to prove the absurdity of the idea of the immutability of language: "Escribe, creyéndolos de cepa clásica pura, vocablos que fueron repugnantes neologismos en la gloriosa lengua de Quevedo, Tirso y Lope" (34). [(Don Perfecto) writes, believing they are of pure classical strain, words that were disgusting neologisms in the glorious language of Quevedo, Tirso, and Lope.] Díaz Rodríguez undoes the notion of linguistic purity and unveils the process of naturalization of words, whose origin is never pure, anticipating his discussion of racial purity in the final chapter. Additionally, like Darío in *Songs of Life and Hope*, he creates the first link between the Spanish Golden Age and modernismo, a connection that will recur in his essay.

On the Subjectivity of Science

From language, Díaz Rodríguez moves to another form of knowledge, science. He accepts the importance of science without hesitation but criticizes the way it had become a form of religious fanaticism to the point of undermining the very methodology that ensures its objectivity, the scientific method. According to Díaz Rodríguez this is a consequence of Anglo American modernity, of the "yanquizarse de la tierra":

> Junto al arribismo y al amor al dólar, *caracteres de nuestro mundo moderno yanquizado, sólo han ido esparciéndose y prosperando, como religión y cultos únicos, la religión y el culto de la ciencia.* Quienquiera que habla hoy en nombre de la ciencia toma ... prestigio de hierofanta, y quienes escuchan, profanos o iniciados, iguales a los fieles de los antiguos credos cuando oían el oráculo, se turban, enmudecen y caen

> de rodillas, como ante el fallo de una divinidad omnipotente, invisible y despótica. (38; my emphasis)
>
> [Together with arrivism and the love for the dollar that characterize our Americanized modern world, the only things that have spread and prospered, and have done so as the only religion and cult, are the religion and cult of science. Whoever speaks today in the name of science attains the prestige of a hierophant; and whoever listens, lay person or initiated, like the followers of ancient creeds when they heard the oracle, gets disquieted, dumbfounded, and falls to his knees as if before the judgment of an omnipotent, invisible, and despotic God.]

Díaz Rodríguez addresses here the issue of prestige, what Bourdieu calls distinction. That is, by connecting money to science, he is pointing at what Bourdieu calls the two principles of hierarchy of the field of power: economic and cultural capital. In so doing, he also exposes how one works in relation to the other, that is, "the conversion of economic capital into symbolic capital, which produces relations of dependence that have an economic basis but are disguised under a veil of moral relations" (Bourdieu, *Logic* 123). The kind of scientific fanaticism that Díaz Rodríguez portrays here functions in a way similar to Bourdieu's symbolic capital, "power that is not perceived as power but as legitimate demands for recognition, deference, obedience, or the service of others" (Swartz 90). By comparing science to religion, Díaz Rodríguez implicitly highlights continuities between the past and the present. While religion served to justify despotism, science seems to silence all dissidence to an equally despotic "mundo moderno yanquizado" [Americanized modern world] and its "amor al dolar" [love of the dollar]. The power of symbolic capital lies in its capacity to pass as disinterested, as unconnected to power. Perhaps nothing was perceived as more objective and unbiased than science in the nineteenth century. What Díaz Rodríguez does in his essay is expose the relationship between scientific discourse and economic power, thus undermining its effect, for, as Bourdieu states, symbolic capital "produces its proper effect inasmuch, and only inasmuch, as it conceals the fact that it originates in 'material' forms of capital which are also, in the last analysis, the source of its effects" (*Outline* 183). In short, scientific discourse and its "objective" explanations of Anglo-Saxon racial superiority and material advancement are revealed in Díaz Rodríguez text as part of the symbolic violence exerted by Anglo American modernity as it emerged as a dominant force in the international field of power.

Díaz Rodríguez examines this relationship further when he connects science to the capitalist division of labor. According to Díaz Rodríguez, science has lost any sense of relativity, an element that is, nonetheless, consubstantial to the very Cartesian method on which it is founded—"La ciencia nos enseña a ser humildes, a dudar del propio saber, a pesarlo, medirlo, relativizarlo todo" (78). [Science teaches us how to be humble, to doubt our own knowledge, to weigh, measure, and relativize everything.] Instead, because the division of labor has created a need for specialization, the scientist is confined to his own small experiment and is prone to believe as universal what is only a partial truth:

> Recluido de esta guisa, el sabio acaba por no amar la ciencia, sino *su* ciencia, por no ver la verdad, sino *su* verdad. . . . Sin conocer otras verdades, no le será posible conocer lo relativo de la propia. . . . Quien ocupa y llena su espíritu con una sola verdad se inclina poco a poco y fatalmente a ver en su humilde verdad o en su corto grupo de verdades toda la Verdad: yendo contra el espíritu mismo de la ciencia moderna. . . . Cegado por su amor, el sabio llegará a no acoger sino los hechos y experiencias que confirmen *su* verdad, en tanto que de modo insensible y sistemáticamente rechazará cuanto a *su* verdad se oponga. (43–45)

> [Secluded like this, the scientist ends up loving not science but *his* science, seeing not truth, but *his* truth. . . . Without knowing other truths, it will not be possible for him to know the relativity of his own. . . . Whoever occupies and fills his spirit with only one truth leans slowly and fatally toward seeing all Truth in his humble truth or his small group of truths, going against the spirit itself of modern science. . . . Blinded by his love, the scientist will end up being receptive only to the facts and experiences that confirm *his* truth, while he will reject insensitively and systematically whatever contests *his* truth.]

Díaz Rodríguez points out the difference between the philosophical engine that gave a new impulse to the modern in the form of the Cartesian method (40), based on methodical doubt, and science as an exclusionary practice, in which a partial truth is universalized as the truth for all, at the expense of silencing all others. He explains that, as a result, those whose truth is excluded are pathologized and rejected as sick (46). The scientist thus has become a new version of the dogmatic and intolerant priest (not an innocent comparison in light of Díaz Rodríguez's later discussion of the Black Legend). Like the priest, however, the scientist is only human and "así como los antiguos creyentes acataban la palabra del sacerdote como la palabra misma del dios, los creyentes actuales también son llevados a confundir la aserción más o menos arbitraria del sabio con el fallo inconcluso de la ciencia" (44) [just as the old believers followed the priest's commands as if they were god's own, believers today are also prone to confuse the more or less arbitrary assertion of the scientist with the inconclusive verdict of science].

In sum, Díaz Rodríguez never doubts the importance of science as a form of knowledge, but he reveals it as subject to both social conditions and human passions. Not only is it not infallible, but also it can become a form of religious fanaticism, of vanity rather than pride, to put it in his terms, and hence more concerned with appearances than with true knowledge. Díaz Rodríguez presents science as the companion of what he calls the modern "yanquizarse" of the globe, a partial and relative version of modernity that through symbolic violence and proselytism presents itself as the universal truth against all others, rewritten now as nonmodern.

It is particularly interesting that Díaz Rodríguez begins and ends this discussion of science reflecting on the way scientific discourse was then being used as a tool to judge art, a topic to which he returns in the last section of his text. Here, he brings the conclusions of his discussion on science as an exclusionary practice to bear on issues of literature and modernismo. Revisiting Max Nordau's still influential *Entartung* (Degeneration) and his aspiration "al imposible de encontrar en la ciencia los elementos esenciales de un criterio seguro para juzgar de un artista y obra" (51) [to the impossibility of locating in science the essential elements of a sure criteria with which to judge an artist and work of art], Díaz Rodríguez reiterates that objective scientific judgment is both biased and contradictory, and exposes it as particularly ill-equipped to enter the literary field (52, 76). He depicts the implications of the imposition of scientific discourse in the realm of art and literature as both disastrous and absurd, as, under the pen of a teutonic Nordau, who hunts and describes stigmas, or of his "perfecto discípulo" [perfect disciple] Don Perfecto, who describes "casos en la literatura que conoce" [cases in the literature that he knows], it works as an exclusionary narrative that labels "toda una primavera del espíritu humano" [an entire springtime of human spirit] as degenerate and sick, and locks them away, condemning them to "los apartamentos altos del castillo" (52, 37) [the high chambers of the castle].

Indeed, the section concludes with a vision of Don Perfecto as a beastly fanatic of the new "religion" of scientific criticism who triumphantly offers up Rubén Darío as a lunatic, piously shutting him away in "una casa de orates" [an insane asylum]. In this final image, Díaz Rodríguez reveals scientific discourse's incursion into culture as the tool of a witch hunt, one that can be wielded to "discover," "denounce," and "justify" the suffocation of another, for it is Don Perfecto's use of an already biased scientific narrative that allows him to drown Darío's voice with his own: "Alza este libro de las *Prosas* en el aire, en medio de un gesto y una sonrisa hechos de triunfo, lástima y desdén, cual si . . . hubiese cazado y ahogado por siempre jamás, entre los torvos gavilanes de su pluma, las tórtolas de oro que van cantando en los versos del poeta" (53). [He holds the book *Profane Prose* up in the air, with a smiling gesture made of triumph, pity, and disdain, as if . . . with the fierce and horrifying hawks of his feather pen, he had hunted and drowned for ever more the golden turtledoves that sing in the poet's verses.] It is the pen of Don Perfecto as mimicking disciple of Nordau and scientific criticism that unjustly and ignorantly writes Darío's work into oblivion. In this way, science provides the basis of legitimation for a narrative that invades the cultural field and erases its self-proclaimed others. Given the connection Díaz Rodríguez has already traced between scientific discourse, economic power, and Americanization, his implicit critique of the northern exclusionary narrative of modernity, wielded to discredit and dominate others, can hardly be missed. Díaz-Rodríguez's defense of culture from the contemporary incursions of a biased scientific discourse might also be read as a first step in mounting a counternarrative that establishes cultural heritage as a superior paradigm for understanding modernity, an implicit invocation of the already well-established Caliban/Ariel opposition. Indeed, this hierarchy is the implicit focus of the following section in *Camino de perfección*.

On Modernism

Building on his earlier discussions, in the third chapter of *Camino de perfección* Díaz Ródriguez develops a notion of culture (in the form of art and literature) as a privileged way of knowing. Explicitly placing it above scientific discourse (and given his demolishing critique of science as an objective epistemological tool), he grants ultimate authority to art and literature as ways of understanding the world and of revolutionizing thought. "En realidad, no es el médico, no es el sabio, sino el poeta o el artista quien sabe el alma de las cosas" (62). [In fact, it is not the doctor, nor the wise man, but the poet or the artist who knows the soul of things.] Moreover, within the art and literature of the Western tradition, he creates a specialized hierarchy of knowledge and epistemological power: that is, contemporary modernists, and perhaps especially Spanish American modernistas, are those most able to identify, understand, and reveal hidden truths—notably, modernistas like himself, we might add, who are confronting Anglo-Saxon definitions of modernity that would seem to write them out of power.

Díaz Rodríguez begins by offering a theory of modernism (here used in a broad sense and not limited to the Hispanic context) as defined by two main forces: the return to nature, understood as simplicity, a going back to the "primitivas fuentes naturales" (55) [primitive natural springs], and mysticism, understood as the revelation of the soul of things. In this way, the author defines modernism against those who condemned it as superficial and suffering from "manía del estilismo" [a mania for stylism], representing it instead as a balance between form (via the return to nature) and content (via mysticism).[39] In fact, Díaz Rodríguez emphasizes the relationship of content and mysticism in this section, as literary mysticism is depicted as an epistemological tool, a way of knowing: "Misticismo es . . . clara visión espiritual de las cosas y los seres." [Mysticism is . . . the clear spiritual vision of things and beings.] Beyond the fact that only the poet or artist (and not the scientist or wise man) can see things for what they are, within this privileged group, the best reach even farther into the world's truths: "Cuanto más alto el poeta o el artista, es tanto mayor la fuerza de adivinación con que él penetra el alma de los seres, y aun el alma de las cosas en apariencia inanimadas" (62).

[The more stature the poet or artist has, the stronger the force of divination with which he penetrates the soul of beings and even the soul of apparently inanimate things.] Notably, it is in contemporary literature that Díaz Rodríguez locates the first flourishing of literary mysticism since the times of the Spanish Renaissance (63), privileging modernists as visionaries and modernism as an innovative and truly revelatory explanatory model.

This genealogical preoccupation permeates the chapter, as the Venezuelan rewrites the history of watershed moments in art and literature, of the return to nature in art, and of mysticism. Tracing a history of the simultaneous appearance of these two tendencies in art and literature (a simultaneity he understands as a prerequisite for artistic revolution), Díaz Rodríguez maps a chronology of renovation in cultural discourse from Plato to modernism that characterizes the latter as the first visionary and revolutionary movement since the Spanish Golden Age.[40] *Camino de perfección* thus writes modernism into the chain of watershed moments in literary history and, like Martí's history of the world in *La Edad de Oro* and Darío's *Cantos de vida y esperanza* before it, represents the modernists specifically as heirs to the revolution in thought that produced the modern age. Thus modernism is at once revolutionary *and* a reconnection to the Renaissance. Moreover, Díaz Rodríguez explicitly repositions the importance of Spain in this story, not only establishing an alternative to the stereotype of a dark and austere Spain, but also locating the roots of *all* literary modernity "en la literatura clásica española" (60) [in Spanish Golden Age literature], marking a continuity between Fray Luis de Granada, Jean Jacques Rousseau, and "modernist art" (60–61). In this way, Díaz Rodríguez constructs a particular understanding of Western contemporary art and literature, subsuming apparently disparate elements under the new concept of modernism and thereby providing a new theoretical framework from which to consider them, and establishing a genealogy of literary modernity anchored in the Hispanic tradition.[41] Thus while Anglo-Saxon modernity is built upon a radically flawed epistemology that naturalizes its unjust exclusions, Hispanic modernity is grounded in a cultural heritage able to reveal hidden truths, to rejuvenate and renovate human understanding.

Within this broad explanation of literary modernity, Díaz Rodríguez stops to discuss Hispanic modernismo specifically. What is interesting is that while the essay so clearly celebrates Spain's past, in the contemporary field the Peninsula suddenly limited the movement and the race. Indeed, it is here that Díaz Rodríguez calls attention to the fact that the movement began in America and transformed the peninsular literary field. Deploying the very colonial language prevalent in the Spanish reception of Spanish American modernismo, he coins the expression "the inverted conquest," reminding the reader of the reversal of influence and the change in the location of cultural authority, as well as the fact that it was "la crítica militante peninsular" [militant peninsular criticism] and "un conocido profesional de las letras" [a known professional writer] who (much like a Don Perfecto) labeled the modernistas sick with a "mania modernista" (61) [modernist mania], a "mania del estilismo" (62) [mania for stylism].

In this gap between "Spain" and the "Peninsula," we may read, on the one hand, the strategic invention of "Spain," that is, Díaz Rodríguez reveals, perhaps more forcefully than Darío himself had done, that his defense of Spain and Spanish modernity is a rhetorical device that has little to do with a nostalgia for empire, a colonialist agenda, or any blind pledge of allegiance to the "madre patria" [motherland]. It was, rather, a discursive construction in a struggle for cultural capital and distinction against the imperialist projects of northern modernities, a struggle in which Spain also stood to gain but in which it had nothing to say. On the other hand, this gap reveals a clear bid for authority in the contemporary field of enunciation, that is, if we are talking about Hispanic modernismo as a privileged epistemological tool within the already privileged field of culture, then it is the Spanish Americans who have the most authority to speak. It is, of course, the Venezuelan Díaz Rodríguez who defines here "los rasgos principales del modernismo verdadero, o si se quiere del modernismo como algunos lo entendemos y amamos" (56) [the main features of true modernism or, if you will, of modernism as some of us understand it and cherish it]. In this sense, Díaz Rodríguez's text suggests that while the modernistas are best equipped to uncover the world's truths, in the Hispanic tradition, Spanish American modernistas hold the greatest authority, are the most gifted visionaries on the contemporary scene. In this regard, the placement of this section is hardly innocent.

Like Darío, who opened *Cantos de vida y esperanza* with a prologue reminding his readers of the "triumph" of modernismo in Spain, Díaz Rodríguez includes a "parenthesis" (as he ironically calls this chapter) that affirms his authority as a Spanish American to speak *for* Spain and Spanish culture, and as a representative of a superior way of knowing (culture versus science) to speak *against* the exclusionary discourse of Anglo American modernity and expose its hidden truths. The positioning of this chapter is deliberate, since Díaz Rodríguez undertakes both tasks in the next and final chapter of *Camino de perfección*.

Against Race: Rewriting Spanish History

Despite its vague title, "Ensayo crítico de la crítica" (Critical Essay on Criticism), the last chapter of *Camino de perfección* focuses largely on race as a critical concept. Díaz Rodríguez does not negate the existence of race, but he sets out to challenge its use as a tool of objective analysis and as an explanatory category for understanding literature and art. For him, it is impossible "hallar entre las razas . . . ninguna en estado de pureza" (80) [to find among races . . . any in a pure state] and, once again in a vein similar to Martí's, it is a "universal causa de error . . . ver un carácter de raza en lo que es del fondo humano común a todas las razas y pueblos" (82) [universal mistake . . . to see as a racial characteristic what is part of the human core, common to all races and peoples].[42] Díaz Rodríguez then asserts the limitations of science's attempt to understand human actions, particularly through the category of race:

> En el caso de la síntesis química . . . nos hallamos en presencia de una verdad cuyos austeros lineamientos resaltan en el hecho o el fenómeno que la integran de modo determinado y preciso, en tanto que en el otro caso de una clasificación, por sus caracteres morales e intelectuales, de las diversas razas de hombres, en vez de conquistar una verdad equivalente, apenas ganamos aproximaciones a la verdad, que se resuelven en más o menos arbitrarias y felices conjeturas. (78)
>
> [In the case of chemical synthesis . . . we find ourselves in the presence of a truth whose austere rules stand out in the fact or phenomenon that integrates it in a clear and precise manner, while in the case of a classification of the diversity of human races by their moral and intellectual characteristics, rather than conquering an equivalent truth, we hardly gain approximations to the truth that lead to more or less arbitrary and happy conjectures.]

What Díaz Rodríguez foregrounds are the limits of the social sciences, whose emergence in the nineteenth century had affected almost every aspect of life, from politics and imperial projects based on social Darwinism to literature and the arts, which had been dominated for over half a century by realism and naturalism and their claim to objective and scientific observation. Given that Díaz Rodríguez is specifically addressing the limited capacity of the social scientist to explain literary and cultural phenomena, at its most basic level his text stakes a claim for the autonomy of the literary and cultural fields. Conversely, in so doing, he is furthering the critique he made in the previous chapter regarding the relative lack of autonomy of the social scientific field, tied as it is to public applause and political and economic forces.[43]

More importantly, Díaz Rodríguez's critique of the objective and autonomous basis of the social sciences is also a critique of the concept of modernity that this same scientific discourse helped create and impose at the expense of all other conceptions of the modern. Indeed, Díaz Rodríguez concludes that the scientific use of the category of race is inadequate because it depends on the judgment of an observer who is never impartial, an observer biased by his own worldview: "Por espíritu de casta, o aún de campanario, quizás el observador vea con vidrios de aumento, o no vea del todo, o lo vea todo confuso." [Because of a spirit of caste, or plain parochialism, the observer may see with a magnifying glass, or may not fully see, or may see it all blurry.] He develops this conclusion by calling attention to how northern modernity and its accompanying scientific discourse are ultimately part of a self-justifying narrative based on the construction of a negative image of the other in order to build a positive image of the self: "Las cualidades y defectos del pueblo extraño serán el simple comentario de las cualidades y defectos del propio, y el cuadro hecho del primer pueblo quedará como simple cuadro negativo del último" (82). [The qualities and defects of foreign people will always be a mere commentary on the qualities and defects of their own, and the portrait of the former will remain a simple negative picture of the latter.]

To prove his point, the Venezuelan author turns Spain into his case study. For most of the remainder of the chapter, Díaz Rodríguez embarks on a rewriting of Spain in which, far from being the dark premodern country that racial theories and what he calls the "clisé histórico" [historical cliché] have constructed, it becomes the first modern nation. Elaborating a long list of traits that have been associated with Spain and the Spanish race, he describes

> hombre *fanático y limitado*, incapaz para la crítica, la política y la ciencia, nada apto para el vuelo del alta especulación, inhábil para mantenerse en lo justo del término medio por su temperamento extremoso . . . , secular presa de la ignorancia y la desidia, la víctima del tiránico formalismo religioso, regulado por la máquina infernal de la Inquisición, que es la mejor disciplina de mando, o el mejor complemento de gobierno en una monarquía teocrática y absoluta. (86–87)

> [a fanatical and limited man, incapacitated for criticism, politics, and science, completely inept for high philosophical speculation, unable to stay in the fairness of the middle ground because of his extreme temperament . . . , for centuries prey to ignorance and idleness, victim of tyrannical religious formalism, regulated by the infernal machine of the Inquisition, which is the best tool for discipline and control, or the best complement of government in a theocratic and absolute monarchy.]

Against the darkness, fanaticism, and austerity projected by the racial view of an observer that he has already disqualified, Díaz Rodríguez delineates a different image of Spain and Spanish history, contesting one by one the main elements of the Black Legend, images that, as DeGuzmán and others have pointed out, were so effectively being used by northern Europe and the United States to erase the Hispanic Atlantic from the modern. The first image that Díaz Rodríguez undermines is the fiction that there is a single Spain. He refers to the many "Spains" within Spain, a diversity that is not limited to the Peninsula (from the Basques to the Andalusians) but also encompasses those "nacidos en otra latitud, al calor de otro clima y con la ley de otro régimen" [born in another latitude, under a different climate and a different political regime], that is, the Spanish Americans. This diversity requires, according to Díaz Rodríguez, a new "geografía crítica" (88) [critical geography].

Commenting on representations of the Spanish literary tradition, the Venezuelan writer contests influential French critic and historian Hippolyte Taine's portrayal of Spanish literature and art as dominated by sobriety and austerity, an extension of José de Ribera's tenebrist baroque paintings. Without denying the existence of this vein, Diaz Rodríguez reclaims a different one from the humor of the Arcipreste de Hita and his Trotacoventos to Góngora's poetry, encompassing the work of the mystics, the writings of Leon Hebreo, the *comedias*, and the paintings of Murillo (89–91). For example: "La sonrisa de Trotaconventos atraviesa el nublado de humo de los autos de fe y la lluvia de sangre de las empresas heroicas. Es una verdadera sonrisa, flor de ironía y fineza, que nada tiene que ver con la gran risa rabelesiana" (88–89). [Trotaconventos' smile cuts through the smoky fog of the Inquisition's executions and the rain of blood of the heroic enterprises. It is a true smile, a flower of irony and finesse, that has nothing to do with the great Rabelaisian laughter.] And of Góngora: "Ninguno como él refleja el exquisito y leve matiz de la gracia" (89). [No one like him reflects the exquisite and light nuance of grace.] Díaz Rodríguez then concludes that "la sonrisa y la gracia no son, como algunos insinúan, . . . ajenas a la índole española" (91) [laughter and grace are not, as some insinuate, extraneous to the Spanish nature].

Moving from literature to politics, Díaz Rodríguez sets out to dismantle the image of absolutism as "un monstruo exclusivamente indígena de España" (92) [a monster that is exclusively indigenous to Spain]. For him, absolutism was indeed paralyzing for Spain, but the reduction of Spanish political history to that form of government was accomplished only by erasing others:

> *Se ignora, o no se recuerda, si acaso de propósito no se calla,* que antes de la España absolutista y romanista hubo una España gótica, de franca vida comunal, celosa de su autonomía y de sus fueros. En pro y en contra del absolutismo se luchaba en Inglaterra, cuando ya habían definido y promulgado sus derechos los plebeyos y los nobles de Castilla. Un siglo antes de establecerse en otro pueblo de Europa el régimen político representativo, existían las cortes castellanas. (92; my emphasis)
>
> [*Some ignore, or do not remember, if not perhaps simply hush up on purpose,* that before absolutist and Romanist Spain there was Gothic Spain, with a frank communal life and zealous about its autonomy and its charters. There were fights for and against absolutism in England at a time when Castilian commoners and aristocrats had already defined and promulgated their rights. A century before a representative political system was established in any other European nation, it existed in the Castilian assemblies.]

In a climactic gradation, he goes from ignorance, to a lack of historical memory, to purposeful silencing. The source of this apparent forgetfulness or premeditated silence is implied in Díaz Rodríguez's text, as he insists on correcting a history that has been distorted by racial bias. Thus, when he refers to "España la secular precursora de Inglaterra en el gobierno representativo" (93) [Spain, the centuries-old predecessor of England in representative government], he implicitly points at those historians who were most invested in writing history differently. Like Martí, Rodó, and Darío, Díaz Rodríguez creates an alternative, but not before demanding an explanation for this silencing of history: "Los que ven la tendencia al absolutismo como propia de la raza española, debieran explicarnos por qué fue España precisamente la primera nación europea que implantó el régimen político más avanzado" (93). [Those who see the absolutist tendency as inherent to the Spanish race should explain to us precisely why Spain was the first European nation to implement the most advanced political system.] Furthermore, turning the tables, Díaz Rodríguez presents absolutism not only as a system "foreign" to the Hispanic people, but also as imposed by northern Europe. Referring to Emperor Charles V:

> Contra lo que se podría suponer, dada la más corriente y divulgada psicología de la raza española, quien sofocó las libertades del pueblo . . . no fue un seco y avellanado español de alma solar, sino un hombre del Norte, graso y barbitaheño germano de ojos azules. Fue este germano, rodeado de una corte de flamencos, el que predispuso al absolutismo el ambiente de España. (94)
>
> [Against what one might presume, given the most commonly divulged view of the psychology of the Spanish race, it was not a dried up and wizened Spaniard with a sunny soul, but a man from the North, a fat German with red beard and blue eyes, who suffocated the liberties of the people. . . . It was this German, surrounded by a Flemish court, who predisposed the Spanish environment to absolutism.]

The Venezuelan critic performs a rewriting of history by which modern progress in Spain was stalled in the past precisely by the people who claim to be the bearers of progress in the present. Díaz Rodríguez writes of absolutism in Spain as a "tendencia . . . exótica" [exotic tendency] that was never fully able to eliminate the country's "tendencia indígena y libérrima" (94) [extreme indigenous tendency to freedom]. Rather, absolutism seems to be at home only in northern Europe.

Moreover, according to Díaz Rodríguez, nothing in Spanish history resembles the "falange ininteligente y brutal en que hace las veces de inteligencia y carácter una disciplina de autómatas, como en la militarizada Alemania del día" (94) [unintelligent and brutal phalanx where the discipline of automata passes as intelligence and character, as in present-day militarized Germany]. In his argument, the force of this exotic absolutism is also responsible for the emergence of tyrannies in Spain's and Spanish America's recent history, a kind of corruption that, "cuando no es precursora de la muerte definitiva, expresa la exuberancia de los tiempos que Nietzsche apellidó de otoño, y entonces precede y acompaña a los grandes renacimientos" (95) [when it is not the precursor of final death, expresses the exuberance of the times that Nietzsche called autumnal, in which case it precedes and accompanies great rebirths]. What is remarkable about the argument in Díaz Rodríguez's text is not his explanation of events in racial terms, but the turning of scientific racial explanations of history on their head by making the opposite argument and presenting absolutism as a political system indigenous to the North. To the extent that the category of race can be used to explain the same events in diametrically opposed ways, Díaz Rodríguez's text questions the validity of race as a critical concept.

After tracing the northern origin of absolutism and the Spanish origin of representative political systems, the Venezuelan critic undertakes a similar dismantling of the image of Spanish religious intolerance. As in the case of politics, Díaz Rodríguez sets out to argue the opposite of the accepted image: "La tolerancia, al revés de lo que de ordinario se cree, parecería, según ciertos orígenes, convenir mejor al espíritu de la raza" (95). [Contrary to what is commonly believed, tolerance would seem to befit better the spirit of the race, according to certain origins.] He locates those origins in what he represents as the centuries of harmonious and fraternal coexistence of three religions in medieval Spain: "Los cristianos, los musulmanes y los judíos de España cantaban en la misma lengua las mismas canciones, y en la misma lengua fraternalmente disertaban sobre los problemas de la ciencia de esa edad a la sombra del sacro bosque de columnas de la mezquita cordobesa" (95–96). [Christians, Muslims, and Jews in Spain used to sing the same songs in the same tongue and in the same tongue used to dissertate fraternally about the scientific problems of the times under the shade of the sacred forest of columns of the mosque of Cordova.] As he opposed native love of freedom to exotic absolutism, Díaz Rodríguez argues that in a nation where different religions coexisted so peacefully for centuries, religious intolerance could not have been a native trait, one inherent to the Spanish race. Rather than driven by fanaticism, Díaz Rodríguez portrays Spanish religiosity as open-minded and embracing of difference.

The reference to science is not casual, for Díaz Rodríguez suggests that it was precisely this open religious tradition that made possible the development of science in the West, thus tracing a genealogy of "modern" science to Spain and, more generally, the South. By connecting the beginning of intolerance with the beginning of absolutism, he makes the implicit claim that both came from outside, more specifically, from the countries of the Reformation, where religious intolerance took a nastier form: "No fue más cruel y repugnante en España que en los pueblos abrazados a la causa de la Reforma. Su crueldad, al contrario, se reveló en estos países más rígida, áspera y seca" (96). [It was not more cruel and repugnant in Spain than in the nations that embraced the cause of the Reformation. On the contrary, their cruelty turned out to be more rigid, harsh, and dry in these countries.] For him, there is no comparison between Catholic and Protestant intransigence, since the

Catholic version was softened by compassion. Ultimately, Díaz Rodríguez employs the same argument used by thinkers like Montesquieu or Hegel but reaches the opposite conclusion for, as time has shown, "en los pueblos latinos, particularmente en España, . . . toda intransigencia religiosa desapareció de las costumbres, en tanto que en los pueblos anglosajones, que se dicen los más avanzados . . . , persiste en las costumbres, y renueva todos los días . . . el suplicio de los antiguos crucificados" (97) [in the Latin countries, particularly in Spain, . . . all religious intransigence disappeared from their customs, while in the Anglo-Saxon nations, which call themselves the most advanced . . . , it persists in their customs, renewing daily . . . the torture of the crucifixions of old].

In this way, two of the main components of the Black Legend, absolutism and religious intolerance, are not only contested but also traced back to the North. In Spain, on the contrary, the spirit of freedom and "true" religious spirit worked "against" religious intolerance so that "muchas manifestaciones del espíritu religioso lo fueron también del espíritu de libertad" [many manifestations of the religious spirit were also manifestations of the spirit of freedom]. Such was the case of the Jesuits, who proclaimed "lo relativo del conocimiento y lo vano de los conceptos absolutos" [that knowledge is relative and absolute concepts vain] and in which Díaz Rodríguez sees the origin of "la libertad del espíritu moderno" (98) [the freedom of the modern spirit]. That was also the case of Spanish mysticism, which he describes as "la más pura expresión individualista del espíritu de libertad" [the purest individualist expression of the spirit of freedom] and "el más radical movimiento revolucionario de la lengua y de la forma" (101) [the most radical revolutionary movement of language and form]. In religion, as in literature and politics, openness and freedom are the elements that, for Díaz Rodríguez, have moved the history of the Spanish race.

After a discussion of the mystics, Díaz Rodríguez returns to Spanish literature and art in order to demonstrate how *all* modern art finds its roots in the Spanish Golden Age. He undertakes a defense of Spanish drama, concluding that "el teatro de cualquiera gran nación de la tierra puede holgada y seguramente asentarse en los hombros de Tirso" (106) [the theater of any great nation on earth can sit on Tirso's shoulders safely and with room to spare]. The picaresque novel is, for the Venezuelan writer, an embodiment of Spanish freedom reacting against "la doble tiranía temporal y espiritual importada de afuera" (107) [the double tyranny, spiritual and temporal, imported from outside]. Finally, Díaz Rodríguez centers his discussion on the works of Cervantes and Velázquez, seen as two prime examples of artistic genius and two pillars of modern literature and art. As he closes his essay, he offers a final reflection on the decline of Spain:

> Otros objetarán que no se concibe cómo, siendo Velázquez el genio representativo de su raza en la pintura, el arte español se haya más bien alejado de la pintura

> velazqueña. A eso podría responderse que nada hay tan español como el régimen político autonómico y federal y que, sin embargo, España se apartó de él, por obra de Carlos V, y desde entonces anda padeciendo, sin acabarlo de pasar todavía, el tifus largo y peligroso del régimen absoluto. Además, la objeción hecha a propósito de Velázquez, recaería sobre todo el arte literario español, arrastrándonos a negarles condición española a Cervantes y a Quevedo, al vigoroso realismo todo color de los picarescos y a la sabia prosa de los místicos, porque el arte español se alejó también de ellos, para entretenerse, antes y después de un buen paréntesis llenos de accesos de romanticismo, ya indígena, ya exótico, en cultivar con rigidez académica la incolora y eterna ñoñería pseudoclásica. (111)
>
> [Others may object that it is inconceivable that Spanish art has moved away from the painting style of Velazquez, given that he was the most representative genius of his race in this art. To this one could answer that nothing is more Spanish than the autonomous and federal political system, and yet Spain moved away from it because of Charles V and is still suffering, without yet recovering, the long and dangerous typhus of absolutism. Besides, the objection regarding Velazquez would apply to all Spanish literary art, forcing us to deny the Spanish condition to Cervantes and Quevedo, the vigorous and colorful realism of the picaresque, and the wise prose of the mystics, because Spanish art moved away from all of them as well, to entertain itself cultivating with academic rigidity an eternal and colorless pseudo-classic insipidness after a good parenthesis full of both indigenous and exotic Romantic outbursts.]

In this context, for Díaz Rodríguez, modernismo brought about the end of an "insipid" academicism and continued the glory of Spanish art and letters that introduced the modern period.

Díaz Rodríguez concludes *Camino de perfección* by emphasizing that the search for knowledge that is constitutive of the "modern spirit" cannot be based on methods and tools that ignore the relativity and incompleteness of all knowledge and that seek instead to assert an absolute truth that, although partial, is imposed as universal, excluding and silencing those with a different truth. Similar to Martí's treatment in *La Edad de Oro*, modernity here appears as formed not in a homogenous manner, but in the conflict of heterogeneous forces and in the violent contrast between light and dark. For Díaz Rodríguez, Hispanic modernity has been constituted much like the Spanish language: "¿La tizona del Cid no segó las flores para ella de los cármenes moros? ¿No vinieron a ella como trofeos, en la punta de las picas, las bárbaras voces flamencas? ¿No le enriquecieron los tercios de Italia con deliciosos italianismos? ¿No le trajeron los conquistadores la sangre y el perfume de la América india en la medialuna de sus partesanas?" (101–2). [Did the Cid's sword not cut the flowers of the Moorish villas for the Spanish language? Did the barbarous Flemish words not come to it like trophies on the point of spears? Did the troops that fought in Italy not enrich it with delightful Italianisms? Did the conquerors not bring to it the blood and the perfume of Indian America in the half-moon of their partisans?] Diaz Rodríguez articulates the intrinsic otherness of modernity, its perpetual state of conflict and mixture. Thus, he confronts the exclusionary sameness of "yanquizada" modernity and the homogenizing force behind theories of racial purity and supremacy, as well as their fear of hybridity, and proposes a counternarrative of Hispanic modernity that locates its origin in Spain. *Camino de perfección* embodies a narrative that rewrites the history of Spain, the Spanish race, and the history of modernity.

The Glory of Don Ramiro: The Mestizo Origins and Atlantic Future of Modernity

Begun in 1903 and first published in 1908, the same year as Díaz Rodríguez's *Camino de perfección*, Enrique Larreta's *La gloria de don Ramiro* (published in English as *The Glory of Don Ramiro* [1924]) was soon hailed as a masterpiece. It was translated into French by Remy de Gourmont and later into other European languages. In Larreta's novel, perhaps the most widely read and critically acclaimed piece of modernista fiction—although one of the most forgotten today—we find condensed most of the ideas present in the writings of his peers, from Martí to Darío to Díaz Rodríguez. Regarding the last, *La gloria de don Ramiro* could be read as the "way of perfection" of its protagonist Ramiro, a trajectory in which race plays a central role.

The novel is set in the late sixteenth and early seventeenth centuries, a time of Spanish imperial decadence that is presented as progressively dominated by commerce and the obsession with gold. This is not only a transposition of nineteenth-century discussions on decadence to the seventeenth century, as has been noted, but also an implicit reference to the beginnings of modernity and the capital accumulation that would make the Industrial Revolution and nineteenth-century modernization possible.[44] A reincarnation of Don Quixote, Ramiro grows up reading chivalry books and lives of saints and listening to stories and legends told by the women of the house. Like Alonso Quijano, he dreams of "los caballeros donceles que en las historias descabezaban endriagos, vestiglos y fieros leones, redimiendo princesas, desbaratando encantamientos y maleficios" (47) [the young knights who in the stories used to behead dragons, monsters, and fierce lions, rescuing princesses, undoing enchantments and curses]. Ramiro is desperate to find glory like that of these heroes of old, but he is also touched by a certain mysticism. Wanting him to join the Church, his mother sends him to the priest Vargas Orozco to prepare for the priesthood. Instead, this fanatic priest convinces Ramiro to spy on the *moriscos* (converted Muslims) to discover an alleged conspiracy. Thus begins a journey for the young hidalgo that leads him to kill the two women he loves (Beatriz, who betrays him with Gonzalo after learning of Ramiro's father, and the *morisca* Aixa, whom he betrays to the Inquisition). He then leaves his native Avila and goes south to Cordova, where he learns the truth about his origins, and travels to Cadiz, where he embarks for Peru. Only there will he finally find his "gloria" some years later as he is attended to by Saint Rosa of Lima on his deathbed.

La gloria de don Ramiro is the tale of a journey that is both interior and exterior: the story of Ramiro is the narrative of his path to self-knowledge and salvation as he travels geographically first from north to south (from Avila to Toledo, Cordova, and Cadiz) and then from east to west (from Europe to America). The two journeys are intimately related. Ramiro is born into an environment where the concept of "purity of blood" has become an obsession, a Spain that, like Ramiro's grandfather and his mentor Vargas Orozco, is intent on erasing its own past and building a fantasy of racial purity. The families of both Ramiro and Beatriz, the daughter of his grandfather's only friend, are racially mixed, but both live in active denial of their past and are set on destroying its traces—"En la librería del palacio . . . aparecieron varios librotes arábigos, que [el abuelo de Ramiro] hizo quemar al pronto, en medio del patio, en presencia de un canónigo" (25). [In the library of the palace . . . several big Arabic books were found which (Ramiro's grandfather) immediately burned in the middle of the courtyard in the presence of a priest.] Ramiro is himself a mestizo, the illegitimate son of the Christian doña Guiomar and a morisco whose name is never mentioned. Ramiro does not know of his morisco origins, however, for his mother was prevented from marrying his father, whose identity has been kept from him.

Since childhood, Ramiro is marked by both a quixotic idealism and a spiritual impulse that connects him to his relative Saint Theresa of Avila, from a family of converts herself. Seduced by the fanaticism of Vargas Orozco, however, Ramiro looks for glory in all the wrong places and fights the otherness within. His relationship with Aixa gives him the opportunity to become the hero he dreams of being: he may join the fight for the cause of an oppressed minority and embrace the mystic spirituality that Aixa embodies. Although torn by doubt, he eventually does neither. Instead, he turns Aixa in to the Inquisition and, after killing Beatriz, escapes from Avila and goes to Toledo, where he happens upon and witnesses Aixa's and other moriscos' auto-da-fé. Horrified, Ramiro keeps going, traveling south to Andalusia, where significantly he begins his own process of self-discovery. On the outskirts of Cordova, the capital of the old caliphate, where Ramiro has become a hermit, his father finds and confronts him, telling him the truth of his origins and cursing him for betraying Aixa. Dumbfounded and angry, Ramiro is unable to accept his lineage, unable to digest what he perceives as his own "impurity." Caught in internal conflict, he resolves to escape again. While in Cadiz, he encounters his old page Pablillo, who has become a war hero in Flanders. Able to see only his own heroic failure, Ramiro enrolls in the army and departs for America on Christmas Eve, "tendiendo su mirada, su imaginación y toda su alma hacia la fabulosa esperanza del horizonte" (435) [streching out his gaze, his imagination, and his whole soul toward the fabulous hope of the horizon]. In Peru, however, Ramiro turns from soldier into bandit, torturing and slaughtering Indians.

Finally, when trying to seduce the woman who would later become Saint Rosa of Lima, Ramiro regains the mystic impulse of his youth, through which he discovers himself and finds his heroism. Ramiro repents his past actions and attains the "glory" of the title, not by isolating himself or by killing Indians, but by saving them.[45] He spends the rest of his life helping those he had once harmed and eventually dies doing so, when he takes the place of an ailing Indian to whom he was tending who had been forced, despite his illness, to go back to work in the silver mines. Working in the mines and dressed as an Indian, Ramiro catches a fever and dies. His journey to the South is therefore also a journey to his past. Only by learning about his past can he embark on his future as he travels west to America. Only by accepting his mestizo self can he find his glory. It comes with neither the cruel Christian Beatriz, nor the mystic Moorish Aixa, nor even the faithful gypsy Casilda (although Ramiro looks down upon her, she follows him all the way to Cadiz). Only the mestiza, Saint Rosa of Lima, the first American saint, brings peace to Ramiro and forces him to assume his heroic destiny.

In 1909, Miguel de Unamuno reviewed Larreta's novel and affirmed it as "un generoso y feliz esfuerzo por penetrar en el alma de la España del siglo XVI y por tanto en el alma de la España de todos los tiempos y lugares" (285) [a generous and happy attempt at penetrating the soul of sixteenth-century Spain, hence, the soul of Spain of all times and places]. If he was right, the soul of Spain in *La gloria de don Ramiro* is, like Ramiro himself, mestiza. Unamuno, however, chooses to highlight linguistic sameness over racial difference: "Sean cuales fueren los cruces de razas, sea cual fuere la sangre material que a la primitiva se mezcle, mientras un pueblo hable en español, pensará y sentirá en español también" (285). [Whatever the racial crossings, whatever the actual blood mixed with the primitive one, as long as a people speak Spanish, they will think and feel in Spanish too.]

Yet, race is a central theme of *La gloria de don Ramiro*. Larreta's novel challenges precisely the fantasy of an eternal and immutable Spain that Unamuno emphasizes. The novel proposes, on the contrary, that Hispanicness was formed in both racial conflict and cross-fertilization. Like Martí and Díaz Rodríguez, Larreta does not shy away from showing the violence of modernity in sixteenth-century Spain as he describes in great detail Aixa's auto-da-fé, the final result of the fanaticism of Ramiro's tutor. But, although Spain lost its modern "soul" in self-hatred and self-denial, that modern soul was reinvented in America. If Larreta was transposing to the sixteenth century the theme of decadence dear to the fin de siècle, for him, decadence stayed behind in Europe. An exile like Martí's don Manuel in *Amistad fuesta,* Ramiro finds his purpose and his glory in America. There, he finds and saves himself. Unamuno's review of *La gloria* is as controlling as it is admiring of Larreta's text. Insisting on reading the novel against itself, Unamuno defends the same unchangeable essence of Spain against which Ramiro had to fight. Furthermore, for Unamuno, it did not matter that Larreta was Argentine, because Argentines and all Spanish Americans were ultimately, whether they wanted to be or not, Spanish: "La Argentina . . . también es España, pese a quien pesare" (285). [Argentina . . . is also Spain, even if it may pain some people to hear it.] In the tradition of Valera (with whom Unamuno shares a conflicted and contradictory relationship with Spanish America), for the Spanish intellectual, Spanish America can make sense only from Spain. In Larreta's novel, however, Spain had to be made sense of—reinvented, in fact—in America, and not as an immutable essence, but as an amalgam of cultures and histories often in conflict. In so doing, *La gloria* also contested contemporary theories of racial purity and the racialization of modernity.

One could argue that Unamuno's remarks on *La gloria de don Ramiro* represent an important difference in the way intellectuals on both sides of the Atlantic dealt with the northern discourse of modernity. In Unamuno's view, there is a notion of "essence," what he calls "soul"—be it linguistic, cultural, geographic, or spiritual (ultimately one and the same thing)—that retains a purity, something eternal and transhistorical that is defined by the sameness to itself. This concept resists both difference and diversity (a stance in staunch opposition to that of Spanish American modernistas); it aims, perhaps against Unamuno's explicit political beliefs, to restore an imperial homogenizing project. Unamuno's comments, however unwittingly, are suffused with nostalgia for the past; Spanish Americans rewrote the past to stake a claim for the future. Here may lie a fundamental difference between the focus on Hispanicness or the Spanish race in Spain and in Spanish America at the turn of the nineteenth century, a difference that makes clear the power of the postcolonial gesture of Spanish American modernismo. Unamuno and many of the Spanish modernistas embarked on a search for the "Spanish soul," an exploration of Castile and the "true" essence of Spain. Spanish American modernistas, on the contrary, assumed from the start the lack of any essential and pure element and valued, instead, hybridity and otherness. Unamuno's comment is centripetal, while modernismo created a decentered and expansive Spain. Rather than a true essence to be sought in the landscapes of Castile, Spain was a discursive artifact, a symbolic construct to be deployed in the global struggle for capital, power, and distinction against the racial discourse of northern modernity. Most Spanish American modernistas were moved by cosmopolitan concern for defending global diversity, while many of their peninsular peers became obsessed with the isolating task of defining national sameness.

For many writers in Spain, like Unamuno, modernismo took the form of imperial nostalgia, caused to a considerable extent by their unwillingness to recognize the "inverted conquest" that had shaped their writing in the first place. On the contrary, Spanish American modernismo and its reinvention of Spain and Hispanicness was driven by anti-imperialist hope. Darío, whose "indigenousness" so disturbed Unamuno and his peers, could have been replying to them when he said: "Español de América y americano de España, canté, eligiendo como instrumento el hexámetro griego y latino, mi confianza y mi fe en el renacimiento de la vieja Hispania, en el propio solar y del otro lado del Océano, en el coro de las naciones que hacen contrapeso en la balanza sentimental a la fuerte y osada raza del norte" ("Historia" 151). [A Spaniard from America and an American from Spain, I sang (choosing as my instrument the Greek and Latin hexameter) my confidence and faith in the renaissance of old Hispania, both in its own land and on the other side of the ocean, in the chorus of nations that offer a counterweight, in the sentimental balance, to the strong and daring northern race.] Modernismo redefined the former imperial relationship with Spain, dismantling it and reversing the location of authority. It both altered the Hispanic literary field and rejuvenated the Atlantic as a diverse geocultural space from which to imagine a different, more egalitarian, and nonimperial relationship between culture and power, a space from which to resist the symbolic violence exerted by the homogenizing discourses of new empires.

Notes

INTRODUCTION

1. This is made explicit, for instance, in Astradur Eysteinsson's *The Concept of Modernism*, as Anthony Geist and José Monleón have rightly noted. Fifteen years after that book, in 2007, Eysteinsson repeats the same gesture (6) in the introduction to the monumental *Modernism*, co-edited with Vivian Liska. Despite the inclusion of well-informed essays on Spanish American, Catalan, and Spanish modernisms in its second volume, Edward Mozejko, in the opening essay of the collection, has no qualms about citing a work from 1966, not just as his only scholarly source, but as an "*irreplaceable* source of information on Hispanic modernismo" (15; my emphasis), effectively disregarding forty years of scholarship on the subject.
2. Jameson, however, goes on to make the scandal less so by downgrading modernismo to "clearly enough a synonym for a style elsewhere identified as *symbolism* or *Jugendstill*" (100) and lamenting the inability of Spanish to keep up with his own "precociousness" by opposing modernismo to *vanguardismo* rather than, as in English, high modernism to avant-garde (it remains unclear why the adjective "high" makes such a big difference). Jameson also assumes, mistakenly, that there existed a "Generation of '98" in Spain *before* the advent of Spanish American modernismo.
3. Here, I use "Latin America" only when the discussion pertains to the entire region. Otherwise, I will favor "Spanish America" ("Hispanoamérica" in Spanish) for two reasons: first, because this book deals mostly with Hispanic modernismo, a literary term that has a different meaning in the Portuguese-speaking world; second, because a large part of my argument has to do with transatlantic relations between Spanish America and Spain (but not necessarily Brazil and Portugal or Haiti and France, etc.), so that by using "Latin America" I would run the risk of absorbing and erasing the specificities of the Luso-Brazilian and other transatlantic contexts. Likewise, I have tried to avoid the terms "America" and "American" to refer to the United States (even when it has resulted in cumbersome phrasing) because in the nineteenth century, these terms in the Hispanic context designated Latin America or both North and South America, and because in this period and for the ethnoracial and political reasons I discuss in this book, "America" progressively came to designate only the United States while the South came to be known as "Latin America." I have also tried to avoid using "North America" to refer to the United States, to prevent conflating that country with Canada, which in this period was still a colony of Britain. Finally,

"the Americas" designates the entire American continent (as it is usually considered in the Spanish-speaking world) or continents (as they are usually considered in the English-speaking world).

4. Spanish modernismo occupies a strange critical position that is, in many ways, a product of its history. Although born out of Spanish American modernismo and, thus, part of a larger Hispanic phenomenon, Spanish modernismo has been studied largely within the European context and as part of European literature, even when the other European critical traditions have consistently ignored or downplay its existence. For instance, Bradbury and McFarlane's classic *Modernism: A Guide to European Literature, 1890–1930*—which, despite its title, includes the United States—mentions a few Spanish writers, even if briefly, but no Spanish American writer. Thus, Jiménez, Unamuno, and García Lorca are included, but not Rubén Darío, who in many ways made the writing of the other three possible.
5. I use "literary authority" and "cultural authority" interchangeably throughout this book because, for all intents and purposes, they were synonymous at the time. This is so because of the centrality of literature and language to the concept of national (and international) cultural production in the nineteenth century, and more specifically because of their centrality in the formulation of national identities. Literature and language were thought to be the expression of a people in a much more forceful and clear way than were any other arts. Nonetheless, a study of the state of transatlantic relations in the artistic and other cultural fields is also necessary and would complement the analysis I present in this book.
6. "Francophiles" (*afrancesados*) and "patriots" was a division generated by the Napoleonic invasion of the Iberian Peninsula. Although the word *afrancesado* predates the invasion, it was during the war that it became an entirely pejorative term to denote those who had supported the Napoleonic court or those who simply had advocated the need for reform. In Spain, after Ferdinand VII returned to power, many intellectuals considered *afrancesados* were persecuted and went into exile.
7. Although things would, of course, change drastically, political independence for the United States did not mean immediate economic independence: still in 1820 a Speaker of the British House of Representatives could claim that the United States were "independent colonies of England," that is, "politically free . . . [but] commercially slaves" (qtd. in Marshall, introduction 23).
8. I am circumscribing my discussion here to the Hispanic context, but of course the first Latin American revolution took place in Haiti in 1791, not even two full years after the French. Hobsbawm seems to grant no importance to this revolution, which, however, had a significant impact not only on other African American liberation movements (Gilroy, *Black* 17), but also on the attitudes of white creoles toward independence and slavery. On another level, the Haitian Revolution is also linked to the beginnings of U.S. expansionism, as the defeat of France in Haiti played a part in Napoleon's decision to agree to the Louisiana Purchase.
9. In order to avoid the cumbersome use of quotes every time the word comes up, I want to clarify that I will be referring to the term "race" throughout this book in the way it was used in the nineteenth and first half of the twentieth centuries, that is, as

a conflation of ethnocultural elements (hence Anglo-Saxon, Spanish, Latin "races"). Although today we know the category of race to be a social and ideological construct of extraordinary importance in social and political life but considered irrelevant, for the most part, in biological terms, that was, of course, not the case in the nineteenth century when scientific discourse developed an entire justificatory system for racial inequalities and social Darwinism was the order of the day. In this book, I am less interested in the actual construction of racial categories at the time (as there is already an extensive and rich bibliography on the subject) than in how their use became central in matters of national and transnational identities and power struggles across the Atlantic.

10. In his theorization of the "Hispanic Atlantic," Joseba Gabilondo has similarly critiqued Homi Bhabha's definition of the postcolonial: "Bhabha does not elaborate the geopolitical and thus historical particularism of his theory: the Indian postcolonial experience. When he universalizes the postcolonial condition of any non-Western society through general rhetorical tropes as 'the other question' or 'third space,' he ends up, by default, universalizing Western modernity" (introduction 97). Gabilondo, however, gets caught in the semantic trap of the term "Western." What Bhabha universalizes is not "Western" but rather the particulars of British modernities and colonialisms.

11. I do not mean to say that there has been any conscious effort on the part of postcolonial studies to exclude Latin America. Paraphrasing what Spivak says about Sartre, postcolonial theorists' "personal and political good faith cannot be doubted" (171).

12. As Walter Mignolo notes, the meaning of modernity remains geopolitically divided and disputed: "From the European perspective, modernity refers to a period in world history that has been traced back either to the European Renaissance and the 'discovery' of America (this view is common among scholars from the South of Europe, Italy, Spain, and Portugal), or to the European Enlightenment (this view is held by scholars and intellectuals and assumed by the media in Anglo-Saxon countries—England, Germany, and Holland—and one Latin country, France)" (*Idea* 5). The concept of modernity in southern European and Latin American circles has seen, however, an increased tendency toward the post-Enlightenment definition.

13. On the role of the Spanish Empire in the construction of the British Empire and its imaginary, see also Armitage (8–9). Unless otherwise noted, ellipsis dots in quotations have been added by me to indicate an omission from the original quote.

CHAPTER 1

1. All translations are mine unless otherwise noted.

2. Modernismo is one of the most studied areas of Hispanic literature and, after years of scholarship mostly centered on issues of form and style (of undeniable importance), the last few decades have witnessed the publication of some groundbreaking studies that have largely changed and improved our understanding of the movement, the period, or Spanish American literary modernity in general. Gerard Aching,

Aníbal González Pérez, Rafael Gutiérrez Girardot, Noé Jitrik, Cathy Jrade, Graciela Montaldo, Octavio Paz, Françoise Perus, Ángel Rama, Julio Ramos, and Susana Rotker are among the most notable. See also Cardwell and McGuirk's collective volume and Orringer's edited issue of the *Bulletin of Spanish Studies.*

3. Rafael Gutiérrez Girardot's *Modernismo* (1983) stands out as an exception, as he reads the movement within the general changes undergone by modern art in Western societies. There is a still a very strong conviction in his work that modernismo meant the "europeization" (i.e., "universalization") of Hispanic literature, to be sure (his explicit links to Jiménez and Onís's view of modernismo may also be his biggest liability; for more on this see Chapter 3). However, although Girardot's critique of dependency theories is at times quite unfair, his sense that too strong an emphasis on simple models of center/periphery could impoverish the understanding of modernismo while ignoring the contradictions of the metropolitan center is commendable. More recently, Cathy Jrade's *Modernismo, Modernity, and the Development of Spanish American Literature* is exceptional in a different but related way. Although she seems to accept the common critical opposition between a Spanish American imperfect modernization and a homogeneously perfect European one, she finds it irrelevant for the study of modernismo, for "regardless of the extent to which Spanish American countries have diverged from the Anglo-European route to development or to which they continue to exhibit a 'Garciamarquesian' fusion of premodern, modern and postmodern influences, [modernista writers] believed that they were confronting, in a noble struggle, the most acute issues of modern life" (2). In a field that often seems stuck in formulating variations of the "modernism without modernization" conundrum, this is indeed a salutary move. Yet, her otherwise excellent study relies heavily on the European influence model, reproducing at times the view of Spanish America as delayed receptor of Europe's historical and cultural agency.

4. I owe the term "myths of modernity" to the formulations of both Enrique Dussel (a self-narrative originated in Europe) and Carlos Alonso (the perception that modernity/modernization resides in Europe), which are two sides of the same coin. Both meanings are included in my usage. To this I add a third meaning: the idea of Anglo European modernization as a homogenous process in the nineteenth century, an idea that tends to be the point of departure of most studies on "peripheral" modernities and modernisms and that is usually implied in the phrase "Western modernity/modernization."

5. See Dussel (*Invention* 63–72) for a discussion of "modernity" and "development" in Ginés de Sepúlveda's arguments in favor of the conquest and in the first critique of modernity carried out by Bartolomé de las Casas, both in the sixteenth century. See also Patricia Seed for a genealogy of the word "modern" as signifying a break from the past. Seed shows us not only how the use of the term predates the eighteenth century, but also how it moved from Renaissance Italy and Spain northward to France and northern Europe.

6. According to Habermas, modernization theory decontextualized modernity in renaming it from its historically grounded "European" context and turned it into a culturally/historically neutral model (*Philosophical Discourse* 2). For a related discus-

sion of cultural versus acultural understandings of modernity, see Taylor, and for a discussion of Taylor in the context of Latin America, see Moreiras (3–4).

7. For the sake of clarity and to avoid the cumbersome use of "first stage" and "second stage," throughout this book I use "nineteenth-century modernity" or "modernization" to refer to the second (stage of) modernity.

8. Shortly before Paz, Ángel Rama had already offered in his *Rubén Darío y el modernismo* (1970) a very influential study of modernismo and the turn-of-the-century in Spanish America. Rama's, however, was not a study of modernity per se as much as a reflection on the work of Rubén Darío and the constitution of modernismo in the context of developing global economic forces that placed Latin America in a neocolonial peripheral position. Rama assigned a more active role to the modernista reception of European literary trends than previous formalist critics had done (even more than Paz himself), understanding it, rather than as a copy, as an example close to transculturation, a concept coined by Cuban ethnographer Fernando Ortiz that Rama would develop later in other studies, most notably in his *Transculturación narrativa en América Latina* (Narrative Transculturation in Latin America).

9. In coining the concept "modernism of underdevelopment," Berman, like Paz before him with regard to Spanish America, differentiates between the "real" experiences of Baudelaire (and French, German, British, and U.S. modernism) and the "fantasy," "dream," or "mirage" that allegedly defines the experience of modernity for Dostoyevsky. Without much of an explanation, Berman extends this idea beyond the specifics of Russia, turning it into an anachronistic model: "Russia wrestled with all the issues that African, Asian and Latin American peoples and nations would confront *at a later date*. Thus we can see nineteenth-century Russia as an archetype of the emerging twentieth-century Third World" (175; my emphasis).

10. While for Ramos, as we will see in Chapter 2, an uneven modernization generates a heterogeneous literary discourse, for Alonso an inconsistent modernization generates a cultural discourse marked by "rhetorical incongruity" (*Burden* 4).

11. One such implication would be that the "narrative of futurity" on which Spanish America's independence was built and upon which Alonso builds his own argument might prove to be irrelevant, since such a narrative was not at work (or at least not in the way Alonso describes it) in Spain.

12. See also Torrecilla's *España exótica*.

13. For instance, Iarocci favors Larra's Madrid over Baudelaire's Paris, for it "speaks to the question of modernity in a way that Baudelerian *flanerie* and its subsequent theorization have tended—perhaps too easily—to overlook" (177). There is a certain romanticization of the other in this kind of critical gesture. In analyzing the so-called modernism of underdevelopment, Berman does something similar regarding Russia: "But the bizarre reality from which this modernism grows, and the unbearable pressures under which it moves and lives—social and political pressures as well as spiritual ones—infuse it with a desperate incandescence that Western modernism, so much more at home in its world, can rarely hope to match" (232).

14. In his groundbreaking study *How to Write the History of the New World*, historian Jorge Cañizares-Esguerra makes this point quite clearly and forcefully: "It is my con-

tention that the term 'West' in 'America' . . . works its magic through negation, policing the boundaries of what is appropriate for others to study. These boundaries have also, so to speak, rendered many academics in the United States intellectually 'colorblind': . . . these academics dismiss those pursuits that blur our sharp mental cultural geographies as either improperly Latin Americanist or not sufficiently Europeanist. . . . [In the United States] I have learned that the public expects from historians of [Latin America] cautionary tales of revolutionary violence and, if socially conscious, stories of cunning peasants resisting treacherous oligarchs. I am a storyteller of a different kind, who believes that there ought to be other tales for the public to consume" (11).

15. An alternate effect has been to ignore modernismo altogether. It is notable that some of the most groundbreaking studies on nineteenth- and twentieth-century Latin American literature that have tackled the issue of modernity in one way or another have left modernismo unaddressed. That is the case, for instance, with Doris Sommer's *Foundational Fictions*, Roberto González-Echeverría's *Myth and Archive*, Mary Louise Pratt's *Imperial Eyes*, and Alonso's own *The Burden of Modernity*.
16. See Alan Pitt for a study of the important place that England and the United States had in the French political imaginary in the nineteenth century—"England and America have served as important symbols in French thought since the early eighteenth century. There came a moment, however, between 1870 and 1914, when America and the collective term 'Anglo-Saxon' came to dislodge the place previously occupied by England alone in French thought. The scale of the impact, even if it was to some extent based upon illusory assumptions, of England and America in French political debate is such that it seems appropriate to speak of it as a prominent feature of French political mythology" (151).
17. Perhaps the only other instance is that which inaugurated modernity itself: the conquest and colonization of the Americas and the intellectual debates these generated in the sixteenth century.
18. "The number of entities treated as sovereign states anywhere in the world was rather modest. . . . Outside the Americas, which contained the largest collection of republics on the globe, virtually all of these were monarchies" (Hobsbawm, *Empire* 23).
19. "Constitutionally the German empire [1871–1918] was far from being a liberal state" (Joll 4). In Italy, on the other hand, "although Italian liberals had realized one of their great ideals with the achievement of unity, the Republicans were disappointed with the maintenance of the monarchy, and parliamentary life, based as it was on a franchise which, even after the reform of 1882, included only 2,000,000 out of some 30,000,000 citizens, soon became a struggle for power and personal advantage in which it was hard for even the most high-minded to maintain their principles" (8). On Italy, see also Davis.
20. According to Pierre Rosanvallon, Bonapartism "would remain a recurring frame of reference, reincarnated or reappropriated in various shapes and sizes, from democratic Caesarism in the Second Empire to liberal Caesarism in the Fifth Republic" (697). The way Rosanvallon characterizes French democracy does not seem too

unlike the way other democracies have been described, both in Europe (Spain, for instance) and Latin America, that is, "simultaneously precocious and delayed. Unlike English gradualism, in which the progress of liberty and democracy can be analyzed as cumulative and sedimentary, French history seems to be divided between new beginnings, stutters, and generous, utopian dreams" (698).

21. Regarding Britain, the British parliamentary system included the House of Lords, which, according to James Joll, "became a major political issue in the first years of the twentieth century, [since] the existence of a chamber composed of members of a hereditary aristocracy seemed a direct challenge to the principles of liberalism and of a constitution based on universal suffrage" (117). Indeed, it was not until 1999 that the hereditary peer system in Parliament was finally ended. Still today, however, lords are not elected and serve for their lifetime. Another way in which the House of Lords does not seem to quite live up to standard understandings of "modern" political systems (and its alleged separation of church and state) is the existence of twenty-six lords spiritual, that is, twenty-six senior bishops and archbishops of the Church of England who are also life members of the House of Lords (the queen herself being head of the church and of the state). However much the House's powers may have been curtailed in the last two centuries, this is not a symbolic institution, as the monarchy arguably is, but an active component of the British political and judicial systems.

22. Chasteen offers a similar assessment: "By century's end, liberalism served, in one form or another, as the official ideology of every Latin American country. A powerful consensus reigned among the region's ruling classes, seconded by its urban middle classes" (174).

23. On the participation of American delegates in Cadiz, see Astuto, Rodríguez, and Rieu-Millán.

24. The impact that the Spanish American revolutions had on the thought and politics of Europe and elsewhere deserves further study. It is striking that despite establishing a connection between the wars of independence on both sides of the Atlantic, Spanish America remains mostly absent from Álvarez Junco's revisionary history of nineteenth-century Spain. For instance, on the significance of May 2, 1808, in Spain (the beginning of the uprising against the French in Madrid), his immediate points of reference are not, as one might expect, the Mexican "grito de dolores" [the cry of Dolores] or the May Revolution in the River Plate. Instead, the Spanish historian goes north: "El Dos de Mayo español equivalía, pues, al Cuatro de Julio norteamericano, al Catorce de Julio francés, o a cualquier otra de las fechas fundacionales de la nación" (32). [The Spanish May Second, then, was the equivalent of the North American Fourth of July, the French Fourteen of July, or any of the other foundational dates of nation.] See Gabilondo ("Historical") and Schmidt-Nowara for discussions of the place (or rather lack thereof) of Latin America in Spanish historiography of the nineteenth and twentieth centuries.

25. Arno Mayer, in *The Persistence of the Old Regime*, states that until 1914, the aristocracy rather than the bourgeoisie was the dominant force in European society. See

also Perry Anderson's classic essay "Modernity and Revolution" on the relationship between the continuities of the Old Regime and the development of modernism in Europe.

26. Guardino also notes: "Our knowledge of early-nineteenth-century Mexican politics has advanced in recent years. Nevertheless, most studies continue to leave out the role of the working classes, both urban and rural, in political struggles. Sometimes this exclusion is implicit; other times, authors explicitly discount the possibility that lower-class actors participated in or had any effect on political conflict. . . . The empirical record does not justify this confidence in the ability of Mexico's elite to contain political conflict and to exclude large sectors of the population from politics" (6).
27. The factors that led to such dramatic urban growth are those typically associated with modernization: "population growth and an acceleration in the pace of urbanization; the more effective integration of the Latin American economies into the world economy as primary producers; the beginning of industrial growth in some areas; improved transportation and public services; national political integration and administrative centralization; increased social differentiation; and, not least, the gradual move of elite groups away from their traditional locus near the main plaza towards outlying suburbs" (Scobie 237).
28. Even sleepy towns became urban cities overnight, as was the case for Torrejón, México, whose population soared from only a few hundred inhabitants in the 1870s to close to fifty thousand at the turn of the century (Scobie 240).
29. The case of France is particularly relevant not only because of its prestige in the nineteenth century, but also because for most scholars of modernismo France embodies the epitome of the modern metropolitan center, against which Spanish America's nineteenth-century modernity is hopelessly uneven or flawed. It is not without irony that a similar debate about France's own lack of modernization and its alleged "backwardness" (what Crouzet calls "the 'retardation/stagnation' thesis" [215]) has been under way for decades in French historiography. Not surprisingly, in the context of this book, British and U.S. scholars were largely responsible for setting the tone of the debate: "The problem of French 'backwardness' was set—and solved—by foreign scholars. In this context, an eminent Briton . . . launched the 'stagnationist' thesis. The leading idea is simple: 'France never went through an industrial revolution. There was a gradual transformation,' but it was slow and incomplete" (Crouzet 216). And soon after, U.S. scholars "could not but be struck by the contrast between the wealth of America and the poverty, squalor, and decrepitude which prevailed in France" (217). It is difficult to miss the similarities in the way Latin American and Spanish histories have been written. See Crouzet as well for an account of how much the understanding of nineteenth-century France has been mediated by the degree of France's modernization at the time historians set out to study the past.
30. Moreover, the social and cultural realities were quite similar for a large number of nineteenth-century Europeans in rural areas, where still at the beginning of the twentieth century "most of the peasants of Europe, in spite of the spread of compulsory education, the construction of railways and the invention of the bicycle, still accepted without question the beliefs of their Church and the stability of the existing social

order unless, as happened in Spain in 1892 and 1903, in Sicily in 1893 and in Russia in 1905, economic conditions became so intolerable that the peasants burst out in a largely undirected wave of revolt" (Joll 164). Primarily agricultural, Spain's problems with land distribution have affected much of its contemporary history and surfaced not only in the large estates of the South, run as in Italy by absentee *terratenientes*, but also in the small northern *minifundios*, where nineteenth-century peasants "seemed to foreigners still to live a life of Homeric simplicity; at the western extreme of the northern coast, the Galician peasant scratching a poor existence out of his handkerchief plot reminded English visitors of Irish wretchedness" (Carr 16). It is worth noting here the importance of the foreign gaze in forging the perception of other regions as nonmodern, backward, and Homericly prehistoric. Although Carr does not dwell on it, the effect of the English gaze is double, uniting the Spanish and Irish cases as the "wretched" of European modernity. This is precisely the kind of gaze imposed on Latin America.

31. According to Shubert: "Lines were built according to the interests of the foreign capitalists who controlled the companies, not according to the needs of the Spanish economy. Madrid was the hub of the network, with lines radiating outwards. This pattern 'did not correspond to the traditional channels of commerce,' nor did it facilitate the economic integration of the various regions of the country so they could feed off each other's growth. Nowhere was this truer than in Asturias. Although it was only 200 kilometres from the principal market, the foundries of Vizcaya, the province's coal was consistently undersold by imports from Wales, in large part because of the unreliability and high costs of rail transport" (18).
32. What Jameson calls modernity is what I have been calling nineteenth-century modernity or modernization and what Dussel calls the second (stage of) modernity.
33. Arguably, that was not the case in Britain either, since many in the nineteenth century (and later) saw the United States as the epitome of the modern, while, as we will see in Chapter 4, many in the United States saw Britain as still tied to tradition.
34. The notion that the separation of church and state meant the secularization of the "modern" world is arguably one of the most pervasive myths of nineteenth-century modernity if it is taken to mean, as it usually is, that religion has no place in political life. Hegel rewrote history to a large extent to justify the superiority of the countries of the Reformation over the Catholic countries. In fact, in *The Philosophy of History*, Hegel wonders why the Reformation never took hold in southern Europe and, ironically, finds the main explanation in the Catholic tradition of separation of church and state, which he considered one of the *problems* of Catholic countries (from which he barely saves France): "This is the leading feature in the character of these nations—the separation of the religious from the secular interest, i.e., from the special interest of the individuality; . . . Catholicism does not claim the essential direction of the Secular; religion remains an indifferent matter on the one side, while the other side of life is dissociated from it, and occupies a sphere exclusively its own" (421–22). In contrast, "the development and advance of Spirit from the time of Reformation onwards consist in this, that Spirit . . . now takes it up and follows it out in building up the edifice of secular relations. . . . It is now perceived that Morality and Justice in the

State are also divine and commanded by God, and that in point of substance there is nothing higher or more sacred" (422). Thus, for Hegel, the (Protestant) state is not separate from religion, but always already imbued by it.

35. Dussel also understands that when Hegel explains that America is the land of the future, he means that "Latin America . . . remains outside world history," which although technically true, since the future is not part of history, is not so entirely. First, Hegel refers to "America"—that is, North and South, not only to "Latin America." As a matter of fact, Hegel's whole description of the Americas is but the projection of the division between superior Protestants and inferior Catholics in Europe. Every possible cliché about each is present in his brief account of the new American republics (whose echoes can still be heard in Paz, Berman, Alonso, Mignolo, and others). Second, in such a teleological conception of world history as Hegel's, it is quite clear that America as the land of the future *will* have a central role to play and cannot possibly be equated, as Dussel assumes, with Hegel's view of Africa, which is entirely removed from the past, the present, *and* the future. However—and here Dussel may have a point, albeit indirectly, to the extent that Latin America is related to Catholic Europe—it is quite clear that for Hegel the "future" will belong to North America; he falls short of spelling this out when he speculates that the future may be resolved in a "contest between North and South America" (*Philosophy* 86). This is a significant point because it shows the extent to which in Hegel's mind the matter of modernity was conceived as a fight between North and South, Anglo-Germanic and Latin, Protestant and Catholic, that is, modern versus nonmodern.

36. Mignolo, in fact, presents a vision of modernization that embodies the myth of European modernity in terms quite similar to those used by Paz: "Republicanism and liberalism, in Europe, emerged as bourgeois projects against the monarchy and a despotic form of government; they were also against the Christian church, which was curtailing the sovereignty of the individual; and finally they were against monarchic control of the mercantile economy, which was holding back the benefits that free trade was promising to the emerging social-economic class, the bourgeoisie. None of these conditions obtained in the ex-Spanish and ex-Portuguese colonies" (*Idea* 66).

37. It is not without a measure of irony, and even poetic justice, that the empire so defended by Ginés de Sepúlveda's arguments against the Indians in the Valladolid Debates of the sixteenth century became itself the object of a similar operation of symbolic violence and exclusion in the nineteenth. This should not be surprising, though, since many of the arguments employed in the nineteenth century as proof of Spanish "barbarity" were direct reworkings from the Black Legend that emanated from those very debates between Sepúlveda and Las Casas.

38. President Benito Juárez remained active in exile and eventually succeeded in expelling French troops from Mexico, executing Emperor Maximilian, and regaining his presidency.

39. From the work by such intellectuals as Montesquieu and Hegel to the highly influential theories of Max Weber on capitalism, Protestantism, and modernity, there is but one step. On the "orientalization" of southern Europe in the eighteenth century,

see also Dainotto and Iarocci. Conversely, on the perception of northern Europe by southern Europeans, see Stadius.

40. On the Enlightenment and the Hispanic tradition, see the recent works by Francisco Sánchez Blanco and Jesús Pérez Magallón for Spain, and Ruth Hill and Jorge Cañizares-Esguerra for a broader transatlantic scope. At the other end of the spectrum, see Eduardo Subirats' classic *La ilustración insuficiente*. Subirats, one of the most important, and in many ways exceptional, contemporary Spanish thinkers and one of the few to seriously engage in transatlantic study, interprets not only the Hispanic Enlightenment, but the entire history of Spain and Spanish America since 1492 as a confirmation, rather than a questioning, of the Black Legend.
41. Lily Litvak's seminal study *Latinos y anglosajones: Orígenes de una polémica* remains an obligatory point of reference for understanding how central was the debate over "Latin" versus "Anglo" in Spain and southern Europe. See Pitt for the particulars of France and McGuinness for the case of Latin America.
42. On the romanticization of Spain and its exclusion from "modern Europe," see Iarocci.
43. Martí's "Nuestra América" (Our America) is a good example of this tension between the outside and the inside, and of the repercussions that the North-South racial divide had for internal racial relations in Latin America. For Martí there is a continuum between the "disdain" of the northern neighbor for Latin Americans and that of the internal "letrados artificiales" ["artificial men of letters"], who "se avergüenzan, porque lleva delantal indio, de la madre que los crió" (12) ["are ashamed of the mother that raised them because she wears an Indian apron" (*Selected* 289)]. Both stances are for Martí part of the same mindframe and racial discourse, which ultimately led him to insist that there were no races and that all people were equal, a position that Óscar Montero has linked to recent postracial theories like those put forth by Gilroy in *Against Race*.
44. As Nancy Stepan has shown, the very concept of race was a battleground between Anglo-Germanic and Latin scientists. In her outstanding book on eugenics, Stepan also makes a powerful critique of the way in which Latin American scientific discourse has been dismissed or, most often, ignored for the same reasons that I have discussed regarding Spanish American nineteenth-century modernity and modernismo: "The historical neglect of eugenics in Latin America is, of course, part of the larger neglect of the history of intellectual and cultural life in an area generally presented as being either out of the mainstream or only dimly reflecting European thought. The European bias of the history of ideas is well known, but it is especially strong in science. Latin America is often ignored altogether or it is treated as a consumer and not as a contributor of ideas, and a fairly passive one at that. The implicit assumption is that intellectual historians of Latin America are studying only an attempt to imitate or reproduce a European activity in an 'alien' or 'unscientific' setting. The intellectual gaze always moves from a center outward, toward a problematic 'periphery.' In this book I argue precisely this point, namely that when we study the history of eugenics in Latin America, as a special kind of social knowledge produced out of, and shaped by, the political, historical, and cultural variables peculiar to the area,

our understanding of the meaning of eugenics in general is altered. The terminology of 'center' and 'periphery' loses much of its analytical force" (3–4).

CHAPTER 2

1. The document, published in 2003 and titled *El espacio cultural latinoamericano: Bases para una política cultural de integración* (The Latin American Cultural Space: Bases for a Cultural Politics of Integration), was coordinated by Manuel Antonio Garretón and underwritten by Jesús Martín-Barbero, Marcelo Cavarozzi, Néstor García Canclini, Guadalupe Ruiz-Giménez, and Rodolfo Stavenhagen.
2. José Eduardo González and Jeff Browitt have both pointed out the relevance of Bourdieu's theory for the study of modernismo.
3. Bourdieu's is a description of empirical events as much as a theoretical model from which to understand the relationship between culture (and in the case of his study of Flaubert, literature) and power that is, in principle, applicable to any other national context (Boschetti 148–49). Yet as Toril Moi reminds us, "in order to produce his remarkable investigation of *L'Education sentimentale*, for example, Bourdieu mobilized a huge team of researchers, and it still took him over ten years to finish *The Rules of Art*" (505). I use some of Bourdieu's central concepts as tools to think about modernismo in a way that may help us better understand its relationship with Spanish American and European cultural production in the larger context of forces and struggles for discursive authority at the turn of the century.
4. Regarding homology between cultural fields in a single nation, Bourdieu writes: "If the innovation that led to the invention of the modern artist and art are only intelligible at the level of all the fields of cultural production together, this is because artists and writers were able to use the lags between the transformations occurring in the literary field and the artistic field to benefit, as in a relay race, from advances carried out at different moments by their respective avant-gardes" (*Rules* 132).
5. There exists among the participants, however, an unspoken consensus on the importance of the field itself and on the importance of playing the game by the rules. Bourdieu calls this tacit agreement the "illusio" (*Rules* 227–31).
6. Bourdieu is mostly concerned with class and does not address factors such as gender and race, which are certainly an important component of the habitus, as they clearly affect socialization. In his study of the French literary field at the turn of the century, he pays attention to "geographical origin" mostly in the context of Paris versus the rest of France. Geographical origin, however, is a central aspect of the habitus of agents in a transnational literary field.
7. As David Swartz explains it: "If the dispositions of habitus are the product of class-specific conditions of primary socialization, the action they generate is not, however, a direct expression of this prior class socialization and the accumulation of specific forms of capital it provides. Rather, action is the product of class dispositions intersecting with the dynamics and structures of particular fields. Practices occur when habitus encounters those competitive arenas called fields, and action reflects the

structure of that encounter. Bourdieu's complete model of practices conceptualizes action as the outcome of a relationship between habitus, capital, and field" (141).

8. Although commonly linked in the Kantian-Weberian tradition to eighteenth-century rationalism, autonomy in Bourdieu's theoretical model should be thought of as a process rather than a state achieved at a given point. Bourdieu himself traces the concept back to the Renaissance. A field can have varying degrees of autonomy at different points and not necessarily in a linear progression, that is, it may be less autonomous in a period following another of a high degree of autonomy, since the field is inserted in the field of power and, as any structure, is always changing. According to Bourdieu, the French literary field had a higher level of autonomy at the end of the nineteenth century than at the time he was writing his study. In the case of Hispanic literature, the argument can be made that the autonomy of art has been an operating concept since the Renaissance and the Baroque. The poetry of Luis de Góngora, especially in works such as "La fábula de Polifemo y Galatea" (The Fable of Polyphemus and Galatea; 1612) and "Soledades" (Solitudes; 1613), is a well-known example of the claim that poetry is subject to its own rules and justifies itself without appealing to external forces. Another interesting example can be found in Mexican Sor Juana Inés de la Cruz's famous "Respuesta a Sor Filotea" (Answer to Sor Filotea; 1691), in which Sor Juana appeals to what we may call with Bourdieu "the rules of art" as she defends her poetry from accusations by the Bishop of Puebla: "pues una herejía contra el arte no la castiga el Santo Oficio, sino los discretos con risa y los críticos con censura," "for a heresy against art is not punished by the Holy Office but rather by wits with their laughter and critics with their censure" (44, 45)]. That is, Sor Juana argued that only other agents in the artistic field, not the Church, should have a say about art itself. Both modernismo and later avant-garde literary movements heralded Sor Juana and, especially, Góngora as forerunners of their artistic autonomous impulse. While this has been well documented in the case of the "Generation of '27" in Spain (whose very name comes from a poetic commemoration of Góngora's death), Góngora already had a prominent place in the modernista imaginary. As we will see in Chapter 4, Díaz Rodríguez gives him a central role in the genealogy of modernist art, and Darío paid homage to him in his poetry collection *Cantos de vida y esperanza* (Songs of Life and Hope). Amado Nervo wrote an influential book on Sor Juana and Gabriela Mistral, a lyrical portrait.

9. If Góngora and Sor Juana could be examples of a pre-Enlightenment impulse for autonomy in the first sense, Spanish playwright Lope de Vega is a paradigmatic example of heteronomy (itself, allegedly a post-Enlightenment phenomena), since he declared in his *Arte nuevo de hacer comedias* (1609; published in English as *New Art of Writing Plays*) that the demands of the public superceded the rules of art. As Lope stated regarding his playwriting: "Escribo por el arte que inventaron / los que el vulgar aplauso pretendieron, / porque, como las paga el vulgo, es justo / hablarle en necio para darle gusto (vv. 45–48). ["I write in accordance with that art which they devised who aspired to the applause of the crowd; for, since the crowd pays for the comedies, it is fitting to talk foolishly to it to satisfy its taste" (*New Art* 24–25)]. Well

before the eighteenth century, in the Spanish literary field Lope de Vega the popular playwright and Góngora the sophisticated poet are polar opposites, as are the two genres of theater and poetry for Bourdieu, inhabiting the two extremes of heteronomy and autonomy, respectively.

10. See Bourdieu 29–73.
11. For Anna Boschetti, autonomy is even more polysemic: "Many researchers, for example, misunderstand the notion of autonomy as they fail to distinguish between its various forms: autonomy as power of defining intellectual and artistic legitimacy does not necessarily coincide with financial independence or with political freedom" (149). These various forms are not fully clear in Bourdieu's work itself, for example, his analysis of the intellectual. For Bourdieu, it was precisely the commercial (market-driven and hence heteronomous) success of Zola, often considered the first "modern" intellectual, that allowed him to claim the autonomy of the literary field as a space of authority from which to intervene in the public sphere and indict the French government during the Dreyfus Affair. Yet, this notion of autonomy is complicated by the fact that Zola's naturalism found its explicit authority—and the authority of literature more generally—outside itself, in scientific discourse. So much for art's self-justification. Bourdieu's dismissal of this issue—claiming that Zola did not quite believe the tenets of the naturalism he created—is not a sufficiently convincing argument (and ultimately irrelevant). It is, thus, quite clear that any concept of the autonomy of the literary field based on a single aspect (sales or lack thereof, the authority of aesthetics, or whatever it may be) is bound to be problematic, since the relationship between the literary and the public spheres has always been (and still is) muddy. Some scholars have challenged the idea that Zola was the first intellectual (see Storm and Kauppi). See Patterson for a study of the complex relationship between literature and politics in the United States in the nineteenth century.
12. Even when Bourdieu deals with the transnational, he does so in terms only of "fields of reception" rather than of production, and is still heavily dependent on national fields. In his essay "The Social Conditions of the International Circulation of Ideas," Bourdieu makes central to international circulation the issue of translations and publishing houses but does not consider the many instances when translation is not necessary, as in the reception of French texts in the rest of the educated West in the nineteenth century, where part of the habitus of most agents in the literary field included knowledge of French, a sign of distinction and of cultural capital. Pascale Casanova has offered a model for thinking of literature transnationally in *World Republic of Letters*, which, although insightful in many respects, is ultimately permeated by a fairly obvious franco/eurocentrism. From a different theoretical framework, Franco Moretti has interpreted literature (especially the novel) as a global system. See Sánchez-Prado's edited volume for a collection of excellent articles on Casanova's and Moretti's models from a Latin American perspective.
13. As Boschetti (149) has noted, Bourdieu does not acknowledge how other national fields and power relations contributed to the situation of the French literary field at the turn of the century.
14. On women writers, nation, and transnationalism, see Pratt ("Mujeres," "Women")

and Masiello. The transnational dimension should also be extended northward to the United States, as Silva-Gruesz has shown in her study *Ambassadors of Culture: The Transamerican Origins of Latino Writing*, and, as we shall see, eastward to Spain in an all-encompassing Hispanic literary field.

15. It is not without irony, then, that British poet Elizabeth Barrett, who in 1846 had told Robert Browning that "since she had read the works of Balzac, she had said farewell to the English novel" (Starkie 19), complained to a friend that "the Italians seem to hang on translations from the French—as we find from the library—not merely of Balzac, but Dumas, your Dumas, and reaching lower—long past De Kock—to the third and fourth rate novelists. What is purely Italian is, as far as we have read, purely dull and conventional. There is no breath nor pulse in the Italian genius" (153). Barrett's double-talk points to the web of discursive practices and power relations that affect cultural production and reception across nations, as well as the formation of stereotypes that accompanies them and that, in turn, affect successive production and reception.
16. See Torrecilla's *La imitación colectiva*.
17. See Brian Nelson, *Naturalism in the European Novel*. See also Montaldo (47–48) on what she calls the "diverse contaminations" that took place, especially with regard to language itself, once the Romantic system broke down as an "aesthetic certainty" (48). She rightly places modernismo and its renovation of the Spanish language in this context.
18. The role of translations in the workings of the transnational literary field is also extremely relevant, as is the dissemination of international writings in literary journals and magazines. See, for instance, Anthony Pym's "Cross-Cultural Networking: Translators in the French-German Network of *petites revues* at the End of the Nineteenth Century." As Pym explains: "A network of small literary periodicals distributed the principles of Paris-based Aestheticism throughout the industrialized world at the end of the nineteenth century. These publications formed clear links across national borders, and those links were often manifested as translations that helped disseminate knowledge and form a sense of artistic belonging. However, the relations within the network could also be actively negative, as various receptive strategies used translations and commentaries to defend national rather than international aesthetics. In periods of political tension between France and Germany, such relations were further complicated by use of a wider intercultural space. From 1871, cross-cultural links in the network significantly drew on intermediaries from Belgium, Holland, Alsace and Switzerland, cultural spaces between the main centers of the French-German network" (1). On the nineteenth-century book trade as necessarily transnational, see Rukavina.
19. Another myth that has haunted the study of Spanish American literature is that of its delay. Mistakenly, I believe, literary criticism tends to repeat that literary trends in Spanish America were always late to arrive and lasted longer, unfortunately perpetuating the general image of dependency and tardiness that seems to beleaguer the continent. A cursory look at the way nineteenth-century aesthetics developed beyond France, however, throws a different light on this inherited apparent truism. While

romanticism may have begun at the end of the eighteenth century in Germany and England, it did not develop in southern Europe until the 1830s, around the same time as in Spanish America. Further, the realism of Chilean Alberto Blest Gana's *Martín Rivas* (1862) is but three years away from what is generally considered the introduction of realism in Britain, George Eliot's *Adam Bede* (1859), and, in fact, precedes by almost a decade the earliest works of one of Europe's most important realists, Spanish writer Benito Pérez Galdós (*La fontana de oro*, 1870). Realism was not introduced in the United States until after its Civil War (1861–1865). Despite putting naturalism into practice since the 1870s, Zola did not actually theorize it until 1880 in *Le roman experimental* (The Experimental Novel) and some of his most renowned and influential texts (such as *Nana* and *Germinal*) are from this decade. It was in the 1880s, then, that Zola's "scientific" approach to literature spread beyond French boundaries and into much of Europe and the Americas, where it would have a lasting impact into the early twentieth century.

20. As a result of the power shift discussed in the previous chapter, the cultural capital of Europe also shifted north, so that Iberian cultural production became peripheral—when not simply erased—in the new modern archive. In Spanish America, however, the Spanish cultural archive was not lost even when for most liberals it lost much of its prestige.
21. See also Paul Giles on the importance of U.S.-Britain relations for understanding U.S. literary culture in the nineteenth and twentieth centuries.
22. Referring to the views of the so-called Lost Generation of the 1920s and 1930s, Malcolm Cowley wrote: "Everywhere, in every department of culture, Europe offered the models to imitate—in painting, composing, philosophy, folk music, folk drinking, the drama, sex, politics, national consciousness—indeed some doubted that [the United States] was even a nation" (qtd. in Lasky 77). Regarding Gertrude Stein and the Lost Generation's relationship with Europe and the silence of scholarship on the subject, see also Casanova 86–87.
23. For readings of the United States in relation to postcoloniality, see also Singh and Schmidt, King, Schueller, Cohn, and Cohn and Smith.
24. A very clear example of how "foreign" agents do matter in national fields can be found in cinema today. The role that the U.S. film industry plays in virtually all other national fields worldwide is well known. The effects are multiple, from governmental attempts at regulating and imposing quotas on U.S. film to protect home productions to (and perhaps more importantly) changes in the conception of film-making and the kind of movies produced. Hollywood, much like Paris a century ago, is the ultimate granter of prestige in film. The U.S. cinematic field today may also be a good analogy to the French literary field at the turn of the century, that is, a field more concerned with itself than with foreign products. Yet, even in such an extreme case of self-reliance as the U.S. film industry, the influence of certain foreign agents (directors, movies, actors) is also notable. On Hollywood and Latin American national cinemas in a transnational context, see Poblete ("New").
25. See Eugenia Roldán Vera's excellent study on the role of foreign books in postindependence Spanish America. As she explains: "Imported books constituted a consider-

able part of the printed objects in circulation in independent Spanish America. Although foreign books had entered the Spanish American territories throughout the colonial period, they began to arrive in large quantities at the beginning of the 1820s" (22).

26. According to Roldán Vera, early in the century many of the imported foreign books were already in Spanish (she analyses, in particular, the important presence of Rudolph Ackermann publishing house in the 1820s), "often thanks to the large number of exiled Spaniards [in Britain and France] that could be employed as translators" (22).

27. On *folletines*, or serial novels, in Spanish America, see also Barros-Lémez, Castro Ibarra, Sarlo, and Wolf and Saccomanno.

28. Although fewer, novels by other Latin American authors were serialized in addition to European and national texts. For instance, *Guatimozín*, by Cuban writer Gertrudis Gómez de Avellaneda, was published in installments in Chile in 1847, only a year after its publication in Spain, where Gómez resided at the time (Moseley 276).

29. In Blest Gana's *Martín Rivas*, both upper-class and lower-middle-class characters like Doña Francisca and Edelmira are avid readers of romantic novels. On the proliferation of serial historical novels after 1850 in Chile, see Cánepa-Hurtado; for both a broader and more in-depth analysis of readership and the circulation and consumption of literature in relation to nation building in nineteenth-century Chile, see Poblete, *Literatura*; and for a history of the book in Chile, see Subercaseaux.

30. For example, in José Martí's *Amistad funesta* (1885), the characters do not read Chateaubriand or European romances, but Isaacs's *María* and other Latin American romances like José Marmol's *Amalia* (193–94).

31. When thinking about literature and the market, we should not forget the important place of popular literature at the most heteronomous pole of the field, often ignored in the canonization and explanation of literary culture but important to the development of the literary field and the avatars of the reading public. For instance, neither the aforementioned library statistics about reading trends nor the anonymous newspaper article lamenting the lack of national authors took into consideration such thriving parts of Argentine literary production as the extremely successful *folletines* of Eduardo Gutiérrez and other "criollista" texts. As Prieto argues, the increasing book bias of the "high culture" over other forms of literary production and distribution at the end of the century has left literary history blind to such important areas of literary production and reception. To landmarks like the works of Gutiérrez, we would need to add another element of popular culture: popular poetry. From the *corridos* in Mexico to the *gauchesca* in the River Plate, often printed in *pliegos sueltos* and always connected to public readings, popular poetry was thriving in the nineteenth century. For a study of the manifestations and importance of print culture and its strong connection to popular literature in Argentina and Uruguay, see Acree.

32. Ramos's assertion that modernistas were the first to hold a degree of specifically aesthetic authority is questionable, for, as Alonso has rightly pointed out, by focusing on Bello and Sarmiento, Ramos's argument "necessarily pays little attention to the many significant works from the first half of the nineteenth century—especially but

not limited to poetry—in which there is an evident and even defiant literary intention" (*Burden* 45). There is indeed a certain amount of apriorism in Ramos's selection of texts: "Si no hemos reducido la lectura a materiales más homogéneamente literarios, es porque pensamos, precisamente, que la categoría de la literatura ha sido problemática en América Latina" (15). ["If this study is not restricted to the reading of more homogeneously literary materials, it is precisely because the category of literature has continued to be a problematic one in Latin America" (xliv).] Thus, his selection of texts seems to be predetermined by that which his study is supposed to prove, the heterogeneity of Latin American literature.

33. I quote from John D. Blanco's translation, to which the page numbers refer, but in some cases, as here, I have altered his translation to reflect more closely the wording of the original. In the case of this quote, for instance, Blanco translates the active "habría que insistir" (which clearly implies a conscious critical will to read Spanish American literature a certain way) as the passive "one is confronted" (which assumes a larger degree of objectivity: Spanish American literature *is* that way and the critic must simply explain why). Similarly, Blanco translates "extrañeza" (strangeness) as "particularity," a much more neutral term.
34. As mentioned, for Ramos, this situation distinguishes modernista writers from earlier writers like Bello and Sarmiento, in whose work literature allegedly served a state function. For him, modernismo was the first instance in Spanish America where the "will to autonomy" was manifested. Following this line of thought, Ramos offers a convincing critique of Ángel Rama's influential transhistorical category of the *letrado* (man of letters) in his classic *La ciudad letrada* (The Lettered City).
35. See Unzueta for the case of Bolivia, and Poblete (*Literatura*) on readership in Chile.
36. On periodicals published abroad, see Silva-Gruesz, Pineda Franco, and Mejías-López ("Conocer"). Such was the readership in Spanish America and the importance of its periodicals at the end of the nineteenth century that even writers from Spain sought to publish there and became paid contributors. According to Venezuelan novelist Manuel Díaz Rodríguez, Spanish novelist Emilia Pardo Bazán said that were it not for Spanish American readers, writers and editors in Spain would starve (110).
37. On Gutiérrez's novels and their readership, see also Dubatti and Laera.
38. It is important to note that 1000 print-copies was certainly not a low number by 1830s standards. Some examples from Europe and the United States may help place Echeverría in perspective. William Wordsworth, who published *The Excursion* in 1814, "had to wait more than ten years before [its] cumulative sales reached a 1,000, made up of two, highly priced editions of 500 copies in which Wordsworth took an equity share" (St Clair 375). Walt Whitman, a journalist for much of his life, had to pay for the first two editions of his *Leaves of Grass* (1855) himself before he managed to have a third edition five years later—with a print-run of 1000 copies—done by a Boston publisher that filed for bankruptcy shortly after. Paul Verlaine, who self-published 500 copies of his *Wisdom* in 1881 and only sold 8, took over 20 years for the other 482 copies to sell (it was, in fact, through the success of his newspaper articles that he could find a publisher who took care of his books, past and present). With regards to the novel, the print-run of Stendhal's *Le Rouge et le Noir* (1830), for instance,

was of 750 copies. As Lyons humorously comments: "Stendhal dedicated his work to 'The Happy Few': it is hard to say if his readers were happy but they were certainly few" (3).

39. Copyright laws have existed in Spanish America since the eighteenth century. The *Cortes de Cadiz* further stipulated in 1812 that authors could sell or donate their works as their sole owners, and most Spanish American republics implemented similar laws after independence. See Roldán Vera 17–18.

40. "Free reproduction" refers to international copyrights, a matter of international debate in the nineteenth century. The United States, for instance, refused to pay copyrights to foreign authors, so pirate editions of European works, mostly English works that did not require translation, were very common, prompting numerous complaints by such different authors as Benjamin Disraeli and Charles Dickens. According to Phillip Allingham: "American publishers continued to regard the work of a foreign (i.e., non-resident) author as unprotected 'common' property. Thus, although the Berne Convention greatly simplified the copyright process among European nations [in 1886], numerous unauthorized American re-prints continued to appear until 1891, when the United States finally agreed to discontinue sanctioning literary piracy." Not until 1896 did the U.S. Congress join the international copyright union. The situation in Spanish America was actually not much different. As Roldán Vera explains, there was a notable increase in the importation of foreign books after independence, which "were not protected by any sort of international copyright agreement and thus some of them began to be reprinted in the Spanish American countries themselves as early as the 1820s" (18).

41. In addition to sales, the increasing role of public libraries must also be taken into account when estimating readers (if not buyers). A contemporary description of daily readers in the Biblioteca Municipal Bernardino Rivadavia of Buenos Aires states: "Nada más interesante que el espectáculo que presenta el vastísimo salón de la biblioteca del municipio, en las horas de mayor concurrencia, particularmente en las largas noches de invierno, que es cuando más afluyen los lectores, con sus mesas de lectura ocupadas por personas de todas las edades y de todas las posiciones sociales, desde el modesto jornalero con las manos encallecidas en el rudo trabajo de todos los días, hasta el hombre de fortuna dedicado a gustos literarios, o el joven estudiante sediento de verdad o llena la cabeza con la terrible preocupación del próximo examen; todos con la vista clavada sobre las páginas abiertas de un libro" (qtd. in Prieto 47). [Nothing more worth seeing than the spectacle of the municipal library's vast reading room during the high-traffic hours, especially during the long winter evenings which is when more readers come: all the tables are occupied by people of all ages and social standings, from the modest worker with hands calloused from working hard every day, to the man of fortune dedicated to literary pleasure, or the young student thirsty to learn or terribly worried about the next exam; they all have their eyes fixed on the open pages of a book.]

42. For a further comparison with the situation in the United States, Richard Brodhead explains that before the Civil War, "American literature had the character very largely of an unsupported activity" (467). This was not because there was no reading public

nor because literature did not occupy a place in U.S. social life, but rather because, as in Spanish America, *European literature* occupied that place. According to Brodhead: "The sizable consumption of literary works did not much extend, at first, to native productions. Indigenous institutions of the sort that would eventually be able to produce and support an indigenous American literature—publishing houses, literary magazines, and so on—begin to be founded in the early decades of the nineteenth century, but typically these institutions were, well into the 1840s, geographically limited, economically vulnerable, and short-lived; of all the American writers only one, James Fenimore Cooper, was able to support himself wholly by the proceeds of his literary labors prior to 1850" (467–68). Furthermore, for most of the nineteenth century, as Janice Radway explains, "even if book publishers had learned to rely parasitically on the distribution networks of the few national magazines, which had, after all, relatively constant readerships, it is doubtful that the size of the audience they could thus have reached would have been large enough to make a book-production venture profitable. The mass-market portion of the industry languished, consequently, even throughout the first third of [the twentieth] century. It revived only with the invention of even more efficient presses and with the creation of more extensive and effective distribution networks" (25).

43. In addition to his own novel, Martí was also a translator of foreign novels. His translation of Helen Hunt Jackson's *Ramona* (1887), which he thought could be "tal vez la base de mi independencia" (qtd. in Ramos 89) [perhaps the basis of my independence], had sold two thousand copies in Buenos Aires *before* it was published and saw a second edition the year it appeared that soon sold out (Ramos 89). The year before, in 1886, Martí published his translation of Hugh Conway's *Called Back* (*Misterio*); according to Martí himself, "en La Habana al menos, la gente ha comprado sin tasa" (qtd. in Ramos 89) [in Havana, at least, people have bought it without measure]. Martí had actually considered a career as a translator, first during his exile in Spain, and then in Mexico, where he translated Victor Hugo's *Mes fils* (*Mis hijos*) and published it in installments in 1875, not even a year after it had come out in France. For Martí as translator, see De la Cuesta.

44. It is also significant that Ramos relates the European modern public to the novel, but most of his cited comments about a lack of readers in Spanish America were made by poets about poetry. These complaints should not be surprising, since poetry (with the possible exception of popular poetry) had become a minority genre completely divorced from large audiences. As Bourdieu explains: "Although the break between poetry and the mass readership has been virtually total since the late nineteenth century (it is one of the sectors in which there are still many books published at the author's expense), poetry continues to represent the ideal model of literature for the least cultured consumers" (*Field* 51). This aura of poetry is due, in fact, to its distance from the market.

45. The same connections can be made regarding the intersection of the journalistic, the literary, and the political. As Aníbal González Pérez explains: "Until [the end of the century], particularly in French- and Spanish-speaking countries, journalism had been closely allied with politics" (*Journalism* 88).

46. Without any reference to the southern European tradition, both Ramos and Susana Rotker also assume the United States as the model of "modern" journalism against which modernista texts are considered.
47. Chalaby overemphasizes its "objective" fact-based character and largely ignores the existence of the literary in Anglo-Saxon journalism. So called "Literary journalism" in England and the United States has received increased critical attention in recent years. However, when this genre is studied in the United States, rather than a symptom of underdevelopment, it is considered a "modern" form in its own right, as in John Hartsock's recent study *A History of American Literary Journalism: The Emergence of a Modern Narrative Form*. See also Kerrane and Yagoda's compilation *The Art of Fact*.
48. The case of Carlos Reyles is interesting in this regard because he began his career writing a naturalist novel, *Beba*, but soon changed his literary creed and joined the ranks of the modernistas, becoming one of the most outspoken members. The prologue to his *Academias*, an example of position taking itself, was to have a significant impact in Spain, as I discuss in the next chapter. In Bourdieu's terms, Reyles was able to foresee and capitalize on the ascent of modernismo versus a sinking naturalism.
49. While Darío may be the most emblematic example of how modernista work cannot be conceived of within the limits of national fields, the case of José Martí is particularly significant given his revolutionary cause, Cuban independence. Despite Martí's clear investment in Cuban nationhood (for which he died), the vast majority of his production is far more concerned with Latin America as a cultural and geopolitical space than with the particulars of each nation. His "Nuestra América" (1891) is from its first sentence a wake-up call against nationalist thought. In his prologue to Pérez Bonalde's "Poema al Niágara" in 1882, he had stated: "Otros fueron los tiempos de las vallas alzadas; este es tiempo de las vallas rotas. Ahora los hombres empiezan a andar sin tropiezos por toda la tierra" ("Poema" 144). ["Gone are the days of high fences; now is the time of broken fences. Now men are beginning to walk across the whole earth without stumbling" (*Selected* 45).]
50. For a lucid critique of the idea that modernista cosmopolitanism was a mere replica of the elite's consumption of European products, see Rotker 80–90.
51. See Aching (*Politics* 115–43) for an analysis of the modernista creation of "transnational cultural literacy" through their journals.
52. Northern African cultures are usually included under the "orientalist" rubric; on what has been termed modernista orientalism, see Tinajero and Morán. Sub-Saharan Africa, if notably less present, was not entirely absent from the modernista imaginary.
53. Not all chronicles were reports from abroad, although many of the best known were. Under crónicas falls a miscellaneous and varied body of journalistic writings written both at home and from abroad on an extremely wide range of topics. Although this large body of work remains understudied, it is the subject of some of the best recent works on modernismo: in addition to Ramos's, see González Pérez (*Crónica*) and Rotker. Andrew R. Reynolds's current dissertation work on the crónica offers an insightful reexamination of this heterogeneous genre and promises to be a solid contribution to the field of modernista studies.

54. A possible exception might be Catalan *modernisme*, which developed in Barcelona in the 1890s, were it not for the limitations imposed by a minority language. The movements, however, had much in common. I believe that, in a similar fashion to Spanish American modernismo, Catalan modernisme was largely grounded on a synthesis of regionalism (Catalanism in this case), cosmopolitanism, and modernity. On Catalan modernisme, see also note 2 of Chapter 3.
55. See the early works by Ivan Schulman and Manuel Pedro González on the centrality of these authors and poets (who used to be relegated to the category of "precursors") to the modernista movement.
56. Silva's novel offers an early reference to what Ortega y Gasset would later theorize as a new relationship between modern art and the public in *La deshumanización del arte* (1925). Silva's image of the "lector mesa/piano" also precedes by a few decades the far better known but unfortunately gender-biased formulation of Julio Cortázar regarding *lectores macho* and *lectores hembra* (male and female types of readers).
57. On *De sobremesa*'s innovation and experimentation as well as on its engagement with nineteenth-century modernity, see González Pérez (*Novela*; "Estómago") and Mejías-López ("Perpetuo"). Although Silva's text is unfortunately entirely under the radar of modernism studies (and for a long time of modernismo studies also), *De sobremesa* is without a doubt one of the earliest, most fascinating, and self-conscious examples of modernist/modernista narrative.
58. The *folletines* (romances and mystery novels) written by modernistas such as Gutiérrez Nájera, Martí, and Darío in the 1880s had a similar function. Gutiérrez Nájera published *Por donde se sube al cielo* in installments in 1881, the first modernista novel on record. Martí's *Amistad funesta* (*Lucía Jérez* in the projected book form) was published also in installments in 1885; Darío and Eduardo Poirier cowrote *Emelina* in 1886, which was published first in book form. Beyond the strictly literary, another impact of modernista language on popular culture is its influence on popular music like the tango and the bolero. On the bolero, see Muñoz Hidalgo; on the influence of Rubén Darío on Argentine tango, see Barcia.

CHAPTER 3

1. Valera makes explicit his literary authority and that of his Spanish peers: "Apenas hay libro que se escriba y se publique en América que no nos lo envíe el autor a los que en España nos dedicamos a escribir para el público. Yo, desde hace seis o siete años, recibo muchos de estos libros, pocos de los cuales entran aún en el comercio de librería, aquí desgraciadamente inactivo" (*Obras* 3:213). [There is hardly a book written and published in America that is not sent by the author to those of us who write for the public in Spain. In the last six or seven years, I have received many of these books, few of which actually make it into the book selling business, so inactive here, unfortunately.]
2. I refer to "modernismo" in the sense that the term would take when used to designate the movement in 1888. The term "modernisme" would also be used in Spain by a group of Catalan artists and writers that sought to renovate Catalan expression and

cultural life at the end of the nineteenth century. Although the term "modernisme" had appeared once in 1884 in the journal *L'Avens*, it was used with the general meaning of modern or new: the editors expressed their support for the production in Catalonia "d'una literatura, d'una ciencia y d'un art essencialment modernistas" (qtd. in Marco 24). More specifically, however, these editors were using *modernista* in reference to Naturalism, conceived of as the latest trend in the literary realm. It is not until around 1892 and in the second period of *L'Avens* that modernisme came to clearly denote its current literary and artistic meaning and became solidified in the first Festa Modernista (Modernist Festival) celebrated in Sitges in September 1892. Rubén Darío would eventually become close friends with some of the Catalan modernistas (most notably with Santiago Rusiñol) and would consistently praise the innovation of Catalan artists in his writings in *España contemporánea*. On Catalan modernisme, see Valentí Fiol, Marco, and Cacho Viu. See also Quintian on Rubén Darío's relationship with Catalonia.

3. In his analysis of Valera's review, Robin Fiddian does an excellent job of identifying some of the text's most striking imperial elements but presents them as monolithic and unequivocal, an authoritative ideological block imposed on an unresisting text. As a result, Fiddian fails to see the hesitations and contradictions that make Valera's text both interesting and a prime example of the anxieties driving the imperial nostalgia of Spanish discourse at the time.
4. A clarification may be necessary here. The term "hispanoamericano/a" was sometimes used to denote "pan-Hispanic," that is, belonging to both Spanish America and Spain (a definition that, although obsolete for quite a while, still appears as the main one in the *Spanish Academy Dictionary*). It is quite clear, however, that Valera's meaning in his reference to Darío is the one current nowadays, "Spanish American." There are many other examples of this use in his letters as, for instance, when he explains: "La innegable diferencia entre los yanquis y los hispanoamericanos de cualquier república que sean [reside] en que una América, civilizada ya, procede de ingleses y de españoles otra" (3:243). [The undeniable difference between the yankees (U.S. Americans) and the Spanish Americans from any republic (resides) in that, already civilized, one America comes from the English and the other from the Spanish.]
5. Years later, when modernismo was dominant in Spain, Nájera's comments would resonate in Díaz Rodríguez's forceful critique of Spanish intellectuals (see the last section of this chapter).
6. The term "ultramarino," literally, "from overseas," had a strong connection to commerce and the import, mostly, of foodstuff. Until very recently, "tienda de ultramarinos" meant "grocery store" in Spain. Gutiérrez Nájera employed a similar economic metaphor in the previously cited essay "El cruzamiento en literatura": "Mientras más prosa y poesía alemana, francesa, inglesa, italiana, rusa, norte y sud americana etc., importe la literatura española, más producirá y de más ricos y más cuantiosos productos será su exportación. Parece que reniega la literatura de que yo le aplique estos plebeyos términos de comercio; pero no hallo otros que traduzcan tan bien mi pensamiento" (289–90). [The more German, French, English, Italian, Russian, North and South American, etc., poetry imported by Spanish literature, the richer and

more plentiful the products it will export. It seems that literature resists my use of these plebeian terms of commerce, but I cannot find others that translate my thinking as well.] These market metaphors not only show awareness of the existence of what Bourdieu calls the market of symbolic goods, but also prove how closely related culture, politics, and economics were thought to be in the transnational arena and its power struggles.

7. Clarín, who died that year and had relentlessly attacked Darío, dedicated one of his last reviews to criticizing Darío's *España contemporánea*.

8. For a detailed account of Clarín's animosity toward Darío, see Ibarra. Clarín began writing insulting remarks about Darío in 1890 and would never relent in his violent criticism of the Spanish American poet. In 1899, Clarín was still joking about Darío's "pórtico" for Rueda, who had now himself written a prologue for Gregorio Martínez Sierra's *Diálogos fantásticos* (Fantastic Dialogues), prompting Clarín to make fun of "esos *pórticos, atrios, peristilos y propileos* que escriben para los libros de los mozos principiantes" (qtd. in Ibarra 536) [those porticos, atrium, peristyle and propylaeum that are now written for the books of young writers]. Prologues, prefaces, letters, essays—all are important forms of position taking in Bourdieu's model of the literary field. Behind Clarín's joke, there is the awareness of the unstoppable modernista revolution in Spain, happily announced by Rueda in 1892, gaining momentum and receiving the increasing support of younger generations.

9. Considering that this text appeared only nine months after José Martí published his "Nuestra América" in the pages of the same journal, Valera's remarks also signal the reception of Martí's essay in Spain and may be read in dialogue with it.

10. This lengthy and heated discussion spanned several months and drew in novelists such as Pardo Bazán, Jacinto Octavio Picón, and, of course, Leopoldo Alas (Clarín), as well as literary critics like Gómez de Baquero and Rodó himself. For a more detailed description of the different positions, as well as the specific chronology of events, see Morby, the first scholar to pay attention to this debate, and Meyer-Minnemann, who corrects and completes Morby's account.

11. I do not mean to imply that Reyles's novel should be considered of the same significance as *Azul*. My interest here is neither aesthetic judgment nor the validity of Valera's appraisal of literary value, but rather the way that appraisal was presented and the tensions it reveals.

12. Naturalists like Jacinto Octavio Picón and Emilia Pardo Bazán had to disagree with Valera's classicism but sided with him regarding Reyles as a poser, accusing him, as Pardo Bazán did, of a "falta de discernimiento y sobra de servilismo en imitar a los autores de moda" (qtd. in Morby 132) [lack of discernment and an excess of servilism by imitating fashionable authors]. Clarín, for his part, dismissed Reyles as an "American modernista" and compared him to the "señoritas de pueblo cursis a las modas" (qtd. in Meyer-Minnemann 134) [small-town misses tuned in to fashion].

13. Despite her aesthetic differences with Valera, Pardo Bazán shared both his interest in and imperial view of Spanish American letters: "Las *Cartas americanas* no las juzgaré con la severidad con que suelen serlo, al contrario . . . En ellas existe, no sólo copia de información útil sobre temas y asuntos americanos, poco o nada conocidos aquí, sino

una continua y noble vindicación de España en su papel histórico de descubridora, conquistadora y colonizadora de las que se llamaron *sus* Indias" (qtd. in Hilton 147; ellipses in original). [I will not judge the *American Letters* as harshly as they usually are judged, on the contrary . . . Not only do they provide a lot of useful information on American topics and events that are little known or unknown here, but also a noble and relentless vindication of Spain in its historical role as discoverer, conqueror and colonizer of what used to be called *her* Indies.]

14. Saint Sylvester was pope during the time of Emperor Constantine and the Council of Nicea, where the Nicene Creed originated.
15. As we shall see in the next chapter, to fill the empty vessel of Spain with meaning from across the Atlantic constitutes one of the central strategies of modernismo in the discursive battles of modernity.
16. Unamuno would apologize for all his animosity after Darío's death. For a wonderful anecdote regarding Ramón del Valle-Inclán's intermediary role between Darío and Unamuno in the aftermath of this remark, see García Sabell. Fogelquist's early study on the modernistas in Spain is a mandatory point of reference for the reception of modernismo and especially of Darío in Spain. See also Alazraki, Pike (*Hispanism*), and Salgado.
17. Still, years later, in 1960, poet Luis Cernuda would notoriously say: "Darío, como sus ancestros frente a los españoles, estaba dispuesto a dar el oro nativo a cambio de cualquier baratija" (qtd. in A. Rama, *Rubén Darío* 121). [Darío, like his ancestors before the Spaniards, was willing to trade native gold for a bunch of beads.]
18. Robert Spires has argued that 1902 marks the beginning of modernism (in its English meaning) in Spanish narrative, and Germán Gullón has called 1902 the "miraculous year" of Spanish narrative, noticing that these four Spanish novels represent a transition from realist to modernist aesthetics. What neither critic explicitly says is that this shift was possible only because of the impact of Spanish American modernismo.
19. As late as 1929, Venezuelan Rufino Blanco Fombona would say, referring to the "Generation of '27," that "la influencia de escritores americanos sobre escritores jóvenes de la península es visible. A todos nos lee la generación española que hoy está entre los veinticinco y los cuarenta años" (qtd. in Fogelquist 88) [the influence of American writers on the young writers of the Peninsula is visible. All of us are read by the Spanish generation that is now between twenty-five and forty years old].
20. Although the revolution that modernismo brought about in Hispanic letters and its transformation of the Spanish literary field may be the most groundbreaking instance and, certainly, the most glaring gap in scholarship, the argument can easily be made that the reversal of influence—that is, the "inverted conquest"—carried out by modernismo did not end with it. In 1918, Chilean poet Vicente Huidobro's arrival in Madrid signals the beginning of the avant-garde in Spain, as Spanish poet Rafael Cansino-Assens immediately recognized. Of course, as with modernismo, many in Spain (including Cansino himself) ultimately credited French poets like Guillaume Apollinaire and Pierre Reverdy, contemporaries and friends of Huidobro, rather than fully acknowledging the Chilean himself, who has remained in literary history a

catalyst, a moon to the French sun. The end of the Spanish Civil War saw an exodus of writers and intellectuals to Latin America. In the 1960s the Latin American narrative "boom," largely connected to Spanish publishing houses, reaffirmed the preeminence and centrality of Spanish American literature over that of the Peninsula. Some groundbreaking work has been done recently on the presence of the boom in Spain, which generated debates reminiscent of the ones I have described regarding modernismo. See Mario Santana's *Foreigners in the Homeland*, Adrián Rivera's *Novela española y boom hispanoamericano* (The Spanish Novel and the Spanish American Boom), Alejandro Herrero-Olaizola's *The Censorship Files*, and the volume *La llegada de los bárbaros* (The Arrival of the Barbarians), edited by Joaquín Marco and Jordi Gracia. There is, however, still little scholarship on the unquestionable presence of the Spanish American boom in today's canonical Spanish novelists like Antonio Muñoz Molina, whose narrative production cannot be fully understood without it.

21. See also Thomas Harrington, Joan Ramón Resina, and Sebastiaan Faber, although their studies deal with the broader topic of Hispanism rather than specifically with Spanish national identity. (Harrington and Resina come very close to considering them the same thing.) Spanish America is entirely absent from Harrington's analysis of Spanish nationalism, while Resina ("Whose Hispanism?") refers to Latin America first as an absence (a territorial loss that prompted Hispanism as a compensatory strategy) and then as an accomplice of (163, 172), subject to bribery by (169), and a blind follower of (172) a quite monolithic and ever violent Spanish state. See also his "Hispanism and Its Discontents," from which Spanish America is explicitly excluded. A notable exception is Sebastiaan Faber's work on Spanish exiles, which succeeds in demonstrating the often contradictory and multifaceted character of Hispanism by placing it within a wider context, showing its relevance for both Spaniards and Americans, and paying attention to how the view of many Spanish Republican exiles was affected by their host countries, especially Mexico. See also Escudero for an analysis of how little Spanish official discourse about Latin America has changed between the Franco regime and the subsequent democratic governments, and James Fernández for an insightful analysis of the figure of the *indiano* in Clarín. Fernández was one of the earliest critics to point out the need to study the place of Spanish America in the Spanish national imaginary. On nineteenth- and early twentieth-century Hispanism, see the pioneering studies by Van Aken and Pike. The latter, however, although useful for the wealth of information it contains, is ultimately a book on how fundamentally undemocratic Spaniards and Latin Americans are. As Pike makes quite explicit in his article "Making the Hispanic World Safe from Democracy," the opposition Anglo-Saxon/Hispanic is alive and well in his work. For a wide, more contemporary range of interpretations of Hispanism, see the recent collection *Ideologies of Hispanism*, edited by Mabel Moraña. Finally, it is worth noting that—and wondering why—modernismo is largely absent from most of this scholarship on Hispanism.

22. A related silence over the place and role of Spanish Americans in Spanish national histories has recently been noted by Christopher Schmidt-Nowara in relation to Cuba, Puerto Rico, and the Philippines: "Ironically, while remaining virtually silent

on the nineteenth-century colonies, historians have pondered at length the meanings of decolonization, as 1898 has become an iconic date in Spanish history. In other words, while talking incessantly of the loss of the colonies, historians have generally remained mute about the colonies themselves" (*Conquest* 8). Schmidt-Nowara's excellent study on the rewriting of imperial histories in Spain and its remaining colonies in the nineteenth century is particularly relevant here, for it shows how central empire was to the construction of the Spanish national imaginary (and its relationship with the new empires of northern Europe) before 1898 and how that imaginary was being contested by colonial intellectuals. See also Feros.

23. G. Gullón acknowledges Spanish American modernismo, but its presence is otherwise minimal in his study, where "rubendarianismo" (Ruben Darío–like style) is always presented in a negative light.
24. See Shaw for a good overview of these processes and debates regarding Spanish American fiction. For a good overview of recent critical discussions regarding Spain, see Harrison and Hoyle.
25. I cite Azorín as the main source because, although he was not the first to speak of a "generation" associated with the events surrounding 1898, his essays were the most influential and the basis of all future criticism. I say "loosely based" on Azorín because, when dealing with the topic, literary critics "corrected" or changed Azorín's first formulation in various ways, the most glaring and significant of which being the erasure of Rubén Darío, significantly included originally in the group by Azorín. Before settling on the term "Generation of '98," Azorín called it the "Generation of '96"—interestingly enough, the year of the publication of Darío's *Prosas profanas* and Reyles's *Academias*, as well as that of the polemic that ensued over the modernista novel.
26. See Alfred Coestner's early review of Onis's anthology for a perceptive identification of its Spanish bias. Although praising Onis's work, Coestner shows puzzlement about his selection, the weight given to Jiménez (placed at the same level as Darío), and the notorious absence of poets such as Gutiérrez Nájera in favor of more obscure alleged Spanish "precursors."
27. Admittedly, this denial is not limited to the Peninsula. Many Latin American intellectuals themselves would later reproduce the Generation of '98/modernismo divide, often to the benefit of the former, even when foregrounding the importance of the latter. Even a critic of colonialism like Fernández Retamar, in his otherwise insightful essay on the significance of 1898 and the relationship of both Latin American and Spanish culture to underdevelopment and anti-imperialism ("Modernismo"), concludes by favoring the term "Generation of '98" as more appropriate also for Spanish American modernistas.
28. Rubén Darío is arguably the exception to the rule, the ghost that Spanish literary history could not fully repress and instead soon incorporated into itself. In other words, stripped of origin and company as if his was a one-man operation and not part of a much larger Spanish American enterprise, Darío became part of Spanish literary history as a virtual "Spanish writer," one of the modernista group that also included Valle-Inclán, Juan Ramón Jiménez, Antonio Machado before the latter three moved on to more "serious" writing, namely *esperpento*, pure poetry, and *noventayochismo*,

respectively, thus leaving Darío ultimately alone. It should also be noted, however, that concomitant to the "erasure" of modernismo's impact and implications, there has been consistent praise of Rubén Darío's role (again, mostly alone) in the development of Spanish poetry. From Federico García Lorca to Carlos Bousoño, José Hierro, and Francisco Umbral, Spanish poets have repeatedly paid homage to Darío's groundbreaking role in Spanish poetry. See Acereda and Guevara (62–86).

29. Max Henríquez Ureña would later use the same metaphor, albeit completely neutralized, in his essay "El retorno de los galeones" (The Return of the Ships).
30. For an analysis of Díaz Rodríguez's important essay as a construction and defense of Hispanic modernity, see Chapter 4.
31. In the same essay, Díaz Rodríguez does not forget to mention economic dependency in the form of the "trágica y funesta sangría del emigrante" (142) [tragic and deadly bleeding of emigrants] to América.

CHAPTER 4

1. Jiménez would publish Rodó's letter praising his *Rimas* in the journal *Renacimiento* in 1907, a clear instance of position taking in the field that shows to what extent the reversal of authority was complete: the validation of a Spanish American writer was now a sign of consecration in the Spanish literary field.
2. As with many publications at the time, *La Revista* had originally been linked to commerce. It was founded and owned by Panama-born and New York–based Elías de Losada, businessman and owner of Thurber-Wyland and Co., an import/export company with which the magazine was first associated. Since 1886, the magazine had progressively focused less on commerce and more on culture and literature, turning into a monthly magazine modeled after *Harper's* and the *Atlantic Monthly*. According to Mercedes Caballer, it had nine thousand subscribers in Latin America, with subscriptions at three dollars a year. (Caballer does not provide numbers regarding the United States or Spain, where, as her study shows, the magazine was well known among Spanish writers, many of whom contributed to its pages.) See also the invaluable work done by Vernon Chamberlin and Ivan Schulman in rescuing the magazine from oblivion.
3. See also Marshall, "Britain."
4. The Rhodes scholarship was created based on the notion of Anglo-Saxon superiority and the desire to secure Britain's central place in that racial imaginary. Rhodes, in fact, lamented the independence of the United States and hoped to "recover" it as part of a plan to bring the world under Anglo-Saxon rule. In his first will, written in 1877, he stated: "I contend that we are the finest race in the world and that the more of the world we inhabit the better it is for the human race. Just fancy those parts that are at present inhabited by the most despicable specimens of human beings, what an alteration there would be if they were brought under Anglo-Saxon influence, look again at the extra employment a new country added to our dominions gives. I contend that every acre added to our territory means in the future birth to some more of

the English race who otherwise would not be brought into existence. Why should we not form a secret society with but one object: the furtherance of the British Empire and the bringing of the whole uncivilised world under British rule, for the recovery of the United States, for the making of the Anglo-Saxon race but one Empire. What a dream, but yet it is probable, it is possible" (qtd. in Flint 249–50). The purpose of the society Rhodes envisioned was to train the finest Anglo-Saxon men to reach influential posts, not only of government, but in every area: "The Society should inspire and even own portions of the press for the press rules the mind of the people. The Society should always be searching for members who might, by their position in the world, by their energies or character, forward the object" (251).

5. Anglophobia had been present in the postindependence United States to be sure, but U.S. culture had been largely anglophile for most of the century (see Chapter 2). As Tennenhouse states: "It does not necessarily follow from [political independence] that the colonists renounced their British identity in other respects simply because they rejected British government. Political separation did not in fact cancel out the importance of one's having come to America from Great Britain. Indeed the literary evidence indicates that the newly liberated colonists became if anything more intent on keeping the new homeland as much as possible like the old one in terms of its language, literature, and any number of cultural practices" (2).

6. According to Love, racism in the form of Anglo-Saxon superiority was a more powerful engine *against* U.S. imperialism than in its support. Here, however, I am interested only in showing the extent and pervasiveness of the Anglo racist discourse. See also Beisner.

7. Although Carl Schurz was German, he conceived of his adopted country as Anglo-Saxon. In opposing the annexation of Cuba, Puerto Rico, and the Philippines in the aftermath of the Spanish-American War of 1898, he stated: "And under the influences of their tropical climate they will prove *incapable of becoming assimilated to the Anglo-Saxon*. They would, therefore, remain in the population of this republic a hopelessly heterogeneous element—in some respects more hopeless even than the colored people now living among us. We shall transform the government of the people, for the people, and by the people, for which Abraham Lincoln lived, into a government of one part of the people, the strong, over another part, the weak. Thus the homogeneousness of the people of the republic, so essential to the working of our democratic institutions, will be irretrievably lost; *that our race* troubles, already dangerous, will be infinitely aggravated" (Schurz, *American Imperialism* 9, 11; my emphasis). For him, then, democracy is the realm of the Anglo-Saxon people. In his racial imaginary, Schurz, who served as ambassador to Spain under Lincoln, goes on to establish a parallel between the racial context in the Americas and that of Europe: " 'But we must have coaling stations for our navy!' Well, can we not get as many coaling stations as we need without owning populous countries behind them that would entangle us in dangerous political responsibilities and complications? Must Great Britain own the whole of Spain in order to hold Gibraltar?" (28). The racial divide is also a geographical divide between North and South Atlantic, modern and premodern.

8. At another point in her text, Mansilla notes that Anglo Americans aspired to be more English than the English, while Spanish Americans tried to distance themselves from Spain. For an analysis of Mansilla's travel narrative, see Urraca.
9. The issue of naming has been a symbolic gesture of no small importance since independence in the Americas. If Latin Americans felt they had an equal claim to the name America, for Anglo Americans that claim was a reminder of all that was still not theirs. As Edgar Allan Poe put it: "*We* may legislate as much as we please, and assume for our country whatever name we think right—but to us it will be no name, to any purpose for which a name is needed, unless we can take it away from the regions which employ it at present. South America is "America" and will insist upon remaining so" (qtd. in DeGuzmán 10). In 1885, an editorial in *El Latinoamericano*, a Latin American magazine published in New York, decried a proposal by General Lew Wallace to change the name of the United States of America to simply America. See Mejías-López ("Conocer").
10. Many French intellectuals have perceived the modernization of France since the last third of the nineteenth century as "Americanization" (see Chapter 1). On the growing use of the term "Americanization" in this sense at that time, see also Rydell and Kroes. For the persistence of the term throughout the twentieth century in Europe, especially after World War II, see Kuisel for France, Nolan for Germany, and Armstrong, Fagge, and Lockley for Great Britain. See also Stephan's collected volume *The Americanization of Europe*. In Spanish America, for the reasons discussed regarding the name America, "Americanization" was not used. Instead, Rodó called it "nordomanía" and Díaz Rodríguez "yanquizarse de la tierra." Note the parallel with debates a century later over the relationship between Americanization and globalization.
11. Martí wrote the entire magazine, which was published monthly in New York from July to October 1889. Enrique J. Varona reviewed the first issue on August 2, and Gutiérrez Najera wrote a long and glowing review for Mexico's *El Partido Liberal* in September, stating: "*La Edad de Oro* es muy buena porque enseña fuera de la escuela y lo que no enseñan en la escuela; ¿Dan al niño en la escuela nociones antropológicas y etnográficas e históricas, como las que le da *La Edad de Oro* en 'La historia del hombre contada por sus casas'? Así quisiéramos los hombres que nos enseñaran muchas cosas que no sabemos! ¡Así me ha enseñado *La Edad de Oro* mucho que ignoraba!" (Arias 50–51). [*The Golden Age* is very good because it teaches outside school that which is not taught in school; Do they teach children in school notions of anthropology, ethnography, and history like those taught in *The Golden Age* in pieces like "The History of Mankind Told by Their Houses"? That is how men would like to be taught many things we do not know! That is how *The Golden Age* has taught me much of which I was ignorant!]
12. See Ramos's and Montero's thorough readings of "Coney Island." See also Faber's insightful reading of this and other crónicas by Martí in connection with Rodó's *Ariel* and the ideas of Spanish writers Ángel Ganivet and Joaquín Costa ("Beautiful").
13. All "Coney Island" translations are from Martí's *Selected Writings*, translated by Esther Allen.
14. On Martí and race, see Montero (60–85), Martínez-Echazábal, and Aching, "Against."

15. Classic Greek and Latin cultures had a central place in the Western educational system at the time. Indeed, one of the books that Martí translated for Appleton was a school manual on Greek civilization. Hegel discusses Socrates' demon in the section devoted to ancient Greece in *The Philosophy of History*. See Gutiérrez Grova on Martí and Greek culture.
16. For more on this formulation of desire in modernismo and its representation in Silva's *De sobremesa*, see Mejías-López, "Perpetuo."
17. The text establishes a symbolic connection between the children, who are compared to "mariposas marinas" (127) ["marine butterflies" (91)], and those with a sublime inner demon following the "rebelde mariposa libre" (126) ["free, rebellious butterfly" (92)].
18. In an unfinished letter to Manuel Mercado written the day before his death, Martí said, referring to the United States: "Viví en el monstruo y le conozco las entrañas" (*Obras* 161). [I lived in the monster and I know its entrails.]
19. I return to the importance of language in modernismo in my analysis of Manuel Díaz Rodríguez's *Camino de Perfección* later in this chapter.
20. Although the quoted translation ("barren stretches") is perfectly correct in this context, it loses some of the meaning of the original "soledad" (solitude): loneliness, isolation, lack of human contact, and silence.
21. See Beverley on the concept of "neo-arielismo."
22. Gordon Brotherston (13) cites the notes taken by Rodó on Groussac's 1898 speech on the war. Rubén Darío's essay appeared that same year. This might be yet another instance of Rodó's capitalizing on Darío's position to advance his own, as I mentioned earlier.
23. Fernández Retamar, who famously "corrected" Rodó's choice of symbol in his classic essay on Latin American identity and colonialism, *Calibán* (1971), rightly argues on the contrary that "a pesar de su formación, a pesar de su antijacobinismo, Rodó combate allí el antidemocratismo de Renán y Nietzsche [y] exalta la democracia, los valores morales y la emulación" (33) [despite his education, despite his antijacobinism, Rodó fights in his book Renán's and Nietzsche's antidemocratic positions, [and] exalts democracy, moral values, and emulation]. On the echoes of Rodó's *Ariel* beyond Latin America, see San Román for an interesting (and quite unusual) study on the influence that Rodó's text exerted on British politics.
24. As we saw with the concept of field, Bourdieu's analysis of education, cultural reproduction, and social reproduction is mostly limited to the national, understandable given the central role that education has in state formation and control. On the interconnectedness of post-eighteenth-century notions of culture and the state, see David Lloyd and Paul Thomas. Nonetheless, the argument that cultural reproduction works for social reproduction, that is, to maintain a set of power relations, can certainly be extended to the transnational realm. In this sense, it is illuminating to consider the situation in Spanish America right after independence from Spain: "Apart from religious and political catechisms, the Spanish Americans produced very few textbooks of their own. In the 1820s the dominant tendency was either to translate them or to buy them abroad" (Roldán Vera 37). Roldán studies, in fact, the role

that imported British textbooks had in the formation of national identities in Spanish America. According to Venezky regarding the United States: "The earliest settlers to North America brought with them a variety of English textbooks and continued to import textbooks from England until well into the nineteenth century" (41).

25. In the text, Martí depicts the relation between North and South in gendered sexualized terms (male-female) that evoke rape. Martí was misogynous and prudish well beyond what one might reasonably attribute to the times, but his imaginary of gender and sexuality, far from simple, is full of contradictions. See Ramos, Faber ("Beautiful"), and Montero on the importance of gender in "Nuestra América," "Coney Island," and his work more generally. See also Molloy's classic essays on Martí and Oscar Wilde ("Too Wilde") and Martí and Whitman ("His America") for a discussion of sexuality in his work.

26. In 1899, this fear was expressed in the novel *El problema* (The Problem) by Guatemalan Máximo Soto-Hall. Its culmination takes the form of marriage, like a foundational fiction gone wrong in which at the end the Latin American woman marries the wealthy Anglo American man just as the U.S. annexation of Central America is being signed. At the novel's close and in good modernista fashion, the rejected Latin American Julio charges on his horse, like Don Quixote against the windmills, against the train that carries the newlyweds: "Caballo y caballero, arrojados por la gran mole de hierro, rodaron juntos sobre las bruñidas cintas de los rieles. Se oyó un crujir de huesos, y el ahogado relincho de un caballo, mientras el tren con su cortejo magnífico, arrastrando a una pareja feliz, pulverizaba al último representante de una raza caballeresca y gloriosa" (174). [Knight and horse, thrown out by the great iron mass, rolled around together over the polished lines of the tracks. The crack of bones and the drowned neigh of a horse could be heard while the train, with its magnificent entourage and dragging a happy couple, pulverized the last representative of a knightly and glorious race.]

27. Much better known is the turning of Don Quixote into a national symbol by turn-of-the-century Spanish writers like Unamuno, Azorín, and Ganivet; see Britt-Arredondo's book on the subject. Although Britt-Arredondo does not identify references to Don Quixote in early modernista fiction, he devotes the last chapter of his book to analyzing several rereadings of Cervantes' novel by Spanish American writers and scholars, showing how their progressive ideology stood in sharp contrast to the conservative stance taken by their peninsular counterparts.

28. For a different but intricately related appropriation of Spain, see Nieto-Phillips's excellent study on New Mexico's road to statehood, *The Language of Blood*. On Anglo-Saxon/white ethnicity and the construction of the U.S. national imaginary, see also Guterl, Horsman, Jacobson, and Kaplan.

29. A reflection on Spanish modernity and on the nature of Hispanicness also took place in Spain, of course, where the turn of the century witnessed a proliferation of texts about what was known as "el problema de España." As mentioned, this was one of the defining elements of the so-called Generation of '98. As I have shown, however, the advent of Spanish American modernismo and its removal of literary authority from Spain was one of the most important factors in shaping the way many Spanish intel-

lectuals would rethink Spain and Hispanicness. In addition, Spanish intellectuals were able to find a new language, a new narrative, and to a large extent a new cause thanks to the changes brought about by their Spanish American peers. In her seminal study on the debate over Latin and Anglo races, Lily Litvak explains that "España, al reaccionar contra la supuesta decadencia del mundo latino tomaba mucho en consideración la ayuda que provendría de las jóvenes naciones iberoamericanas" (75) [Spain, reacting against the alleged decadence of the Latin world, would take into much consideration the help coming from the young Iberian-American nations]. See also Faber's excellent essay on Martí's crónicas and the many connections between the ideas of Martí in the 1880s and the regeneracionista ideas of Spanish intellectuals Joaquín Costa and Ángel Ganivet in the 1900s. An in-depth transatlantic study that would consider texts and authors from both sides would be very illuminating in this regard. The last chapter of Britt-Arredondo's *Quixotism* is an important step in this direction.

30. Martí first published the novel in serial form as *Amistad funesta* and later planned an edition in book form under the new title of *Lucía Jerez*. Most modern editions of the novel, including the one cited here, have kept the projected title rather than the published one.
31. There is an unexplained change of name of this character in the novel. Leonor becomes Sol in the third and last chapter. The meaning of Sol is self-explanatory. Leonor is another form of Helen, a name and myth dear to modernistas, which connects the character with aesthetics and Greek culture. In this discussion, I use only the name Sol.
32. The misogyny of the text is also parallel to that of "Coney Island," and the gender-based distinction between Lucía (whose "masculine" attributes are often highlighted by the narrator) and Sol parallel that between the United States and Latin America for Martí, described in terms close to rape in "Nuestra América."
33. The relationship between Juan and his more materialistic friend Pedro is depicted in terms that allude to Quixote and Sancho Panza.
34. Juan is also symbolically related to another important heroic figure in Martí's imaginary of the modern: Bartolomé de las Casas, to whom Martí dedicates an essay in *La Edad de Oro*.
35. The only other U.S. character in the novel is a rich banker, Mr. Floripond, whose daughter Iselda is, significantly, Sol's antagonist at school.
36. A particularly interesting counterpoint to Darío's image of Spain in *Cantos* is his crónica "La España negra" included in *España contemporánea*, in which he presents a critical portrait of the destruction wrought by Spaniards in America.
37. Regarding the term "barbarian": In "Dilucidaciones" (Dilucidations), which serves as prologue to *El canto errante* (The Wandering Song; 1907), Darío insists on his leading role in the imposition of modernismo in Spain "a pesar de mi condición de 'meteco,' echada en cara de cuando en cuando por escritores poco avisados" (693) [despite my condition of "meteco," thrown in my face every so often by dim-witted writers]. "Meteco" is a word of Greek origin that signifies "foreigner, non-Greek," a word thus related to "barbarian."

38. Díaz Rodríguez creates the figure of Don Perfecto, who rejects anything modernista, as a foil to present his ideas in the text. While he certainly functions in this way, Don Perfecto also allows Díaz Rodríguez's essay to simultaneously dismantle common criticisms of modernismo, expose their shortcomings, and rewrite the definition and significance of the movement.
39. This is precisely the stereotype that Díaz Rodríguez is writing against when he entitles the section ironically "Paréntesis modernista o ligero ensayo sobre el modernismo" (54) [Modernist Parenthesis or Light Essay on Modernism] in reference to what he had already noted were condemnatory portrayals of modernismo as superficial and simply concerned with style—"En su estilo [el de Don Perfecto] no caben, como en el de los modernistas, cosas ligeras" (32). [In (Don Perfecto's) style, unlike in that of the modernistas, there is no room for light things.] In fact, this chapter is the only one whose argumentation includes no irony, a tool used time and again in *Camino de perfección* to both critique and dismantle dominant modes of thought. Instead, this section straightforwardly and powerfully lays out a definition of modernism as a revolutionary movement and the most perceptive and accurate epistemological tool available.
40. For Díaz Rodríguez, for instance, nothing in post-Enlightenment romanticism can surpass the prose of sixteenth-century Spanish writer Fray Luis de Granada: "Enfadoso y pedantesco parece y es el *Genio del Cristianismo* de Chateaubriand, cuando se ha platicado con la araña y la abeja y todas las criaturas en el huerto de candores de Fray Luis de Granada" (60). [(Chateaubriand's) *Genius of Christianity* seems, and is, annoying and pedantic when one has spoken with the spider and the bee and all creatures in the garden of candor of Fray Luis de Granada.]
41. Among the modernist writers cited by Díaz Rodríguez in this chapter are Ruskin, Pater, Nietzsche, Baudelaire, Maeterlinck, Verlaine, Rossetti, Ibsen, Tolstoi, D'Annunzio, and Wilde. Among the "large group" (64) of Hispanic modernistas, he highlights Spanish American Darío and Spanish Valle-Inclán.
42. Díaz Rodríguez questions race as a meaningful analytical category. A similar operation can be found in Martí's famous statement at the end of "Nuestra América": "No hay odio de razas, porque no hay razas. El alma emana, igual y eterna, de los cuerpos diversos en forma y en color. Peca contra la humanidad el que fomente y propague la oposición y el odio de las razas" ("Nuestra América" 15). ["There is no racial hatred, because there are no races. The soul, equal and eternal, emanates from bodies that are diverse in form and color. Anyone who promotes and disseminates opposition or hatred among races is committing a sin against humanity" (*Selected* 295–96).] Martí is not proposing that there are not different races, as is apparent elsewhere in the same essay, but advocating color blindness. Montero has suggested that Martí proposed what Paul Gilroy has recently termed "strategic universalism" (61).
43. In this sense, Díaz Rodríguez's text anticipates later twentieth-century critiques from both outside and within social sciences. Bourdieu, himself a sociologist, believed that "social sciences can never achieve the degree of autonomy that natural sciences like biology and physics enjoy because 'internal struggle for scientific authority' in the social sciences is connected to 'external struggles' between social classes in the political

field 'for the power to produce, to impose, and to inculcate the legitimate representation of the social world'" (Swartz 251). Bourdieu speaks in the context of the 1970s, when biology might have been functioning under a different, more autonomous paradigm than a century earlier. In the nineteenth century, however, biology was mediated as much by "external struggles" as by its social counterparts. While human biology was the clearest example and the one with the most disastrous consequences, this was also the case in other areas of biological research, as Gabriela Nouzeilles demonstrates in "Patagonia as Borderland," where she shows how scientific research on dinosaur remnants became entangled in nationalist claims in Argentina and the United States.

44. On the nineteenth- to seventeenth-century transposition, see Goic, Greenfield, and González Pérez (*Novela*).
45. Ramiro had a previous mystic experience in Toledo after he witnessed in horror the "human holocaust" of the auto-da-fé. As a result, he decided to become a hermit and seclude himself in a cave, from which the visit of his father pulls him out into the world again.

Works Cited

Acereda, Alberto, and Rigoberto Guevara. *Modernism, Rubén Darío, and the Poetics of Despair*. Lanham, Md.: University Press of America, 2004.

Aching, Gerard. "Against 'Library-Shelf Races': José Martí's Critique of Excessive Imitation." *Geomodernisms: Race, Modernism, Modernity*. Ed. Laura Doyle and Laura A. Winkiel. Bloomington: Indiana University Press, 2006. 151–69.

———. *The Politics of Spanish American Modernismo: By Exquisite Design*. Cambridge: Cambridge University Press, 1997.

Acree, William G. *From Reading to Reality: Print Culture, Collective Identity, and Nationalism in Uruguay and Argentina*. Ph.D. diss., University of North Carolina, 2007.

Alazraki, Jaime. "Unamuno, crítico de la literatura hispanoamericana." *Hispania* 49, no. 4 (1966): 755–63.

Allingham, Philip V. "Nineteenth-Century British and American Copyright Law." *The Victorian Web*. *www.victorianweb.org/authors/dickens/pva/pva74.html.*

Alonso, Carlos. *The Burden of Modernity: The Rhetoric of Cultural Discourse in Spanish America*. Oxford: Oxford University Press, 1998.

———. *The Spanish American Regional Novel: Modernity and Autochthony*. Cambridge: Cambridge University Press, 1990.

Álvarez Junco, José. *Mater Dolorosa: La idea de España en el siglo XIX*. Madrid: Taurus, 2001.

Álvarez Junco, José, and Adrian Shubert. *Spanish History since 1808*. Oxford: Oxford University Press, 2000.

Anderson, Benedict. *Imagined Communities: Reflections on the Origin and Spread of Nationalism*. 2nd ed. London: Verso, 1991.

Anderson, Perry. "Modernity and Revolution." *New Left Review* 144 (1984): 96–113.

———. *The Origins of Postmodernity*. London: Verso, 1998.

Appiah, Kwame Anthony. *Cosmopolitanism: Ethics in a World of Strangers*. New York: W. W. Norton, 2006.

———. "Race." *Critical Terms for Literary Study*. 2nd ed. Ed. Frank Lentricchia and Thomas McLaughlin. Chicago: University of Chicago Press, 1995. 274–87.

Arias, Salvador, ed. *Acerca de La Edad de Oro*. La Habana: Centro de Estudios Martianos/Letras Cubanas, 1989.

Armitage, David. *The Ideological Origins of the British Empire*. Cambridge: Cambridge University Press, 2000.

Armstrong, Catherine, Roger Fagge, and Tim Lockley, eds. *America in the British Imagination*. Newcastle, UK: Cambridge Scholars, 2007.

Astuto, Philip. "A Latin American Spokesman in Napoleonic Spain: José Mejía Lequerica." *The Americas* 24, no. 4 (1968): 354–77.

Azorín (J. Martínez Ruiz). "La generación del 98." *Obras completas*. Vol. 1. Madrid: Aguilar, 1975. 1125–35.

Balibar, Etienne. "Racism and Nationalism." *Race, Nation, Class: Ambiguous Identities*. Etienne Balibar and Immanuel Wallerstein. London: Verso, 1991. 37–68.

Barcia, Pedro Luis. "Rubén Darío, entre el tango y el lunfardo." *Boletín de la Academia Argentina de Letras* 70, no. 277–78 (2005): 93–118.

Barrett-Browning, Elizabeth. *The Letters of Elizabeth Barrett-Browning*. Ed. Frederick Kenyon. London: Smith, Elder, 1898.

Barros-Lémez, Alvaro. *Vidas de papel: El folletín del siglo XIX en América Latina*. Montevideo: Editorial Monte Sexto S.R.L., 1992.

Beasley, Edward. *Mid-Victorian Imperialists: British Gentlemen and the Empire of the Mind (British Foreign and Colonial Policy)*. London: Routledge, 2005.

Beisner, Robert L. *Twelve against Empire: The Anti-Imperialists, 1898–1900*. New York: McGraw-Hill, 1968.

Berge, William H. "Voices for Imperialism: Josiah Strong and the Protestant Clergy." *Border States. Journal of the Kentucky-Tennessee American Studies Association* 1 (1973). *spider.georgetowncollege.edu/htallant/border/bs1/berge.htm*.

Berman, Marshall. *All That Is Solid Melts into Air: The Experience of Modernity*. New York: Penguin Books, 1988.

Bethell, Leslie, ed. *The Cambridge History of Latin America*. Vols. 4–5. C. *1870 to 1930*. Cambridge: Cambridge University Press, 1986.

Beverley, John. "Calibán después del comunismo." *Roberto Fernández Retamar y los estudios latinoamericanos*. Ed. Elzbieta Sklodowska and Ben A. Heller. Pittsburgh, Pa.: Instituto Internacional de Literatura Iberoamericana, 2000.

Bhabha, Homi. *The Location of Culture*. London: Routledge, 1994.

Borges, Jorge Luis. "A Conversation with Jorge Luis Borges." *Habitus: A Diaspora Journal* 3 (2007). *www.habitusmag.com/index.php?id=43*.

Boschetti, Anna. "Bourdieu's Work on Literature: Contexts, Stakes, and Perspectives." *Theory, Culture, and Society* 23, no. 6 (2006): 135–55.

Bourdieu, Pierre. *Distinction: A Social Critique of the Judgement of Taste*. Trans. Richard Nice. Cambridge, Mass.: Harvard University Press, 1984.

———. *The Field of Cultural Production: Essays on Art and Literature*. Ed. and intro., Randal Johnson. New York: Columbia University Press, 1993.

———. *The Logic of Practice*. Trans. Richard Nice. Stanford: Stanford University Press, 1990.

———. *Outline of a Theory of Practice*. Trans. Richard Nice. Cambridge: Cambridge University Press, 1977.

———. *The Rules of Art: Genesis and Structure of the Literary Field*. Trans. Susan Emanuel. Stanford: Stanford University Press, 1996.

———. "The Social Conditions of the International Circulation of Ideas." *Bourdieu: A Critical Reader*. Ed. Richard Shusterman. Oxford: Blackwell, 1999. 220–28.

Bourdieu, Pierre, and Jean Claude Passeron. *Reproduction in Education, Society, and Culture*. London: Sage, 1990.

Bradbury, Malcolm, and James McFarlane. *Modernism: A Guide to European Literature, 1890–1930*. New York: Penguin, 1978.

Britt-Arredondo, Christopher. *Quixotism: The Imaginative Denial of Spain's Loss of Empire*. Albany: State University of New York Press, 2005.

Brodhead, Richard H. "Literature and Culture, 1865–1910." *Columbia Literary History of the United States*. New York: Columbia University Press, 1988. 467–81.

Brooks, Peter. *Reading for the Plot: Design and Intention in Narrative*. Cambridge, Mass.: Harvard University Press, 1992.

Brotherston, Gordon. Introduction to *Ariel*. José Enrique Rodó. Cambridge: Cambridge University Press, 1967. 1–19.

Browitt, Jeff. "Modernismo, Rubén Darío, and the Construction of the Autonomous Literary Field in Latin America." *Pierre Bourdieu and the Field of Cultural Production*. Ed. Jeff Browitt and Brian Nelson. Newark, N.J.: University of Delaware Press, 2004. 113–29.

Buell, Lawrence. "Postcolonial Anxiety in Classic U.S. Literature." *Postcolonial Theory and the United States: Race, Ethnicity, and Literature*. Ed. Amritjit Singh and Peter Schmidt. Jackson: University Press of Mississippi, 2000. 196–219.

Bushnell, David, and Neill Macaulay. *The Emergence of Latin America in the Nineteenth Century*. 2nd ed. Oxford: Oxford University Press, 1994.

Butt, John. "The Generation of 98: A Critical Fallacy." *Forum for Modern Language Studies* 16, no. 2 (1980): 136–53.

Caballer Dondarza, Mercedes. *La narrativa española en la prensa estadounidense: Hallazgos, promoción, publicación y crítica (1875–1900)*. Madrid/Frankfurt: Iberoamericana/Vervuert, 2007.

Cacho Viu, Vicente, ed. *Els modernistes i el nacionalisme cultural: Antologia*. Barcelona: La Magrana/Diputación de Barcelona, 1984.

Calhoun, John C. "Conquest of Mexico." 1848. *teachingamericanhistory.org/library/index.asp?document=478*.

Călinescu, Matei. *Five Faces of Modernity: Modernism, Avant-Garde, Decadence, Kitsch, Postmodernism*. Durham, N.C.: Duke University Press, 1987.

Cánepa-Hurtado, Gina. "Folletines históricos del Chile independiente y su articulación con la novela naturalista." *Revista de crítica literaria latinoamericana* 15, no. 30 (1989): 249–58.

Cañizares-Esguerra, Jorge. *How to Write the History of the New World: Histories, Epistemologies, and Identities in the Eighteenth-Century Atlantic World*. Stanford: Stanford University Press, 2001.

Carbonell, Marta Cristina. "La polémica en torno a las *Cartas americanas* (1889) de Juan Valera." *Actas del XXIX Congreso del Instituto Internacional de Literatura Iberoamericana*. Barcelona: Publicaciones de la Universidad de Barcelona, 1994. 157–73.

Cardwell, Richard, and Bernard McGuirk, eds. *¿Qué es el modernismo? Nueva encuesta,* *nuevas lecturas*. Boulder, Colo.: Society of Spanish and Spanish-American Studies, 1993.

Carr, Raymond. *Modern Spain, 1875–1980*. Oxford: Oxford University Press, 1980.

Casanova, Pascale. *The World Republic of Letters*. Trans. M. B. Debevoise. Cambridge, Mass.: Harvard University Press, 2007.

Castro Ibarra, Germán. "Justo Sierra O'Reilly: pionero de la novela histórica y de folletín en México." *Caleidoscopio* 8, no. 16 (2004): 125–35.

Chalaby, Jean K. "Journalism as an Anglo American Invention: A Comparison of the Development of French and Anglo American Journalism, 1830–1920." *European Journal of Communication* 11, no. 3 (1996): 303–26.

Chamberlin, Vernon, and Ivan Schulman. *La Revista Ilustrada De Nueva York: History, Anthology, and Index of Literary Selections*. Columbia: University of Missouri Press, 1976.

Chasteen, John C. *Born in Blood and Fire: A Concise History of Latin America*. New York: W. W. Norton, 2001.

Coestner, Alfred. "Review of *Antología de la poesía española e hispanoamericana (1882–1932)* by Federico de Onís." *Hispania* 18, no. 2 (1935): 236–37.

Cohn, Deborah: "U.S. Southern and Latin American Studies: Postcolonial and Inter-American Approaches," *Global South* 1, no. 1 (Winter 2007): 38–44.

Cohn, Deborah, and Jon Smith, eds. *Look Away! The U.S. South in New World Studies*. Durham, N.C.: Duke University Press, 2004.

Cortés Conde, Roberto, and Stanley J. Stein, eds. *Latin America: A Guide to Economic History, 1830–1930*. Berkeley: University of California Press, 1977.

Crouzet, François. "The Historiography of French Economic Growth in the Nineteenth Century." *Economic History Review* 56, no. 2 (2003): 215–42.

Cruz, Sor Juana Inés. *The Answer/La Respuesta*. Ed. Electa Arenal and Amanda Powell. New York: Feminist Press, 1994.

Dainotto, Roberto M. "A South with a View: Europe and Its Other." *Nepantla: Views from South* 1, no.2 (2000): 375–90.

Darío, Rubén. *Azul . . . Prosas Profanas*. Ed. Andrew P. Debicki. Madrid: Alhambra, 1985.

———. "D.Q." *Páginas desconocidas de Rubén Darío*. Ed. Roberto Ibáñez. Montevideo: Biblioteca de Marcha, 1970. 142–45.

———. *Epistolario Selecto*. Ed. Pedro P. Zegers and Thomas Harris. Santiago, Chile: LOM, 1999.

———. *España contemporánea*. Madrid: Alfaguara, 1998.

———. "Historia de mis libros." *La vida de Rubén Darío contada por él mismo*. Caracas: Ayacucho, 1991. 135–57.

———. *Poesías Completas*. Mexico City: Fondo de Cultura Económica, 1952.

———. *Selected Poems*. Trans. Lysander Kemp. Austin: University of Texas Press, 1965.

———. *Songs of Life and Hope: Cantos de vida y esperanza*. Trans. Will Derusha and Alberto Acereda. Durham, N.C.: Duke University Press, 2004.

———. "El triunfo de Calibán." Ed. Carlos Jauregui. *Revista Iberoamericana* 64, no. 184–185 (1998): 451–455.

Darío, Rubén, and Ricardo Jaimes Freyre. *Revista de América*. Ed. Boyd G. Carter. Buenos Aires: Imprenta Nacional, 1967.

Davis, John A., ed. *Italy in the 19th Century, 1796–1900*. Oxford: Oxford University Press, 2001.

DeGuzmán, María. *Spain's Long Shadow: The Black Legend, Off-Whiteness, and Anglo American Empire*. Minneapolis: University of Minnesota Press, 2005.

De la Cuesta, Leonel-Antonio. *Martí, traductor*. Salamanca: Universidad de Salamanca, 1996.

Deleuze, Gilles, and Felix Guattari. *Anti-Oedipus*. Vol. 1 of *Capitalism and Schizophrenia*. Minneapolis: University of Minnesota Press, 1983.

———. *A Thousand Plateaus*. Vol. 2 of *Capitalism and Schizophrenia*. Minneapolis: University of Minnesota Press, 1987.

Della Paolera, Gerardo, and Alan M. Taylor, eds. *A New Economic History of Argentina*. Cambridge: Cambridge University Press, 2003.

Díaz Rodríguez, Manuel. *Camino de perfección y otros ensayos* [The Way of Perfection]. Caracas-Madrid: Edime, 1968.

Dubatti, Jorge Adrián. "Contribución a la historia del lectorado argentino del siglo XIX: los lectores de Eduardo Gutierrez." *La periodización de la literatura argentina: Problemas, criterios, autores y textos. Actas del IV Congreso Nacional de Literatura Argentina. Mendoza, Argentina. 23–27 de noviembre, 1987*. Vol. 2. Ed. Fernando Devoto and María Inés Barbero. Mendoza, Argentina: Universidad Nacional de Cuyo, Facultad de Fiolosfía y Letras, Instituto de Literaturas Modernas, 1989. 109–23.

Durán, Manuel. *Genio y figura de Amado Nervo*. Buenos Aires: Editorial Universitaria de Buenos Aires, 1968.

Dussel, Enrique. "Beyond Eurocentrism: The World-System and the Limits of Modernity." *The Cultures of Globalization*. Ed. Fredric Jameson and Masao Miyoshi. Durham: Duke University Press, 1998. 3–31.

———. "Europe, Modernity, and Eurocentrism." Trans. Javier Krauel and Virginia Tuma. *Nepantla: View from South* 1, no. 3 (2000): 465–78.

———. *The Invention of the Americas: Eclipse of "the Other" and the Myth of Modernity*. Trans. Michael D. Barber. New York: Continuum, 1995.

Escudero, María. "Hispanist Democratic Thought versus Hispanist Thought of the Franco Era: A Comparative Analysis." *Bridging the Atlantic: Toward a Reassessment of Iberian and Latin American Cultural Ties*. Ed. Marina Pérez de Mendiola. New York: State University of New York Press, 1996. 169–86.

Eysteinsson, Astradur. *The Concept of Modernism*. Cornell, N.Y.: Cornell University Press, 1992.

Eysteinsson, Astradur, and Vivian Liska, eds. *Modernism*. Amsterdam and Philadelphia: John Benjamins, 2007.

Faber, Sebastiaan. "The Beautiful, the Good, and the Natural: Martí and the Ills of Modernity." *Journal of Latin American Cultural Studies* 11, no. 2 (2002): 173–93.

———. "Contradictions of Left-Wing *Hispanismo*: The Case of Spanish Republicans in Exile." *Journal of Spanish Cultural Studies* 3, no. 2 (September 2002): 165–85.

———. " 'La hora ha llegado': Hispanism, Pan-Americanism, and the Hope of Spanish/ American Glory (1938–1948)." *Ideologies of Hispanism*. Ed. Mabel Moraña. Nashville: Vanderbilt University Press, 2005. 62–104.

Feijoo, Benito Jerónimo. "Mapa intelectual y cotejo de las naciones." *Teatro crítico universal*. Vol. 2. Madrid: Joaquín Ibarra, 1779. 299–321.

Fernández, James. "America Is in Spain: A Reading of Clarín's 'Boroña.' " *Bridging the Atlantic: Toward a Reassessment of Iberian and Latin American Cultural Ties*. Ed. Marina Pérez de Mendiola. New York: State University of New York Press, 1996. 31–43.

Fernández Retamar, Roberto. *Calibán: Apuntes sobre la cultura en nuestra América*. 1971. Repr., Mexico City: Diógenes, 1974.

———. "Modernismo, Noventiocho, Subdesarrollo." *Actas del Tercer Congreso Internacional de Hispanistas*. Mexico City: Colegio de Mexico, 1970. 345–53.

Feros, Antonio. "Spain and America: All Is One. Historiography of the Conquest and Colonization of the Americas and National Mythology in Spain c. 1892–c. 1992." *Interpreting Spanish Colonialism: Empires, Nations and Legends*. Ed. Christopher Schmidt-Nowara and John M. Nieto-Phillips. Albuquerque: University of New Mexico Press, 2005. 109–34.

Fiddian, Robin. "Under Spanish Eyes: Late Nineteenth-Century Postcolonial Views of Spanish American Literature." *Modern Language Review* 97, no. 1 (January 2002): 83–93.

Flint, John. *Cecil Rhodes*. London: Hutchinson, 1976.

Fogelquist, Donald F. *Españoles de América y americanos de España*. Madrid: Editorial Gredos, 1968.

Forment, Carlos A. *Democracy in Latin America, 1760–1900*. Vol. 1, *Civic Selfhood and Public Life in Mexico and Peru*. Chicago: University of Chicago Press, 2003.

Gabilondo, Joseba. "Historical Memory, Neoliberal Spain, and the Latin American Postcolonial Ghost: On the Politics of Recognition, Apology, and Reparation in Contemporary Spanish Historiography." *Arizona Journal of Hispanic Cultural Studies* 7 (2003): 247–66.

———. Introduction to the special section, "The Hispanic Atlantic." Ed. Joseba Gabilondo. *Arizona Journal of Hispanic Cultural Studies* 5 (2001): 91–113.

García Canclini, Néstor. *Culturas híbridas: Estrategias para entrar y salir de la modernidad*. Mexico City: Grijalbo, 1989.

García de Cortázar, Fernando, and José Manuel González Vesga. *Breve historia de España*. Madrid: Alianza Editorial, 1994.

García Morales, Alfonso. "Juan Ramón Jiménez, crítico de José Asunción Silva: Sus anotaciones manuscritas." *Thesaurus: Boletín del Instituto Caro y Cuervo* 46, no. 1 (January–April 1991): 88–110.

García Sabell, D. "Valle-Inclán y las anécdotas." *Valle-Inclán y su tiempo hoy: Catálogo de la Exposición en Circulo de Bellas Artes (18 march/20 april 1986)*. Madrid: Ministerio de Cultura, 1986. 119–30.

Garretón, Manuel Antonio et al. *El espacio cultural latinoamericano: Bases para una política cultural de integración*. Santiago, Chile: Fondo de Cultura Económica, 2003.

Geist, Anthony L., and José B. Monleón, eds. *Modernism and Its Margins: Reinscribing Cultural Modernity from Spain and Latin America*. New York: Garland, 1999.
Giles, Paul. *Transatlantic Insurrections: British Culture and the Formation of American Literature, 1730–1860*. Philadelphia: University of Pennsylvania Press, 2001.
———. *Virtual Americas: Transnational Fictions and the Transatlantic Imaginary*. Durham, N.C.: Duke University Press, 2002.
Gilman, Sander L. *Jewish Self-Hatred: Antisemitism and the Hidden Language of the Jews*. Baltimore: Johns Hopkins University Press, 1990.
Gilroy, Paul. *Against Race: Imagining Political Culture beyond the Color Line*. Cambridge, Mass.: Harvard University Press, 2000.
———. *The Black Atlantic: Modernity and Double Consciousness*. Cambridge, Mass.: Harvard University Press, 1993.
Goic, Cedomil. *Historia de la novela hispanoamericana*. Valparaiso, Chile: Ediciones Universitarias de Valparaiso, 1972.
Gómez de Baquero, E. "Dos novelas: *Promisión* por Carlos María Ocantos y *El extraño* por C. Reyles." *La España Moderna* 106 (October 1897): 131–40.
González, José Eduardo. "Modernismo y capital simbólico." *Bulletin of Spanish Studies* 79 (2002): 211–28.
González Echevarría, Roberto. *Myth and Archive: A Theory of Latin American Narrative*. Durham, N.C.: Duke University Press, 1998.
González Pérez, Aníbal. *La crónica modernista hispanoamericana*. Madrid: Porrúa-Turanzas, 1983.
———. " 'Estómago y cerebro': *De sobremesa*, el *Simposio* de Platón y la indigestión cultural." *Revista Iberoamericana* 63, no. 178–79 (1997): 233–48.
———. *Journalism and the Development of Spanish American Narrative*. Cambridge: Cambridge University Press, 1993.
———. *La novela modernista hispanoamericana*. Madrid: Editorial Gredos, 1987.
Greenfield, Sumner. "Larreta, Valle-Inclán y el pastiche literario modernista." *Nueva Revista de Filología Hispánica* 32 (1983): 80–95.
Guardino, Peter. *The Time of Liberty: Popular Political Culture in Oaxaca, 1750–1850*. Durham, N.C.: Duke University Press, 2005.
Gullón, Germán. *La novela moderna en España (1885–1902): Los albores de la modernidad*. Madrid: Taurus, 1992.
Gullón, Ricardo. *Direcciones del modernismo*. Madrid: Alianza Editorial, 1990.
———. "La invención del 98." *La invención del 98 y otros ensayos*. Madrid: Gredos, 1969. 7–18.
Guterl, Matthew. *The Color of Race in America*. Cambridge, Mass.: Harvard University Press, 2002.
Gutiérrez Girardot, Rafael. *Modernismo*. Barcelona: Montesinos, 1983.
Gutiérrez Grova, Alina. "José Martí sobre el teatro clásico griego." *Universidad de La Habana* 231 (1990): 33–46.
Gutiérrez Nájera, Manuel. "El cruzamiento en literatura." *Revista azul* 1, no. 19 (9 September 1894): 289–93.

———. "La novela del tranvía." *Cuentos frágiles*. Ed. Ana Elena Díaz Alejo. Mexico City: UNAM, 1993. 33–42.

Haberly, David T. "Bags of Bones: A Source for *Cien años de soledad*." *Modern Languages Notes* 105, no. 2 (1990): 392–94.

Habermas, Jurgen. "Modernity—An Incomplete Project." Trans. Seyla Ben-Habib. *Postmodern Culture*. Ed. Hal Foster. London: Pluto Press, 1985. 3–15.

———. *The Philosophical Discourse of Modernity: Twelve Lectures*. Trans. Frederick G. Lawrence. Cambridge, Mass.: MIT Press, 1987.

———. *The Theory of Communicative Action*. Vol. 1. *Reason and the Rationalization of Society*. Trans. Thomas McCarthy. Boston: Beacon Press, 1984.

Hale, Charles A. "Political and Social Ideas in Latin America, 1870–1930." *The Cambridge History of Latin America*. Vol. 4. *C.1870 to 1930*. Ed. Leslie Bethell. Cambridge: Cambridge University Press, 1986.

Harrington, Thomas. "Rapping on the Cast(i)le Gates: Nationalism and Culture-Planning in Contemporary Spain." *The Ideologies of Hispanism*. Ed. Mabel Moraña. Nashville: Vanderbilt University Press, 2005. 107–37.

Harrison, Joseph, and Alan Hoyle. *Spain's 1898 Crisis: Regenerationism, Modernism, Post-colonialism*. Manchester, UK: Manchester University Press, 2000.

Hartsock, John C. *A History of American Literary Journalism: The Emergence of a Modern Narrative Form*. Amherst, Mass.: University of Massachusetts Press, 2001.

Hegel, G. W. Friedrich. *The Philosophy of History*. New York: Dover, 1956.

Henríquez Ureña, Max. *Breve historia del modernismo*. 2nd ed. Mexico City: Fondo de Cultura Económica, 1962.

———. *El retorno de los galeones*. Madrid: Renacimiento, 1930.

Herrero-Olaizola, Alejandro. *The Censorship Files: Latin American Writers and Franco's Spain*. Albany: State University of New York Press, 2007.

Hill, Ruth. *Sceptres and Sciences in the Spains: Four Humanists and the New Philosophy (ca. 1680–1740)*. Liverpool: Liverpool University Press, 2000.

Hilton, Ronald. "Pardo Bazán and the Americas." *The Americas* 9, no. 2 (1952): 135–48.

Hobsbawm, Eric J. *The Age of Empire, 1875–1914*. New York: Vintage Books, 1989.

———. *The Age of Revolution, 1789–1848*. New York: Vintage Books, 1996.

Horsman, Reginald. *Race and Manifest Destiny: Origins of American Racial Anglo-Saxonism*. Cambridge, Mass.: Harvard University Press, 1981.

Hulme, Peter. "Including America." *Ariel: A Review of International English Literature* 26, no. 1 (1995): 117–23.

Iarocci, Michael. *Properties of Modernity: Romantic Spain, Modern Europe, and the Legacies of Empire*. Nashville: Vanderbilt University Press, 2006.

Ibarra, Fernando. "Clarín y Rubén Darío: Historia de una incomprensión." *Hispanic Review* 41, no. 3 (1973): 524–40.

Iwasaki, Fernando. "Rubén Darío en Sevilla." *ABC*, 31 May 2008. *www.abc.es/hemeroteca/historico-31-05-2008/sevilla/Home/ruben-dario-en-sevilla_1641903813360.html*.

Jacobson, Matthew F. *Whiteness of a Different Color: European Immigrants and the Alchemy of Race*. Cambridge, Mass.: Harvard University Press, 1999.

James, Henry. *The Notebooks of Henry James*. Ed. F. O. Mattiessen and Kenneth B. Murdock. New York: Galaxy Books, 1961.

Jameson, Fredric. *A Singular Modernity: Essay on the Ontology of the Present*. London: Verso, 2002.

Jáuregui, Carlos. "Calibán, ícono del 98: A propósito de un artículo de Rubén Darío." *Revista Iberoamericana* 64, no. 184–85 (1998): 441–49.

Jitrik, Noé. *Las contradicciones del modernismo*. Mexico City: Colegio de Mexico, 1978.

Joll, James. *Europe since 1870: An International History*. New York: Harper and Row, 1973.

Jrade, Cathy L. *Modernismo, Modernity, and the Development of Spanish American Literature*. Austin: University of Texas Press, 1998.

Kaplan, Amy. *The Anarchy of Empire in the Making of U.S. Culture*. Cambridge, Mass.: Harvard University Press, 2005.

Kauppi, Niilo. "The Sociologist as *Moraliste*: Pierre Bourdieu's Practice of Theory and the French Intellectual Tradition." *SubStance* 93 (2000): 7–21.

Kerrane, Kevin, and Ben Yagoda, eds. *The Art of Fact: A Historical Anthology of Literary Journalism*. New York: Simon and Schuster, 1998.

King, Richard, ed. *Postcolonial America*. Urbana-Champaign: University of Illinois Press, 2000.

Klor de Alva, Jorge. "Colonialism and Postcolonialism as (Latin) American Mirages." *Colonial Latin American Review* 1, no. 1–2 (1992): 3–23.

Kuisel, Richard F. *Seducing the French: The Dilemma of Americanization*. Berkeley: University of California Press, 1997.

Laera, Alejandra. *El tiempo vacío de la ficción: Las novelas argentinas de Eduardo Gutiérrez y Eugenio Cambaceres*. Mexico DF/Buenos Aires: Fondo de Cultura Económica, 2004.

Larreta, Enrique. *La gloria de don Ramiro*. Barcelona: Sopena, n/d.

Lasky, Melvin J. "America and Europe: Transatlantic Images." *Encounter* (January 1962): 66–78.

Legrás, Horacio. "Lectura y pasaje en el fin de siglo." *Revista Iberoamericana* 72, no. 214 (2006): 19–34.

Litvak, Lily. *Latinos y anglosajones: Orígenes de una polémica*. Barcelona: Puvill-Editor, 1980.

Lloyd, David, and Paul Thomas. *Culture and the State*. London: Routledge, 1998.

Lope de Vega y Carpio, Felix. *Arte nuevo de hacer comedias*. Ed. Enrique García. Madrid: Cátedra, 2006.

———. *New Art of Writing Plays*. Trans. William T. Brewster. New York: Dramatic Museum of Columbia University, 1914.

Loureiro, Angel. "Spanish Nationalism and the Ghost of Empire." *Journal of Spanish Cultural Studies* 4, no. 1 (2003): 65–76.

Love, Eric T. *Race over Empire: Racism and U.S. Imperialism, 1865–1900*. Chapel Hill: University of North Carolina Press, 2004.

Lyons, Martyn. *Readers and Society in Nineteenth-Century France: Workers, Women, Peasants*. New York: Palgrave-Macmillan, 2001.

Marco, Joaquim. *El modernisme literari i d'altres assaigs*. Barcelona: Edhasa, 1983.

Marco, Joaquim, and Jordi Gracia, eds. *La llegada de los bárbaros: La recepción de la literatura hispanoamericana en España, 1960–1981*. Barcelona: Edhasa, 2004.

Marshall, P. J. "Britain without America—A Second Empire?" *The Oxford History of the British Empire*. Vol. 2. *The Eighteenth Century*. Ed. P. J. Marshall. Oxford: Oxford University Press, 2001. 576–94.

———. Introduction to *The Oxford History of the British Empire*. Vol. 2. *The Eighteenth Century*. Ed. P. J. Marshall. Oxford: Oxford University Press, 2001. 1–27.

Martí, José. "Coney Island." *Escenas americanas*. Barcelona: Linkgua, 2006. 103–8.

———. *La Edad de Oro*. Ed. Roberto Fernández Retamar. Mexico City: Fondo de Cultura Económica, 1992.

———. *Lucía Jerez [Amistad funesta]*. Madrid: Cátedra, 1994.

———. "Nuestra América." *Nuestra América*. Buenos Aires: Losada, 1939. 11–23.

———. *Obras Completas*. Habana: Instituto de Ciencias Sociales, 1975.

———. "El poema del Niágara." *Nuestra América*. Buenos Aires: Losada, 1939. 139–62.

———. *Selected Writings*. Trans. Esther Allen. New York: Penguin, 2002.

Martínez Albertos, José Luis. *Curso General de Redacción Periodística*. Barcelona: Mitre, 1983.

Martínez-Echazábal, Lourdes. "Martí and Race: A Reevaluation." *Re-reading José Martí (1853–1895): One Hundred Years Later*. Ed. Julio Rodríguez Luis. Albany: State University of New York Press, 1991.

Masiello, Francine. *Between Civilization and Barbarism: Women, Nation, and Literary Culture in Modern Argentina*. Lincoln: University of Nebraska Press, 1992.

Mathy, Jean-Phillipe. *Extrême-Occident: French Intellectuals and America*. Chicago: University of Chicago Press, 1993.

Mayer, Arno J. *The Persistence of the Old Regime: Europe to the Great War*. New York: Taylor and Francis, 1981.

McGrady, Donald. Introduction to *María*. Jorge Isaacs. Madrid: Cátedra, 1986. 13–48.

McGuinness, Aims. "Searching for 'Latin America': Race and Sovereignty in the Americas in the 1850s." *Race and Nation in Modern Latin America*. Ed. Nancy P. Applebaum, Anne S. Macpherson, and Alejandra Rossemblat. Chapel Hill: University of North Carolina Press, 2003. 87–107.

Mejías Alonso, Almudena, and Alicia Arias Coello. "La prensa del siglo XIX como medio de difusión de la literatura hispanoamericana." *Revista General de Información y Documentación* 8, no. 2 (1998): 241–57.

Mejías-López, Alejandro. "Conocer y ser conocido: identidad cultural, mercado y discursos globales en tres revistas latinoamericanas de entre siglos." *Revista Iberoamericana* 72, no. 214 (2006): 139–53.

———. "Del 'Problema de España' a la 'aldea global': Modernismo y Generación del 98 en otro fin de siglo." *El 98 se pasea por el callejón del Gato: Proceso a una generación*. Ed. Pedro Guerrero and José Belmonte. Alicante: Editorial Aguaclara, 1999. 21–32.

———. " 'El perpetuo deseo': Esquizofrenia y nomadismo narrativo en *De sobremesa* de José Asunción Silva." *Revista Canadiense de Estudios Hispánicos* 31, no. 2 (2007): 337–58.

Melo, Jorge Orlando. "El periodismo colombiano antes de 1900: Colecciones, microfilmaciones y digitalizaciones." *Proceedings of the World Library and Information Congress: Seventieth IFLA General Conference and Council*. Buenos Aires. 22–27 August 2004. *www.ifla.org/IV/ifla70/papers/058s-Melo.pdf*.

Meyer-Minnemann, Klaus. *La novela hispanoamericana de fin de siglo*. Mexico City: Fondo de Cultura Económica, 1997.

Mignolo, Walter. *The Idea of Latin America*. Oxford: Blackwell, 2005.

———. *Local Histories/Global Designs: Coloniality, Subaltern Knowledges, and Border Thinking*. Princeton: Princeton University Press, 2000.

Moi, Toril. "The Challenge of the Particular Case: Bourdieu's Sociology of Culture and Literary Criticism." *Modern Language Quarterly* 58, no. 4 (1997): 497–508.

Molloy, Sylvia. "His America, Our America: José Martí Reads Whitman." *The Places of History: Regionalism Revisited in Latin America*. Ed. Doris Sommer. Durham, N.C.: Duke University Press, 1999. 263–73.

———. "Too Wilde for Comfort: Desire and Ideology in Fin-de-Siècle Spanish America." *Social Text* 31–32 (1992): 187–201.

Montaldo, Graciela. *La sensibilidad amenazada: Fin de siglo y Modernismo*. Rosario: Beatriz Viterbo Editora, 1994.

Montero, Óscar. *José Martí: An Introduction*. New York: Palgrave-Macmillan, 2004.

Morán, Francisco. "*Volutas del deseo: Hacia una lectura del orientalismo en el modernismo hispanoamericano*." *MLN* 120 (2005): 383–407.

Moraña, Mabel, ed. *Ideologies of Hispanism*. Nashville: Vanderbilt University Press, 2005.

Morby, Edwin S. "Una batalla entre antiguos y modernos." *Revista Iberoamericana* 4 (1941): 119–43.

Moreiras, Alberto. *The Exhaustion of Difference: The Politics of Latin American Cultural Studies*. Durham, NC: Duke University Press, 2001.

Moretti, Franco. *Graphs, Maps, Trees: Abstract Models for a Literary History*. London: Verso, 2005.

Moseley, William W. "Origins of the Historical Novel in Chile." *Hispania* 41, no. 3 (September 1958): 274–77.

Muller, Dorothea R. "Josiah Strong and American Nationalism: A Reevaluation." *Journal of American History* 53, no. 3 (1966): 487–503.

Muñoz Hidalgo, Mariano. "Bolero y modernismo: La canción como literatura popular." *Literatura y Lingüística* 18 (2007): 101–20.

Nelson, Brian. *Naturalism in the European Novel: New Critical Perspectives*. New York: Berg, 1992.

Nervo, Amado. *Obras completas*. Mexico City: Aguilar, 1991.

Nieto-Phillips, John. *The Language of Blood: The Making of Spanish-American Identity in New Mexico, 1880s–1930s*. Albuquerque: University of New Mexico Press, 2004.

Nolan, Mary. *Visions of Modernity: American Business and the Modernization of Germany*. Oxford: Oxford University Press, 1994.

Nouzeilles, Gabriela. *Ficciones somáticas: Naturalismo, nacionalismo y políticas médicas del cuerpo (Argentina 1880–1910)*. Buenos Aires: Beatriz Viterbo, 2000.

———. "Patagonia as Borderland: Nature, Culture, and the Idea of the State." *Journal of Latin American Cultural Studies* 8, no. 1 (1999): 35–48.

O'Gorman, Edmundo. *La invención de América: El universalismo de la cultura de Occidente.* Mexico City: Fondo de Cultura Económica, 1958.
Olson, Paul R. "Sobre el arte de *Paz en la guerra.*" *Actas del IX Congreso de la Asociación Internacional de Hispanistas.* Coord. Sebastián Neumeister. Vol. 2. 1989. 319–26.
Orringer, Nelson R. "Introduction to Hispanic Modernisms." *Bulletin of Spanish Studies* 79 (2002): 133–48.
Ortega y Gasset, José. *La deshumanización del arte y otros ensayos de estética.* Madrid: Espasa, 1999.
Patterson, Mark R. *Authority, Autonomy, and Representation in American Literature, 1776–1865.* Princeton: Princeton University Press, 1988.
Paz, Octavio. *Children of the Mire.* 1974. Repr., Cambridge, Mass.: Harvard University Press, 1991.
———. *Los hijos del limo.* 1974. Repr., Barcelona: Editorial Seix Barral, 1987.
Pérez Magallón, Jesús. *Construyendo la modernidad: La cultura española en el tiempo de los novatores (1675–1725).* Madrid: CSIC, 2002.
Perus, Françoise. *Literatura y sociedad en América Latina: El modernismo.* Havana: Casa de las Américas, 1976.
Pike, Fredrick. *Hispanism, 1898–1936: Spanish Conservatives and Liberals and Their Relations with Spanish America.* South Bend, Ind.: University of Notre Dame Press, 1971.
———. "Making the Hispanic World Safe from Democracy: Spanish Liberals and Hispanismo." *Review of Politics* 33, no. 3 (1971): 307–22.
Pineda Franco, Adela. *Geopolíticas de la cultura finisecular en Buenos Aires, París y México: Las revistas literarias y el modernismo.* Pittsburgh: Instituto Internacional de Literatura Iberoamericana, University of Pittsburgh, 2006.
Pitt, Alan. "A Changing Anglo-Saxon Myth: Its Development and Function in French Political Thought, 1860–1914." *French History* 14, no. 2 (2000): 150–73.
Plato. *Cratylus.* Trans. C. D. C. Reeve. Indianapolis: Hackett, 1998.
Poblete, Juan. *Literatura chilena del siglo XIX: Entre públicos lectores y figuras autoriales.* Santiago, Chile: Editorial Cuarto Propio, 2003.
———. "New National Cinemas in a Transnational Age." *Discourse* 26, no. 1–2 (2004): 214–34.
Pratt, Mary Louise. *Imperial Eyes: Travel Writing and Transculturation.* London: Routledge, 1992.
———. "Las mujeres y el imaginario nacional en el siglo XIX." *Revista de Crítica Literaria Latinoamericana* 19, no. 38 (1993): 51–62.
———. "Women, Literature, and National Brotherhood." *Women, Culture, and Politics in Latin America: Seminar on Feminism and Culture in Latin America.* Berkeley: University of California Press, 1990. 48–73.
Preminger, Alex, ed. *Princeton Encyclopedia of Poetry and Poetics.* Princeton: Princeton University Press, 1965; 1974 (2nd enlarged ed.).
Preminger, Alex, and T. V. F. Brogan, eds. *New Princeton Encyclopedia of Poetry and Poetics.* Princeton: Princeton University Press, 1993.
Prieto, Adolfo. *El discurso criollista en la formación de la Argentina moderna.* Buenos Aires: Sudamericana, 1988.

Pym, Anthony. "Cross-Cultural Networking: Translators in the French-German Network of *petites revues* at the End of the Nineteenth Century." *META* 52, no. 4 (2007): 744–62.

Quijano, Anibal. "Coloniality of Power, Eurocentrism, and Latin America." *Nepantla: Views from South* 1, no. 3 (2000): 533–80.

Quintian, Andrés. "Rubén Darío y la España catalana." *Cuadernos Hispanoamericanos* 261 (1972): 611–22.

Radway, Janice A. *Reading the Romance: Women, Patriarchy, and Popular Literature*. 2nd ed. Chapel Hill: University of North Carolina Press, 1991.

Rama, Ángel. *La ciudad letrada*. Hanover, N.H.: Ediciones del Norte, 1984.

———. *Rubén Darío y el modernismo (circunstancia socioeconómica de un arte americano)*. Caracas: Ediciones de la Biblioteca de la Universidad Central de Venezuela, 1970.

Rama, Carlos M. *Historia de las relaciones culturales entre España y la América Latina. Siglo XIX*. Mexico City: Fondo de Cultura Económica, 1982.

Ramos, Julio. *Desencuentros de la modernidad en América Latina: Literatura y política en el siglo XIX*. Mexico City: Fondo de Cultura Económica, 1989.

———. *Divergent Modernities: Culture and Politics in Latin America*. Trans. John D. Blanco. Durham, N.C.: Duke University Press, 2001.

Resina, Joan Ramón. "Hispanism and Its Discontents." *Siglo XX/Twentieth Century* 14, no. 1–2 (1996): 85–135.

———. "Whose Hispanism? Cultural Trauma, Disciplined Memory, and Symbolic Dominance." *The Ideologies of Hispanism*. Ed. Mabel Moraña. Nashville: Vanderbilt University Press, 2005. 160–86.

Reyes, Alfonso. "Valle-Inclán y América." *Valle-Inclán y su tiempo hoy: Catálogo de la Exposición en Circulo de Bellas Artes* (18 March/20 April 1986). Madrid: Ministerio de Cultura, 1986. 71–72.

Reyles, Carlos. "Al lector." *Cuentos completos*. Montevideo: Arca, 1968. 7–10.

———. "La novela del porvenir." *Los novelistas como críticos*. Ed. Norma Klahn and Wilfredo Corral. Mexico City: Fondo de Cultura Económica, 1991. 184–87.

Rieu-Millán, Marie Laure. *Los diputados americanos en las Cortes de Cádiz: Igualdad o independencia*. Madrid: Consejo Superior de Investigaciones Científicas, 1990.

Rivera, Adrián Curiel. *Novela española y boom hispanoamericano: Hacia la construcción de una deontología crítica*. Mexico City: UNAM, 2006.

Rivera, Jorge B. *El escritor y la industria cultural*. Buenos Aires: Atuel, 1998.

Robbins, Bruce, Mary Louise Pratt, Jonathan Arac, R. Radhakrishnan, and Edward Said. "Edward Said's *Culture and Imperialism*: A Symposium." *Social Text* 40 (1994): 1–24.

Rodó, José Enrique. *Ariel*. Madrid: Cátedra, 2000.

———. *Obras completas*. Madrid: Aguilar, 1967.

Rodríguez, Mario. *The Cádiz Experiment in Central America, 1808–1826*. Berkeley: University of California Press, 1978.

Rodríguez McGill, Carlos. "Lecturas intertextuales en los folletines gauchescos de Eduardo Gutiérrez: Desde *Juan Moreira* hasta *Los hermanos Barrientos*." *Decimonónica* 5, no. 2 (2008). *www.decimononica.org/VOL_5.2/RodriguezMcGill_5.2.pdf*.

Roldán Vera, Eugenia. *The British Book Trade and Spanish American Independence: Edu-*

cation and Knowledge Transmission in Transcontinental Perspective. Aldershot, UK: Ashgate, 2003.

Rosanvallon, Pierre. "Political Rationalism and Democracy in France in the 18th and 19th Centuries." *Philosophy and Social Criticism* 28 (2002): 687–701.

Rotker, Susana. *Fundación de una escritura: Las crónicas de José Martí*. Havana: Casa de las Américas, 1992.

Rukavina, Alison. "Deleuze, Guattari and Bourdieu: Challenging the National Model in Print Culture." New Histories of Writing, 1: Historiographies. 2003 Midwest Modern Language Association Conference. Chicago. 7–9 November 2003. *www.case.edu/affil/sce/Texts_2003/Rukavinaptr.htm* (accessed 17 February 2007; no longer available).

Rydell, Robert W., and Rob Kroes. *Buffalo Bill in Bologna: The Americanization of the World, 1869–1922*. Chicago: University of Chicago Press, 2005.

Said, Edward W. *Culture and Imperialism*. New York: Vintage Books, 1994.

Salgado, María A. " 'Mi esposa es de mi tierra; mi querida, de París': El hispanismo ingénito de Rubén Darío." *Anthropos* 170–71 (1997): 51–58.

———. "Rubén Darío y la Generación del 98: Personas, personajes y máscaras del fin de siglo español." *Hispania* 82, no. 4 (1999): 725–32.

Sánchez Blanco, Francisco. *La mentalidad ilustrada*. Madrid: Taurus, 1999.

Sánchez-Prado, Ignacio M., ed. *América Latina en la "literatura mundial."* Pittsburgh: Biblioteca de América, 2006.

Sanín Cano, Baldomero. "Literatura americana." *Revista Ilustrada de Nueva York: History, Anthology, and Index of Literary Selections*. Ed. Vernon A. Chamberlin and Ivan A. Schulman. Columbia: University of Missouri Press, 1976. 117–22.

San Román, Gustavo. *Rodó en Inglaterra: La influencia de un pensador uruguayo en un ministro socialista británico*. Montevideo: Asociación de Amigos de la Biblioteca Nacional, 2002.

Santana, Mario. *Foreigners in the Homeland: The Spanish American New Novel in Spain, 1962–1974*. Lewisburg, Pa.: Bucknell University Press, 2000.

Sarlo, Beatriz. *El imperio de los sentimientos: Narraciones de circulación periódica en la Argentina (1917–1927)*. Buenos Aires: Grupo Editorial Norma, 2000.

Schmidt-Nowara, Christopher. *The Conquest of History: Spanish Colonialism and National Histories in the Nineteenth Century*. Pittsburgh: University of Pittsburgh Press, 2006.

———. " 'La España Ultramarina': Colonialism and Nation-Building in Nineteenth-Century Spain." *European History Quarterly* 34, no. 2 (2004): 191–214.

Schueller, Malini Johar. "Postcolonial American Studies." *American Literary History* 16, no. 2 (2004): 162–75.

Schulman, Ivan. *Génesis del modernismo: Martí, Nájera, Silva, Casal*. Mexico City: Colegio de Mexico, 1966.

Schulman, Ivan, and Manuel Pedro González. *Martí, Darío y el modernismo*. Madrid: Gredos, 1969.

Schurz, Carl. *American Imperialism: The Convocation Address Delivered by Hon. Carl Schurz on the Occasion of the 27th Convocation of the University of Chicago*. Chicago: 1899.

———. *Speeches, Correspondence, and Political Papers of Carl Schurz*. Vol. 2. *December 13, 1879–February 27, 1874*. Ed. Frederic Bancroft. New York: G. P. Putnam's Sons, 1913.

Scobie, James R. "The Growth of Latin American Cities." *The Cambridge History of Latin America*. Vol. 4. *C. 1870 to 1930*. Ed. Leslie Bethell. Cambridge: Cambridge University Press, 1986. 233–65.

Seed, Patricia. "Early Modernity: The History of a Word." *CR: The New Centennial Review* 2, no. 1 (2002): 1–16.

Shaw, Donald. "When Was Modernism in Spanish-American Fiction?" *Bulletin of Spanish Studies* 79 (2002): 395–409.

Shubert, Adrian. *A Social History of Modern Spain*. London: Routledge, 1990.

Shumway, Nicolas. *The Invention of Argentina*. Berkeley: University of California Press, 1991.

Silva, José Asunción. *De sobremesa*. Madrid: Hiperion, 1996.

Silva-Gruesz, Kirsten. *Ambassadors of Culture: The Transamerican Origins of Latino Writing*. Princeton: Princeton University Press, 2002.

Singh, Amritjit, and Peter Schmidt. *Postcolonial Theory and the United States: Race, Ethnicity, and Literature*. Jackson: University Press of Mississippi, 2000.

Sinnigen, John H. *Benito Pérez Galdós en la prensa mexicana de su tiempo*. Mexico City: Universidad Nacional Autónoma de México, 2005.

Sommer, Doris. *Foundational Fictions: The National Romances of Latin America*. Berkeley: University of California Press, 1991.

Soto-Hall, Máximo. *El problema*. San José: Ediciones Universidad de Costa Rica, 1992.

Spires, Robert. *Transparent Simulacra: Spanish Fiction, 1902–1926*. Columbia: University of Missouri Press, 1988.

Spivak, Gayatri Chakravorty. *A Critique of Postcolonial Reason: Toward a History of the Vanishing Present*. Cambridge, Mass.: Harvard University Press, 1999.

Stadius, Peter. "Southern Perspectives on the North: Legends, Stereotypes, Images, and Models." *Working Papers of "The Baltic Sea Area Studies: Northern Dimension of Europe."* 3 *BaltSeaNet* (2001): 1–16. */www2.hu-berlin.de/ostseekolleg/virtual/online_pdf/paper3.pdfl*.

Starkie, Enid. *From Gautier to Eliot: The Influence of France on English Literature, 1851–1939*. London: Hutchinson, 1960.

St. Clair, William. Review of William G. Rowland Jr., *Literature and the Marketplace: Romantic Writers and Their Audiences in Great Britain and the United States*. *Review of English Studies*. New Series. 49, no. 195 (1998): 375–76.

Steinbrink, Jeffrey. "Cooper's Romance of the Revolution: *Lionel Lincoln* and the Lessons of Failure." *Early American Literature* 11, no. 3 (1976–1977): 336–43.

Stepan, Nancy L. *"The Hour of Eugenics": Race, Gender, and Nation in Latin America*. Ithaca: Cornell University Press, 1991.

Stephan, Alexander, ed. *The Americanization of Europe: Culture, Diplomacy, and Anti-Imperialism after 1945*. New York: Berghahn, 2006.

Storm, Eric. "The Rise of the Intellectual around 1900: Spain and France." *European History Quarterly* 32, no. 2 (2002): 139–60.

Strong, Josiah. *Our Country: Its Possible Future and Its Present Crisis*. 2nd ed. New York: Baker and Taylor, 1890.

Sturges, Paul. "The Public Library and Reading by the Masses: Historical Perspectives on the USA and Britain, 1850–1900." *Proceedings of the 60th International Federation of Library Associations and Institutions General Conference*. 21–27 August 1994. *www.ifla.org/IV/ifla60/60-stup.htm*.

Subercaseaux, Bernardo. *Historia del libro en Chile (Alma y Cuerpo)*. Santiago, Chile: Andrés Bello, 1993.

Subirats, Eduardo. *La ilustración insuficiente*. Madrid: Taurus, 1981.

Swartz, David. *Culture and Power: The Sociology of Pierre Bourdieu*. Chicago: University of Chicago Press, 1997.

Taylor, Charles. "Two Theories of Modernity." *Public Culture* 11, no. 1 (1999): 153–74.

Tennenhouse, Leonard. *The Importance of Feeling English: American Literature and the British Diaspora, 1750–1850*. Princeton: Princeton University Press, 2007.

Tinajero, Araceli. *Orientalismo en el modernismo hispanoamericano*. West Lafayette, Ind.: Purdue University Press, 2003.

Torrecilla, Jesús. *España exótica: La formación de la imagen española moderna*. Boulder, Colo.: Society of Spanish and Spanish American Studies, 2004.

———. *La imitación colectiva: Modernidad vs. autenticidad en la literatura española*. Madrid: Gredos, 1996.

Unamuno, Miguel de. "La gloria de don Ramiro." *Obras Completas*. Vol. 6. Ed. Ricardo Senabre. Madrid: Fundación José Antonio de Castro, 2004. 283–91.

Unzueta, Fernando. "Periódicos y formación nacional: Bolivia en sus primeros años." *Latin American Research Review* 35, no. 2 (2000): 35–72.

———. "*Soledad* o el romance nacional como folletín: Proyectos nacionales y relaciones intertextuales." *Revista Iberoamericana* 72, no. 214 (2006): 243–54.

Urraca, Beatriz. " 'Quien a Yankeeland se encamina . . .': The United States and Nineteenth-Century Argentine Imagination." *Ciberletras* 2 (2000). *www.lehman.cuny.edu/ciberletras/v01n02/Urraca.htm*.

Valentí Fiol, Eduard. *El primer modernismo literario catalán y sus fundamentos ideológicos*. Barcelona: Ariel, 1973.

Valera, Juan. *Obras completas*. Vol. 2. 2nd ed. Madrid: Aguilar, 1949.

———. *Obras completas*. Vol. 3. Madrid: Aguilar, 1958.

Van Aken, Mark. *Pan-Hispanism: Its Origin and Development to 1866*. Berkeley: University of California Press, 1959.

Venezky, Richard L. "Literacy and the Textbook of the Future." *Literacy: A Redefinition*. Ed. Nancy J. Ellsworth, Carolyn N. Hedley, and Anthony N. Baratta. Hillsdale, N.J.: Lawrence Erlbaum, 1994. 39–54.

Warner, Michael. "Publics and Counterpublics." *Public Culture* 14, no. 1 (2002): 49–90.

Weber, Eugen. *Peasants into Frenchmen: The Modernization of Rural France, 1870–1914*. Palo Alto, Calif.: Stanford University Press, 1976.

Weber, Max. *The Protestant Ethic and the Spirit of Capitalism, and Other Writings*. New York: Penguin, 2002.

Whitaker, Daniel S. *La Quimera de Emilia Pardo Bazán y la literatura finisecular*. Madrid: Pliegos, 1988.

Wilde, Oscar. *The Portrait of Dorian Gray*. *The Complete Works of Oscar Wilde*. New York: Harper and Row, 1989. 17–167.

———. *Selected Journalism*. Ed. Anya Clayworth. Oxford: Oxford University Press, 2004.

Wolf, Ema, and Guillermo Saccomanno. *El folletín*. Buenos Aires: Centro Editor de América Latina S.A., 1972.

Young, Robert J. C. *Postcolonialism: An Historical Introduction*. Oxford: Blackwell, 2001.

Index

www.ingramcontent.com/pod-product-compliance
Lightning Source LLC
Chambersburg PA
CBHW060806310726
48980CB00002B/252

* 9 7 8 0 8 2 6 5 1 6 7 7 0 *